What People Are Say
Anger: Deal with It, H
Stop It from Killing

D0469863

"Through Dr. Bill DeFoore's engaging work with anger and rage, our world is relieved of much of its despair and pain. In this new edition of *Anger: Deal with It, Heal with It, Stop It from Killing You*, Dr. DeFoore illuminates the powerful force of these emotions and how to capture their potent energy for good, for healing and for creating an abundantly successful life."

Carolyn Craft
Executive Director of Wisdom Radio

"A great book that will touch a nerve in everyone. Bill DeFoore gives you a better understanding of yourself and the people around you, as he shares his enormous depth and insight into human nature. I'd like to ask everyone to read this book. Then we would have healthy parents, couples who are able to compromise, and resilient selves."

Connie Tyne
Executive Director of the Cooper Wellness Program,
Cooper Aerobics Center, Dallas

"In keeping with the times, Dr. William DeFoore's revisions to *Anger: Deal with It, Heal with It, Stop It from Killing You* insightfully address the problems of today—anger in schools, on the roads, in our children and at work. Behind every person's anger is a story. Dr. DeFoore can help us understand the stories and empower us to be a part of positive change in ourselves, our homes and our communities."

Cardwell C. Nuckols, Ph.D.
author, *Healing an Angry Heart*

"This powerful new edition of *Anger: Deal with It, Heal with It, Stop It from Killing You* is for anyone who has felt hurt or seen others hurt by unhealthy anger. It is also for those who want to experience and communicate their anger in ways that allow them to gain a sense of personal strength, health and integrity, experience greater intimacy in relationships and attain deeper fulfillment in their lives at every level. It is for all of us wishing to rebuild a world with a safe and healthy future for ourselves and our children."

Jane Middelton-Moz
author, *Boiling Point* and *Good and Mad*

ANGER

Deal with It,

Heal with It,

Stop It from

Killing You

William Gray DeFoore, Ph.D.

Health Communications, Inc.
Deerfield Beach, Florida

www.hcibooks.com

Library of Congress Cataloging-in-Publication Data

DeFoore, Bill, date.
    Anger : deal with it, heal with it, stop it from killing you /
William Gray DeFoore—[Rev.].
        p. cm.
    ISBN-13: 978-0-7573-0111-7
    ISBN-10: 0-7573-0111-8
    1. Anger.   I. Title.

    BF575.A5D45 2004
    152.4'7—dc22

                                                            2003068588

HCI, its logos and marks are trademarks of Health Communications, Inc.

Publisher: Health Communications, Inc.
                3201 S.W. 15th Street
                Deerfield Beach, FL 33442-8190

R-02-06

Cover redesign by Lisa Camp
Inside book design by Dawn Von Strolley Grove

Anyone can become angry—that is easy.
But to be angry with the right person,
to the right degree, at the right time,
for the right purpose,
and in the right way—this is not easy.

Aristotle
The Nicomachean Ethics

CONTENTS

ACKNOWLEDGMENTS

I would like to express my heartfelt appreciation to my beloved wife, Cindy Parker DeFoore, for her encouragement, editing and untiring support during the writing of this revision. I would also like to thank my editor, Allison Janse, for her clear, informed and extremely helpful questions, input and suggestions as to its content. And finally, I offer my appreciation to all of the good people and hardworking souls whose stories are included in some form or version in this book.

INTRODUCTION

Since this book was first released in 1991, anger and violence levels have continued to increase in a variety of different settings. From the loss of everyday civility to incidents of road rage, sky rage and parents brawling at Little League games, it seems that people are becoming more explosive with each passing day. On an even more alarming scale, the tragedy of school and workplace shootings, suicide bombings, terrorist attacks and large-scale wars have impinged upon our reality uninvited. So what do we need to learn, understand and do now and in the future to protect our families, our communities and ourselves?

This revision is devoted to providing some answers to that question.

One thing is for certain. If we only look at what's wrong, what's not working and what needs to be changed, we may end up adding to the problems that we want to solve. It doesn't help to get angry about all of the anger. We must see what's right about our emotions and what's working within and around us in our families, our global community and ourselves. You will find ample positive and uplifting material in this revision.

As an author and a therapist, my understanding of anger and its role in the human process has broadened and deepened in the past thirteen years. I have discovered and utilized many new and effective methods for working with anger in my practice, which I will share with you. Moreover, I have gained some valuable insights and perspectives regarding what's going on in the world, as it relates to our physical, mental, emotional and spiritual wellness.

NEW CHAPTERS IN
THIS REVISED EDITION

You will find four new chapters in this revision. Chapter 7, "Anger Among Our Children," provides insights into understanding and responding to what appears to be a growing level of violence and aggression among our youth. As the shapers of our future, our children are precious to us and vulnerable to our influence in many ways. This chapter challenges you to face these issues head-on and take responsibility for addressing the small-scale and system-wide problems that plague our children nationwide and globally. You will learn of the damaging effects of conscious and unconscious neglect and the power of storytelling for lightening our children's burdens. Finally, you will find in this chapter an abundance of information about what you specifically can do to help children on many different levels. Informative, inspiring and empowering, this material will take you to a new level of freedom and responsibility for the nurturing and care of children.

Chapter 10, "Female Anger: The Emergence of the Powerful Woman," gives some unique perspectives and insights into anger issues as they affect women in particular. The victim-persecutor-rescuer dynamic is discussed in terms of typical male and female roles, and positive and negative stereotypes and mythological images of powerful women are explored to provide an understanding of how we got to where we are now. In conclusion, women are encouraged and inspired to claim the power of presence that surpasses other forms of power that have victimized women throughout history.

New research has been added throughout this revision where relevant, particularly to show the impact of anger-related issues on your health. Chapter 14, "Healthy Anger and Your Health," in particular focuses on the impact of emotions on heart disease, immune function, respiration, circulation and digestion. The emphasis in this material is on building healthy patterns rather than diagnosing dysfunction. Readers are challenged to understand and claim the useful energy of their healthy anger to become proactive and productive in all aspects of their lives.

A metaphorical context is used in chapter 14, taking you from the development of "the warrior spirit" to the evolution of "the spiritual warrior." You will learn about the warrior's "sword" and "shield" and how these energies can work against you—or very much in your favor. You will ultimately find in this information that healthy anger does no harm. Healthy anger is effective action. Healthy anger gets the job done. And you will discover that when it is healthy, anger becomes pure energy that you can use for whatever constructive purpose you choose.

Incidents of workplace violence seem to be at an all-time high as we enter the early stages of the twenty-first century (Bureau of Labor, 2001). In chapter 15, "Overcoming Workplace Violence," you will find information about the psychology of the violent person, coworkers' responsibility and business leaders' responsibility. Practical, useful information, methods and techniques can empower any and all of us to address and attempt resolution of this problem in society. You will learn that the ultimate answer is love, and yet a kind of love that requires tremendous courage.

Throughout this book you'll find affirmations at the end of every chapter that you can use to form empowering positive beliefs about your emotions and yourself. Write them down, say them out loud and expand on them in ways that work specifically for you. If any negative thoughts come up during the process, write them down, too. Replace all negative statements with at least three positive ones. Your thoughts in many ways impact your emotions and your life as a whole. Take charge of this creative process until your thoughts become an asset you can utilize for your own good health and well-being.

NEW MATERIAL
THROUGHOUT THIS REVISION

New methods and techniques for managing, healing and expressing anger and related emotions have been added throughout this revised edition. You the reader will therefore gain more skills that you can use to further your own health and healing process.

If you are to fully embrace and manage your anger and rectify it with your good heart, it is essential that you recognize the nobility and magnificence of the human spirit. To help with this process, you will find more spiritual references in this revised edition, providing a holistic approach to emotional wellness as a key to body, mind and spirit health.

In chapter 8, "Protecting the Child Within," you will learn about the inner child of the past, present and future, and how you can effectively utilize each of these images to enhance your healing and healthy functioning.

Chapter 9, "The Role of Anger in the Grief Process," provides new insights and approaches to the grieving process. Different techniques will help you move through times of loss toward healing, recovery and a return to love.

Perhaps the most important insight gained through in-depth study of anger therapies is that we simply cannot fight anger and win. When we fight, deny, ignore or suppress anger, it just gets stronger and becomes more destructive.

Anger must be understood and embraced if we are to master its energy and be in charge of our own actions.

HOW TO KNOW IF YOU HAVE A PROBLEM WITH ANGER

Many of you already know that you have a problem with anger. For those of you who are not sure, here are some indicators:

- When you get angry, you don't get over it. Sometimes it lasts until you explode, or it may go inside to fuel the fires of your rage. You may be one who "holds a grudge."
- You never get angry. You just don't have the emotion. There are times when you know you should be angry, but the emotion just doesn't seem to come. Your anger is "watered down," and you never fully release it.
- You feel frustrated, disappointed or irritable much of the time, but you just don't ever get angry. Anger may be an unacceptable emotion to you, whereas frustration, disappointment or irritability are more acceptable, however unpleasant. This can interfere with or prevent any meaningful level of fulfillment or joy in life.
- You are sarcastic or cynical about yourself, others or the world around you. You may tease others with "velvet daggers" in some of your "jokes," only to be surprised when they don't want to be around you. You don't openly express anger but it is leaking out all the time.
- You may be depressed frequently and for long periods of time. You don't express anger openly but take it out on yourself, whether you realize it or not. This can lead to suicidal thoughts and behavior or perhaps major illness (Pearsall, 1987).

- Perhaps you are angry all the time. You may be verbally, emotionally or even physically abusive to others in personal and professional relationships. This doesn't mean that you are a bad person, but it certainly means you need to learn to manage your anger. If indeed you have been abusive, it is almost certain that you will need professional help to work through your problems with anger.
- You feel powerless in your own life—powerless to make the changes you choose to reach your goals. Though you may not use the word, you feel like a victim much of the time. You probably have many ways to explain why you can't live your dreams, all of which seem very reasonable to you. The point is that if you are denying your power by denying your emotions, you are getting in your own way. To claim all of your emotions as your allies, and to express them in healthy ways, is to maximize your resources for your own expression of purpose in your life.

If you feel that any of these examples apply to you, then you probably have suppressed anger. You will find helpful plans and suggestions throughout this book that are designed to move you toward emotional health and overall well-being.

THE TEN-STEP PLAN FOR TRANSFORMING ANGER INTO A FORCE FOR POSITIVE CHANGE

This dynamic, practical plan is designed to provide you with a way to structure the content of this book into a process for healing, growth and recovery.

Step One: Call a Truce with Anger

Designed for your protection and safety, anger is originally and ultimately your friend and ally. Until you accept anger as a valid part of who you are, you will be at war with your anger and yourself. Tasks for this step include:

- Understanding the definition of anger as a protective emotion
- Beginning to consider ways in which anger can be useful and positive

Chapter 2 goes into detail about the definition of anger and its basic function. You will read throughout this book about how anger can be destructive and unhealthy. Chapter 14 is entirely devoted to the topic of healthy anger and how it can ultimately help you reach your goals and realize your dreams.

Step Two: Make the Anger-Love Connection

Anger does the most harm when it is disconnected from the other basic emotions. Anger springs immediately from pain and fear, and ultimately from love. When anger is connected with love, it becomes courageous action. Tasks for this step include:

- Recognizing the relationship between anger, fear, pain and love
- Identifying the difference between action motivated by fear and action motivated by love
- Beginning to consider how anger shows up when it is felt and expressed in conjunction with love
- Understanding that courage is a result of the anger-love connection.

Explore these relationships in detail in chapter 2, specifically as illustrated in Figure 2.2 and in the sections entitled "Love is the Fuel for the Fire of Anger" and "That's My Tongue on That Pole." You will find a great example of anger as courageous action based on love in the same chapter in the section entitled "I'm So Mad I Could Lift a Chevy."

Step Three: Rewire Your Hot Buttons

Your hot buttons are your sore spots, your sensitivities, your vulnerabilities, your hang-ups, or your weaknesses that are best known by the ones closest to you. If you don't know your hot buttons, then those who do can work you like a puppet on a string. Rest assured that your spouse, your children, your friends and your closest work associates know your buttons. If these significant people know your sore spots better than you do, you may often feel like a victim in those relationships. So, your tasks for this step include:

- Identifying your hot buttons
  - What are your greatest fears?
  - When do you get the angriest?
  - What makes you the most depressed and/or withdrawn?
  - What actions of others can you just not tolerate?
  - What subjects can you not discuss without getting irrational and/or overemotional?
  - In what situations are you most likely to shut down, pull away, react emotionally or blow up?
  - What is your "Achilles heel"?
- Tracing these current experiences back through your life experience, looking for memories and stories that help to explain these reaction patterns that are uniquely yours.
- Listing these stories chronologically, to the best of your ability.

Through this process, you are tracing the wiring that makes your buttons hot. As you work with and rework these memories through the processes outlined in this book—chapters 8 and 9 are specifically designed to help you with this process—you will be rewiring your hot buttons. This will give you the freedom to:

- Make conscious choices about how to respond when someone pushes your hot button.
- Manage your emotions more effectively so that they are not overwhelming to you.
- Keep your anger level between 0 and 3 (see "Self-Monitoring on the 0–10 Anger Scale" in chapter 13).
- Think clearly and make good decisions even when you are highly emotional.

By rewiring your hot buttons, you are making tremendous strides toward taking charge of your life. You are beginning the process of "turning your dirt into gold" and transforming your weaknesses into strengths.

Step Four: Tell Your Story

Your story is your memory of those life experiences that made you who you are today. It consists of "the best of times and the worst of times." You remember those experiences because of the powerful emotions associated with them, such as deep pain and sorrow or great joy and tremendous love. Those experiences are formative, in that they impact us so deeply that we are literally changed, molded and shaped by them. Here are some suggestions about ways to tell your story:

- Tell it to yourself—write down all of the memories and life experiences you consider significant, meaningful, important, powerful, traumatic, uplifting or inspiring.

- Tell your story to a trusted friend. You can do this in segments, as it is actually a fairly lengthy process. If you already do this, then ask yourself, *What have I not told, and why?*
- Tell your story to a family member. One way to facilitate this is to ask for their stories as well, and then you can do some story-swapping. The board game "Life Stories" can be very helpful in this process (see *www.toysrus.com*).
- Use fairy tales, myths, books or movies that have had special meaning for you as a springboard for your storytelling. You can find your personal myth by weaving your own life story around the themes you discover in these old favorites from your past (McAdams 1997).
- You may choose to work with a personal coach, confidant, mentor or counselor in this process. Depending on the amount of intense emotion and/or confusion you have regarding your stories/memories, you may benefit from having a listener who is objective, supportive and, in some cases, professionally trained.

Consider this a lifelong process. Your life story is a treasure trove of riches for self-knowledge, self-awareness, self-mastery and powerful emotional energy if you choose to use it as such. Unexamined, your past can be a burden of heavy baggage, or you can choose to make it a springboard for future success. The choice is yours.

Step Five: Get Good at Grieving

Much of the anger we see and feel in this world is a result of unacknowledged loss and unresolved grief. Grief is part of life. The older we get, the more we experience death and loss of all kinds. These are facts. It is also a fact that grieving is an act of love. In chapter 9 you will find a full discussion of this topic, including a list of the various kinds of losses we experience in life. You can use the many exercises, rituals and ceremonies provided to facilitate your own grieving process. When you get good at grieving, you will have less fear of loss and therefore less fear of deep love and intimacy. This will give you more personal freedom and flexibility in all aspects of life.

Step Six: Release Toxic Emotions

There is almost nothing worse than feeling or being in the presence of old, toxic anger. Nobody decided to build up those old emotions—it happens very naturally. When we were children we were simply not equipped to process and release all of the feelings that arose on a daily basis. So, many of those emotions have just been sitting there waiting for us to come back and deal with them. The fact is they don't just sit there. They "go bad" and become toxic over time. In the section entitled "Feelings Are Just Like Vegetables" in chapter 3, you will find a full explanation of this process. Here are some indications that you may be carrying a buildup of toxic emotions:

- You don't have enough energy.
- You experience chronic or recurrent illness.
- You suffer from depression.
- You feel irritated, agitated, sad or bitter much of the time.
- You have muscle aches and body pain that cannot be explained medically.
- You react emotionally to situations and don't know why.
- You tend to overreact emotionally in certain scenarios or with certain people.

Of course, there may be medical reasons for many of the above symptoms, but I caution you against taking an exclusively medical approach to dealing with your emotions and emotional issues. In some cases this can amount to simply masking the issue and actually lead to more serious and long-lasting problems.

Chapter 12 is devoted entirely to helping you learn to release your emotions in a healthy manner. It is the buildup of toxic emotion that causes your past to become a burden. It is the clearing and releasing of this toxicity that makes your past lighter, and gives you the opportunity to use it as a resource for growth and success.

Step Seven: Make New Decisions

If your past history or life story is unexamined, chances are that you currently react from and live your life out of old decisions based on childhood emotional experiences. Although some old decisions and/or beliefs are positive and useful, many of them can be self-limiting and destructive. Here are some ways to examine your old decisions and belief systems and transform them into a springboard for positive change:

- Make a list of everything you consider to be a limitation to your health and happiness.
- Examine each of these and determine whether you are powerless to change any of them.
- If so, write down the beliefs about yourself and/or the world that make you powerless. Some of these may indeed be unchangeable, and yet some may simply be self-limiting decisions based on past experience.
- Now you have a list of your old beliefs.
- For each old, self-limiting belief, write at least three positive beliefs. You may draw on positive beliefs you already have or come up with totally new decisions about yourself.
- Use the affirmations at the end of each chapter in this book to assist you with this.

• The affirmations exercise is specifically designed to help you restructure your belief systems and make new decisions.

By doing the work outlined in Steps One through Six, you are laying the groundwork for making new decisions and forming new core beliefs, just as if you were tilling the soil before planting a garden. Preparing the soil is essential if the new seeds are to sprout, grow and blossom. The preparatory process in the first six steps ensures that your new decisions will take root and become new beliefs, setting you free to live the life you choose.

Step Eight: Become an Effective Listener

Chances are that the angriest people you know are not the best listeners. Have you noticed that there are lots of good talkers in the world but not that many good listeners? When you think about it, you may also find that anyone you consider to be a great listener, you will also consider to be a good person.

The skills for effective listening are not complicated or difficult to learn. The challenge is to apply them consistently during emotionally tense communication. In Appendix II you will find "Guidelines for Respectful Communication" for couples and those in close relationships. Appendix III provides a process designed for conflict resolution in the workplace. Both of these exercises will give you practice in the essential tool called reflective listening or active listening. Appendix II will also teach you the skills for expressing empathy, validation and understanding, which are invaluable in emotionally intense communication.

The basic skills you need to master in order to become a great listener are:

- Keeping your mind quiet enough to let the speaker's information enter
- Managing your own emotions and mental activity well enough to set aside any personal agenda, reactions, defenses, explanations or rescue attempts
- Recognizing when communication is simply not feasible due to your own or the other person's anger level, closed-mindedness and/or open hostility
- Developing your attention and memory well enough to repeat the speaker's words back to her/him clearly and accurately in reflective listening
- Being secure enough within yourself that you can hear the speaker make negative references about you without reacting or shutting down
- In reflective listening, maintaining a very respectful and open nonverbal attitude and posture while restating the speaker's words. This is particularly challenging when you feel attacked, accused, criticized or blamed, and yet that may be the most important time to use these skills
- Opening your heart and mind in compassion
- Being willing to see the good in the speaker, and believe in their good intentions
- Holding a vision for a positive outcome to the communication process

Step Nine: Claim Your Power

Power can best be understood in this context as freedom and responsibility. By taking responsibility for your thoughts, feelings and actions, you claim the freedom to make them work for you instead of against you. This takes you right out of the victim role in all of your relationships. Since rage, aggression and violence often emerge directly from a feeling of powerlessness, it follows that you will be avoiding these problems by claiming your power in healthy ways. Your tasks in this step include:

- Accessing and embracing the physical and emotional energy of your anger so that you can use it consciously and willfully to reach your goals and accomplish positive outcomes. Chapters 12, 13 and 14 are particularly designed to help you with this process.
- Having a variety of skills for setting appropriate boundaries and taking care of yourself (see chapters 6 and 13 for more information on boundaries).
- Learning communication skills that enable you to express your emotions freely and openly while respecting your listener. Appendices II and III are designed to help you with this process. The key skill is the use of "I" statements in which you claim:
  - Responsibility for your emotions
  - Authority over your reactions and your behavior
  - Freedom to act independently of your emotional reactions
  - Freedom to express the full power of your passion and emotional energy in ways that you consciously choose

Step Ten: Create a Fabulous Life

Now you are ready to use the creative power of your mind without interference from toxic emotions or self-limiting beliefs. We were given these magnificent minds by our Creator for one reason. We are meant to use them. We have heard all of our lives that most of us only use a small fraction of our mental capacity. It has been my experience that emotional wellness coupled with a powerful faith, optimism and spiritual focus provides us with greater access to the brilliance and power of our minds. Your tasks for this step include:

- Creating a vision of the life you choose, being sure to include the following:
  - Physical health and wellness
  - Emotional wellness
  - Mental clarity, focus and optimism
  - A strong sense of your personal mission and purpose in life
  - Healthy, loving relationships
  - An ongoing, challenging and fulfilling learning and growth process
  - Creative expression that provides you with joy and satisfaction
  - Work and/or service that is in alignment with your mission and purpose in life
  - Financial comfort and/or prosperity that provides you with the freedom and opportunity you desire in order to reach your goals and realize your dreams
- Working with and reworking your vision on an ongoing basis:
  - Write it down
  - Revise it
  - Expand it
  - Make it more focused and specific
- Spending time with your vision in prayer and/or meditation
- Developing a plan and a timeline for realizing your goals:
  - Write out a five-year plan
  - Write reachable goals for each month of the first two years
  - Write reachable goals for each quarter of the second two years
  - Write reachable goals for the last year
- Writing out specific tasks and steps to take for reaching each of your goals. Check them off as you accomplish them.
- Seeing it happening, and feeling it happening. Imagine yourself moving through the world after reaching all of

your goals and realizing all of your dreams. Now move through your world like that. The section entitled "Affirmation, Visualization and Imagination" in chapter 16 will guide you through this process so that you can learn and practice the skills.

1

Anger from a New Angle

Sam had a look of indignant rage in his eyes. The lines of his face curved and formed outlines of his anger, which seemed to flow from his eyes in streams. He was hard to look at. It would have been easy to feel afraid or guilty, looking into those accusing eyes.

When he spoke, I was amazed to hear his mild tone and pleasant voice. It was as if the angry eyes had been lying. His words told the story of a passive man, afraid of his twenty-two-year-old son, afraid of his wife and afraid of facing what he had done to create the misery in his family. Sam's words told me nothing of the anger in his eyes.

He was at war, all right—with himself. "At times," he said, "my chest burns as if there is a red-hot iron piercing my heart." Sam was all-too-well armed with guilt and anger at himself, and his body was the battleground.

In the battle with his wife and son, however, he was unarmed. He was a helpless victim. At least, that's how it seemed to him.

Sam hated his anger. But he couldn't make it go away. It just got stronger and more disturbing. It turned into rage, which began to show up in his son Joe. The rage that was growing in Sam and his family was about to destroy his home.

THE PRESSURE COOKER

Most of us find ourselves exploding from time to time and regretting it later. The explosions occur because we don't like our anger and we try to keep it inside. It works like a pressure cooker. We can only suppress or apply pressure against our anger for so long before it erupts. Periodic eruptions can cause all kinds of problems.

At Sam's house, the pressure cooker was about to blow. No one had "let the steam out" in a long time. The last pressure release had been six months ago when Joe had taken a neighbor's car and run it off a bridge. Joe wasn't hurt, but the car was a total loss. Of course, Joe's parents paid for it. And paid for it. And paid for it. They always paid. But at least the pressure was off—for a while.

It only took a few more months for Joe to reach a boiling point again. He just wasn't as good as Mom and Dad at stuffing feelings. It seemed to be his job in the family to let the steam out of the family pressure cooker. This time he really blew the top off.

Sam and his wife, Margaret, had been out of town visiting relatives for the weekend. They had been very nervous about leaving. As a matter of fact, this had been their first trip together for pure pleasure in quite some time. They were usually far too worried about Joe to leave home for long. Their two daughters were grown, and it seemed now that Joe was all they could think about.

As they were driving home, they were quiet. Each was wondering what their son was going to do next. As they turned down their street, they heard the sirens.

Without knowing why, Sam and Margaret looked at each other and panic filled their eyes. They didn't say a word. Then they saw their house in flames.

The fireman knew who they were by the looks on their faces. He walked up to them slowly and said, "Your son is over there. I'm afraid your home is a total loss. We got here too late. Your neighbor called, and when we arrived we found the house consumed in flames and your son sitting right there acting as if nothing had happened."

They looked where he was pointing and saw Joe sitting on the ground poking at something with a stick. The look on his face didn't make any sense. You would never have known from looking at him that his family's home was burning down just a few hundred feet away.

As they approached they saw that what Joe was holding wasn't a stick. It was a large kitchen knife. On the ground in front of him was a family portrait showing him and his mother with their arms around each other. His father was off to the side with his arms around his two daughters. Everyone in the picture was smiling except Joe. He was stabbing the family portrait while his house was burning. But he didn't feel any pressure. He had started the fire.

Maybe you believe you don't have any anger. You may feel that you have succeeded in stuffing, controlling or stifling that unpleasant part of yourself. This would work fine if there weren't a fire under the pressure cooker. But there is.

Everything we are learning about emotions and health tells us it is unhealthy to stuff feelings. Reports by Reuters Health, 2000, and Vanderbilt University, 1999, for example, indicate that anger suppression may boost blood pressure and/or contribute to depression. Your efforts to control your anger may be hurting you. If you don't blow like an overheated pressure cooker you may have an internal explosion. This usually means depression, self-hatred, major illness or all three.

WHO COULD POSSIBLY LIKE ANGER?

With all of the abuse and conflict in the world, it seems anger is the problem, certainly not the solution. Victims of abuse, perpetrators of abuse and rescuers of abusers all have problems with anger—their own and others. When it comes to abuse, it seems anger is the bad guy.

Anger is usually expressed in ways that make someone a victim. Because of this we often get anger mixed up with aggression and attack. Most people believe anger is just plain bad and the world would be a better place without it. This reminds me of a speaking engagement I had a few years ago.

I had just been introduced to a crowd of about one hundred health-care professionals who had given up three hours of their Saturday morning to learn about "Anger Management and Healthy Emotional Expression."

I requested, "Somebody give me a definition of anger." I love asking this question. Most people don't know what anger is. We think about it, talk about it, feel it and act on it. But we don't know what it is.

No one said anything for about a minute. I could almost see the cogs turning in their minds as they struggled to define something they thought they knew about. I smiled. "Isn't that interesting? It's not easy to define, is it? Just give me some words you associate with anger."

"Rage!" from a woman in the back of the room. I could see it in her eyes.

"Violence" was offered by a small, quiet man in the front row who had one of those strained but permanent smiles on his face.

"Losing control" was the definition proposed by a dignified man in a business suit.

"How do you think the dictionary defines anger?" I challenged them one more time.

A bright, attractive woman offered, "It's an emotion."

"Bingo! That's it! It's just an emotion. It doesn't hurt anybody," I said, enjoying the looks on their faces as they heard this for the first time.

"There's one more part of the definition that is really important. The emotion of anger is for our protection."

No one disagreed. They never do. It was as if they knew, but didn't know that they knew.

"Anger is just an emotion. Emotions are part of who we are, like our heads, hearts and hands. All emotions are okay. The dictionary definition of anger that I like best is, 'A feeling one has toward something that offends, opposes or annoys.' There's nothing malicious or mean in the basic feeling of anger."

"I DON'T WANT TO LOSE CONTROL"

In my counseling practice, I encourage my clients to voice their fears about expressing their anger. One of the most common statements I hear in response is, "But I don't want to lose control."

When we are afraid of losing control, it's not anger we are

afraid of. The wild, destructive force we sometimes feel inside is rage. Rage is a mixture of unexpressed pain, fear and anger that has been building up over a long period of time. It results from being hurt and scared and keeping all the feelings inside. If we return to our story about Sam and his family, maybe we can learn more about the results of suppressed rage and the fear of losing control.

In my counseling sessions with Sam, I made my best effort to ignore the look in his eyes and concentrate on his words. I didn't yet understand the story his eyes told. I thought I'd better listen and see how he explained what was going on behind those eyes.

I learned that Sam was the son of a chronic compulsive gambler and had grown up in a very mixed-up family. His mother was a rageaholic, and the target for her rage was his father.

When his dad wasn't around, however, which was most of the time, Mom took her anger out on Sam. He was victim to his mother's displaced anger. He had learned from a very early age to protect himself and keep peace in his family by being quiet and withdrawn and never showing any emotion. He learned the importance of staying "in control."

Sam had continued to be passive and to control his emotions throughout all of his adult life. This had been necessary in his childhood, but it just wasn't working anymore. In his current family something else was called for.

His son needed him to be strong and take charge of the family, and Sam didn't know how to do it. Joe needed the security of knowing that his dad was in control. Without realizing it, Sam had suppressed his strength and power along with his anger. The rage Sam had seen and been hurt by in his past was a sick distortion of anger mixed with pain and fear. When he suppressed his anger, he lost his ability to claim his strength against anything that threatened him or those he loved. There was no "tough" in his love.

Sam felt totally powerless over the situation at home. As long as he hated and suppressed his anger, he indeed was powerless.

Joe was not in control consciously, but on an emotional and physical level he ruled the family. He lost control on a fairly regular basis, which is exactly what gave him power over his parents.

After their house burned down, Joe began exhibiting violent rage with threats to hurt himself and his parents.

It occurred to me in therapy sessions that Joe was expressing his father's rage along with his own. He was unconsciously "picking up the slack" for his dad and expressing the rage inside the older man that had never surfaced. Joe began abusing alcohol, which seemed to reliably trigger escalating rage attacks.

This was occurring all too frequently. Sam's fear of losing control was causing him to do just that. By suppressing the anger and rage of a lifetime, he had given up his power to gain control over the forces that were destroying his family.

Joe had taken control of his family because he was the only one who released his anger. His parents' fear of his and their own anger was the other part of the equation. This gave him power, however unhealthy it may have been.

The only problem was that Joe was too young to be emotionally in charge of his family. He abused his power and his family as well. He hated himself for what he was doing, but he didn't know how to stop. He needed his parents to take control so that he didn't have to.

Here are some thoughts to consider, or new "angles" on anger:

- Anger is an emotion, and all emotions are okay.
- We have to have anger to survive in a world that is sometimes dangerous, abusive and cruel.
- Anger is a powerful feeling that is natural and exists only for the purpose of self-preservation.
- Anger is emotional energy that we can use to create and maintain healthy boundaries.
- Anger does not have to lead to aggression or attack.
- Anger does not have to hurt anyone.
- Anger is energy and strength to be used for powerful action.
- Anger is based on love.

2

Anger: The Protective Emotion

A feeling of safety and security is important to all of us. Anger is one of the two feelings that come when your safety is threatened. Fear is the other feeling. Fear is the natural first-level reaction to any threat. Anger is the secondary, protective response. Without anger as a protective reaction, all you will have is fear in the face of danger.

We usually think of protection in terms of physical safety. Guns, alarm systems and the martial arts are all for the purpose of protection. In this chapter we will talk about a different kind of protection, one that arises naturally from deep within your emotional self.

9

THAT'S MY LIFE YOU'RE PLAYING WITH!

It is clear that the most dangerous place you can be is fly-ing down the highway in your motorized vehicle. Think about it. There you are, a fairly vulnerable creature sitting in your huge chunk of metal hurling down strips of concrete at breakneck speeds often only inches away from others doing the same thing.

Some of your fellow travelers are a little confused. They think the highway is a video game or a racetrack. To some people, it is actually fun to drive their chunk of metal within inches of your chunk of metal and scare the daylights out of you! But it's not just you—only seconds after they've scared you, they're doing the same to four other motorists because they're going so fast.

And then there are those drivers who are just downright aggressive behind the wheel. Some people actually use the relative anonymity of driving alone in their vehicle as an opportunity to release the anger they are not venting any-where else. That means that all the other motorists are poten-tial victims of anger release from total strangers. This makes the road dangerous for everyone.

Ignoring the flow of traffic, driving slowly in the fast lane, driving too fast in any lane, tailgating, cutting into openings that are not quite big enough, and making last-minute deci-sions that shock other motorists and require them to make sudden adjustments are all aggressive and dangerous moves to make when driving.

You know that rush you feel when you are exposed to one of these situations? That surge of energy that pulses through your body? Well, that is a mix of survival-based fear and anger. Your life is being threatened out there on the open road, and there is virtually nothing you can do about it. The road-rage addicts get off on this rush. The rest of us just want to get where we're going in one piece.

How often do strangers threaten your physical life on a daily basis? If you're like most people, it only happens on the highway. What an excellent opportunity to study your own anger! If these examples apply to you, you can use your driving experience as a sort of laboratory in which to study your anger and anger response patterns.

When you are pushed, crowded, tailgated, honked at or otherwise put at risk on the road, your fear is saying to you, "Danger! Watch out!" and your anger is saying, "I don't like this, and I'd like to do something about it!"

Do you see anything wrong with these reactions? Of course not. They are natural and healthy. The fear is because of the threat, and the anger simply brings the question of what to do about the threat. Anger is designed to spur action to protect life, limb and loved ones. That is its most basic level of functioning.

OPTIONS FOR PROTECTIVE ACTION ON THE HIGHWAY

Unhealthy options include: making an obscene or aggressive gesture, yelling and cursing, following the dangerous driver and running them off the road (becoming a dangerous driver yourself), or in the worst-case scenario, reaching for a weapon in an attempt to retaliate. All of these, of course, add to the problem, and in some cases are against the law. If you're not careful, your anger will make you part of the problem, and then someone else will have to figure out what to do about you!

Healthy options include: calling your free local cell-phone number for reporting dangerous drivers (check with your cell-phone customer service for this number), driving all the more carefully to counter the insanity of the driver who has just endangered your life or silently wishing for that driver to be stopped by a patrolman soon, before he kills someone.

I learned in a defensive drivers class that if someone is tail-gating you—which is one of the most common and frequent ways in which your safety is endangered on the road—you can just slow down to a speed where 1) the driver is very likely to pass you and 2) if an accident happens there will be less damage because of the slower speed. This is an interesting option from the standpoint of learning about anger. Regarding your own anger, it gives you a way of communicating to tailgaters that you don't like what they're doing, and it further shows them that you are not going to be intimidated into driving faster or dangerously to get out of their way. This is a good example of a healthy anger response.

The idea here is that we need lots of options for dealing with our anger. One reason is that anger is so closely connected with the emotion of love, and we want as much love in our lives as possible.

LOVE IS THE FUEL
FOR THE FIRE OF ANGER

Even though anger doesn't look very loving when it comes out, we often feel the most anger in situations where there is the most love. The more love you feel, the more open your heart is. The more open you are, the more vulnerable you become to those you love. This is where the protective emotion of anger comes in.

Any police officer will tell you a sad and sobering reality: that the most dangerous calls they can make are domestic violence calls. When we chose to marry and raise a family, our intentions were only the best. We never intended to harm our loved ones. We happen into these senseless scenarios by being blind to and consumed by our fear and anger. Anger moves into violence when it stimulates retaliation and revenge. This is why you must become emotionally healthy, so that you can be awake, aware and compassionate while feeling strong emotions. Only then can you keep yourself and your loved ones safe in emotionally intense situations.

Each of us was born with a tremendous need for love. This need is just as strong as the need for food and shelter. If we are deprived of love, food or shelter, the results are the same. We get physically or emotionally sick. In some cases we die.

It was our parents' job to meet these needs. However, our need for love was never perfectly met, no matter how wonderful our parents may have been. After all, they were human beings, too, with their own shortcomings and limitations.

Because our need for love is never perfectly met, each of us is hurt as a natural part of growing up. This may have been unintentional, as is the case with much abandonment and neglect. Unintentional abandonment and neglect could result from an unwanted divorce, a parent's illness or a very large family in which there just isn't enough of the parents' love and attention to go around.

Our parents may have had serious problems of their own, however, and they may have deliberately hurt us. Other significant caregivers, such as stepparents, uncles, aunts or grandparents, may also have hurt us. Some of us were hurt by baby-sitters, nannies, church workers, neighbors, family friends, employees in a day-care center or other facility workers.

One way or another, each of us was emotionally hurt as a child because of our vulnerability and our tremendous need for love. The heart of the matter—the center of the circle—is the need to love and be loved.

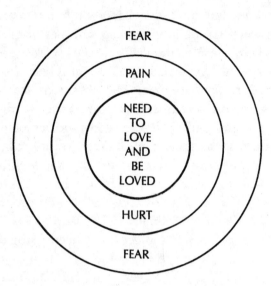

Figure 2.1. The Heart of the Matter

Look at the diagram in Figure 2.1 and follow the circles out from the center as a process of emotional development. Picture these as spheres rather than circles beginning at the center of your being around your solar plexus and moving out into the world.

The essence of who you are is a vulnerable being who needs to give and receive love. Hurting is part of loving, and therefore it is also part of living. There's nothing wrong with feeling hurt. The important thing is what you do about it. Face your pain, and you are free to do something about it. Deny your pain, and you are powerless to stop the hurting, in the present and in the future.

Because you were hurt, you learned to fear being hurt again. Fear is natural. Claim it, and it's yours to motivate pro-tective action. Deny your fear, and it may claim you, govern-ing your thoughts, feelings and actions. By denying or suppressing your fear, you give away all of your power and wind up feeling like a victim in threatening situations. By claiming and embracing your fear as your own, you claim the power to act and to protect yourself when you feel vulnerable.

Another kind of fear is directed inward toward ourselves. When something bad happens, we often fear that it's our fault. This is known as shame. The illogical logic of the child's mind seems to go like this: "If something bad happens to me, it must mean that there's something wrong with me."

THAT'S MY TONGUE ON THAT POLE

It was a typical winter day in Anchorage, Alaska, about five degrees below freezing. I was four years old, over at my friend Rusty's house playing in his carport. I had the good fortune of coming from a basically loving family, so I hadn't yet learned of the cruel edges of the world.

In a friendly manner, Rusty invited me to stick out my tongue and put it on his carport pole. Being a daredevil (and also naive), I complied willingly.

Immediately I knew there was something wrong. I hadn't really planned a long relationship with this pole, but it just wouldn't let go of my tongue. I knew I couldn't stay that way for long. So, "Rrriiip!" and I was free . . . sort of.

I still remember how the top layer of my tongue looked, staring back at me from that pole.

I felt miserable. My tongue was bleeding, and my feelings were hurting even worse than my tongue. It never occurred to me to get mad. I had never learned how. Instead, I felt bad about myself.

Looking back, I can remember thinking, *Why would he do something so mean to me? There must be something wrong with me or else he wouldn't have done that!* Instead of turning outward in anger, I turned inward and questioned myself. This is how shame begins. This childhood experience proved to be an excellent example of the inner-directed fear that "There's something wrong with me."

As children, we just did not know how to put responsibility outside ourselves, so quite naturally we took the blame when something went wrong. This was even truer when our parents caused the harm. We really needed our parents to be "good," so that we could feel safe and secure. So we put the badness in us. This is a way of understanding that some degree of shame is a natural part of being a vulnerable child in this world. Fortunately, we don't have to live with this shame forever. As adults we can see the truth of who was responsible for what happened and didn't happen in our childhood.

Take a look at Figure 2.2. You can see that a new circle has been added, representing the sphere of protection and defense. Anger is the emotion of protection and defense. Without it, all you can do is hide, withdraw and question yourself.

Figure 2.2. The Circle of Protection

Let's summarize this view of emotional development.

Because you need so much love, you get hurt. Because you were hurt, you fear being hurt again or you fear that there's something wrong with you inside. You can't face the world like this, so you develop some kind of protection or defense. This is where anger comes in.

There's the connection between anger and love. Originally, anger is based on a love for comfort and pleasure and a desire to avoid pain. Later, as your love grows and becomes more complex, your capacity for anger grows as well. As adults, of course, we often get angry as a result of our love for others and a desire to protect them from pain.

I'M SO MAD I COULD LIFT A CHEVY!

I remember reading a news account of a woman who lifted the front end of an automobile off her son, who was pinned underneath. Apparently he had been working on the car, and it slipped off the jack and fell on him.

Let's run the clock back a bit. We'll try to figure out what happened that would give a woman the strength to perform a feat that seemed physically impossible. Let's call the mom Joyce and her son Tommy.

When Tommy was born, Joyce was overwhelmed with love for the soft, vulnerable bundle of life and mystery that had somehow grown and emerged from within her womb. Her love for her son was natural and powerful coming from deep within her, through no effort of her own. When Tommy was four, his father died, and Joyce's love for her son grew even stronger.

As she watched him grow, she had to let Tommy go in some ways to allow him to explore, to learn and to develop. Her protective instinct never diminished, however, because it came straight from her love. She was always aware of where he was and what he was doing. She was determined to be available if he ever needed her.

Joyce had just finished the dishes from lunch and was considering an afternoon nap. After all, it was Saturday and she had worked hard all week. She went to the back of the house to see how Tommy was coming along on the repair work he was doing on his car. She could hear the sound of the ratchet wrench and smell the mixture of oil and gas as she opened the door into the garage. At eighteen, it seemed Tommy was more interested in that car than anything in the world—except maybe girls.

As she put one foot into the garage, she saw the car jack leaning dangerously, about to drop thousands of pounds of metal onto the upper body of her son.

It was as if time stood still. All of the love she had ever felt for her son came flooding to the surface and turned to fear. She barely had a chance to say "Tommy!" when it was too late. The jack slipped, dropping the chassis of the car onto her beloved son's chest and shoulder.

There were no thoughts in Joyce's mind. Something deep inside her screamed *No!* in response to her fear. She rushed to the front bumper of the beat-up old Chevy. She never questioned whether she could lift the car or whether she should call for help. All she knew was that her Tommy was in trouble and he needed her. Something tremendously powerful came from deep within her and surged through her hands, arms, shoulders and back. Joyce knew somehow that she would not let that car crush her son.

All of a sudden the car was her enemy, and she channeled all of her emotional energy into removing it from the vulnerable body of her only son. The power that surged through Joyce's body was directed toward this immediate and deadly threat to her son's life. It was a primal raging against the possibility of losing this young man whom she had brought into the world, nurtured and raised with all of her love.

Amazingly, Joyce lifted the car just enough for Tommy to slide out, badly bruised but with no permanent injury. Joyce then released the bumper, letting the car fall. Exhausted and relieved, she went to her son. Later she remembered almost nothing of what happened. She had no idea how she had been able to lift that much weight. She knew she could never do it again . . . unless. . . .

This example demonstrates the physical empowerment of anger motivated by the tremendous love she had for her son. If Joyce had been depressed and lethargic, paralyzed in fear, or disconnected from her emotions, her son could have died under that old Chevy.

No one watching Joyce save her son that day would have described her as angry. Something you will learn again and again in this book is that healthy anger does not look, sound or feel like anger as we have come to know it.

It is natural not to like anger. We have never been taught how to understand it and use it in healthy ways. We have learned that anger is just plain bad and scary.

BUT I'M AFRAID OF MY ANGER

Much of the anger we have seen was expressed in unhealthy ways, which is why there are so many negative beliefs about it. Here are a few I have heard:

- If I show my anger, no one will like me.
- Every time I have been angry in the past I have hurt someone.
- If I let my feelings out, I don't know what will happen.

- I don't have any anger. I decided that a long time ago.
- I don't want to set a bad example for my child.
- Why can't we just solve these problems rationally?
- Can't I just talk about my feelings in a calm, adult manner?
- The world would be a better place if people would just control themselves.
- Every time I get angry, I start crying. I hate that.
- I'm afraid if I really start letting my feelings out, I'll never stop.
- There's something really bad, even evil inside me. If I let my anger out, there's no telling what would happen.
- I hate anger. When my father got angry, my whole family got hurt.

These thoughts and beliefs can rob you of your ability to experience your feelings. As part of an unconscious and dysfunctional protection system, they are designed to separate you from your natural emotional energy. They will also separate you from your strength and power for recovery and success.

Healing is natural. When there is nothing interfering with or blocking your system's natural processes, you heal automatically. When you suppress anger, you also suppress your fear and your pain, which blocks the flow of emotional energy in your system. Suppression of anger, fear and pain also inhibits your ability to experience love.

Love is the source of healing, which comes from the core of your being, and suppressing it slows down or stops the healing process. Just as love was the source of the power experienced by Joyce, it is the source we need in order to heal and empower our lives and ourselves.

Affirmations

- *My anger is for my protection, and I deserve to feel safe and secure.*
- *My anger is a natural emotion.*
- *I need my anger like I need all other natural parts of myself.*
- *I can use my anger to make me stronger and healthier.*
- *I can use my anger to protect and care for those I love.*

3

Buried Anger
Just Won't Stay Down

EMOTIONAL EDUCATION
FROM A SUPPRESSIVE SOCIETY

W e were not educated in our schools as to how to understand, manage and express our emotions. The education we received was an unconscious, indirect message that was well received by most of us. To give you an idea of this pseudo-education and how well you learned its lessons, I'll give you a two-part quiz:

1) The first question is, "How are you doing?"

What is the socially acceptable answer to the first question? You guessed it! The "correct" answer is "I'm fine."

2) The second question is, "What's wrong?"
Right again! The culturally programmed answer is "Nothing."

So that's all you need to know about your emotions. "I'm fine, nothing's wrong."
If that program worked, we wouldn't have the problems with domestic, school and workplace violence that we do, and we would all be healthier, better parents and better spouses. The old program of lying, denying and pretending about your emotions is just not working. It seems to work for a little while, but then those buried emotions just won't stay down.

IF YOU CAN'T SAY SOMETHING NICE . . .

We start learning to bury anger in our childhood. Following are some scenarios that are guaranteed to lead to buried anger:

1. **Your parents suppressed their own anger.** People in your family never raised their voices, but there was a very powerful nonverbal message that said, "Stay in control. We don't act that way here." There was an even stronger message that said, "If you act ugly, we won't love you." What choice does a child have?
2. **It wasn't just anger that was hidden in your home; it was all emotions.** The fear of anger was so great that all of the other feelings were suppressed along with it. The message here is that all feelings are bad. The only problem is that each of us knows at some level that our feelings are part of who we are. Suppression of feelings in this way leads to a feeling of worthlessness and low self-esteem. You just can't suppress your feelings and get away with it.

3. **Mom or Dad specifically punished us for the expression of anger in any form.** "Go to your room until you can act right!" The message to the child is clear: "I'm not supposed to get mad. Mom and Dad won't love me if I act like that." You may also have been physically punished or abused for showing anger. This only has to happen once, in some cases, for the message to come through loud and clear that anger is bad and must be buried.

4. **We were victims of sexual or other kinds of abuse and blamed ourselves, either partly or completely.** This leads to shame and the basic belief that accompanies this feeling, which is, "I have no right to be angry." Shame is inner-directed fear and leads to a deep feeling of worthlessness. This leads to an indirect and yet very powerful suppression of anger.

5. **We were abused physically as a direct result of the anger coming from our abuser.** We learned from this that anger is awful, that it causes the type of fear and pain we felt when we were abused. Our fear would then go something like this: "If I get angry, I will be just like my abuser. By controlling my own anger, I can be sure I will never be like him/her." In this scenario, we would automatically and unconsciously suppress our anger in an effort to be a good person and avoid being like the person(s) who hurt us.

COMPULSIONS, ADDICTIONS AND OTHER SMOKE SCREENS

Compulsions and addictions are great "smoke screens" or distractions from the real issues in our lives. They are also common ways in which we suppress or bury our anger. Here are some examples of compulsive/addictive behavior patterns:

- Obsessive-compulsive behaviors such as
  - Counting
  - Excessive hand-washing
  - Excessive house-cleaning
  - Constant checking and rechecking locks, security systems, etc.
  - Obsessive worrying
- Compulsive busy-ness
- Alcohol and drug abuse
- Codependency
- Love/relationship addiction
- Sexual addiction
- Compulsive overeating
- Anorexia and/or bulimia
- Rage addiction
- Gambling addiction
- Workaholism
- Compulsive shopping
- Television addiction
- Internet compulsion
- Video game addiction

You may know of other disorders that fit in this category. There are many effective programs designed to treat these disorders, including psychotherapy and the many twelve-step programs around the world. Our focus here is on the emotion of anger and how it relates to these thought and behavior patterns.

Compulsive and addictive behaviors are designed to protect you from all of your emotions, and they accomplish this by burying your anger, fear and sorrow deep beneath the complex of dysfunctional patterns. All compulsive/addictive disorders affect body and brain chemistry, providing an unhealthy "self-medication" for emotions.

Buried anger does not go away. We can medicate it, deny it and pretend it's not there for days, weeks, months or even years. It's only a matter of time, however, before it shows up in some form of bitterness, depression, illness, outburst, violent attack or suicide. Buried anger always claims a victim, and the victim is often the person it's buried in.

We tend to react to buried anger in one or both of the following two ways:

1. **We get sick.** Depression can result from buried anger, (see Fava and Rosenbaum 1999 and Elam 2003), and that reduces the effectiveness of our immune system (Scanlan 1999, Schleifer et al. 2002 and McGuire et al. 2002). Physical illness can result from the depression or from the stress caused by the suppressed emotion. The anger does not get expressed, but it makes its presence known. This is sometimes called internalized anger or self-hatred, leading to suicidal thoughts or suicidal behavior. In extreme cases, phobias, delusions and even psychosis can develop over time.

2. **We explode in fits of anger.** These explosions can range all the way from violent rages to minor eruptions. The main point is that we are not in control, and we do things we do not intend to do. We often hurt others and ourselves when our buried anger erupts to the surface. This is the "pressure cooker" syndrome we talked about earlier.

Compulsive and addictive behaviors can develop in either of the two above scenarios. Keeping feelings inside doesn't feel good. It hurts. Drug and alcohol addiction often results from self-medicating the pain that is caused by suppressed emotions.

Rageaholics may use substances or compulsive behaviors to try to control their rage. "I am so relaxed and pleasant when I drink. I only fly into those rages when I'm sober." This is a statement from a woman in denial, using alcohol to attempt to control her rage.

I'M SURE I COULD STOP DRINKING IF I COULD JUST STOP GETTING ANGRY

Clarice's presenting problem was her rage. She would usually start out being upset over some trivial detail around the house and eventually drag in seventeen years of her husband's inadequacy and attack him with it.

"Everything will be going just fine," Clarice explained while staring out the window of my office, "and then I get this feeling. I start out complaining, and the next thing I know I'm screaming at the top of my lungs and throwing things at Foster. I've even hit him in the face with my fists a few times. I don't know why I do that.

"But you know, after I have a couple of glasses of wine, I just calm right down. He even brings me a glass of wine when he gets home sometimes. I guess he's figured it out by now."

Without realizing it, Clarice had mixed two very serious addictions. She was addicted to rage and to alcohol, and the two problems were feeding into each other. She was in total denial about her alcoholism.

"My drinking is not a problem. I'd be in bad shape without it, though. I can quit any time I want to, but I have to learn to control my anger first." From the way Clarice was talking about her drinking, it was very clear to me that it would be pointless to intervene at this stage.

I decided to use her belief that the alcohol was not a problem as a way to get past her defenses.

"I'd like you to abstain from drinking just for a few weeks, while you are in therapy, Clarice. You'll have greater mental clarity and also make much more progress that way. I'll give you some other ways to control your anger, besides drinking."

It was a long shot, but I knew I couldn't help her if she continued drinking while I was working with her.

"Sure, that's no problem. Like I said, I can quit any time I want to." She squirmed a little when she said this. I think her body was telling me the truth she was not ready to admit.

Over the first few days of her abstinence, Clarice's struggle with her rage proved more than she was ready for. Without the alcohol for self-medication, she found herself in either violent rages or serious depression. Her marriage was collapsing rapidly.

Clarice's commitment to recovery was not strong, since she had not acknowledged her powerlessness over alcohol. She returned to drinking and eventually stopped coming to her counseling sessions. The alcohol was an excellent distraction from her emotional problems, and she also happened to be an addict.

This woman was not ready to remove the distraction by dealing with her addiction, so she didn't deal with her buried anger. But it continued to deal with her. It just wouldn't stay down.

I ONLY GET MAD WHEN I'M DRUNK

There are also many cases in which alcohol is the trigger to release the rage. This usually occurs when the person can't let go emotionally. The drinking is an effort to ease the stress of emotional suppression. Extreme suppression often leads to rage. The alcohol provides a false sense of comfort, allowing a release of the rage. The results can be devastating.

This type of problem needs little explanation. Almost all of us know of someone who is only angry and abusive after having a few drinks.

In such cases, the alcoholism treatment must occur before or along with the psychotherapy. The distractions of substance abuse provide a very effective mask for emotional problems. If these addiction issues are not addressed, the emotional issues will never be resolved.

A LONG-OVERDUE RELEASE

Remember Joe, Sam's son, whom we discussed earlier? His alcoholism was the first problem addressed when he went into treatment.

Focusing on his alcoholism gave Joe some security, as drinking was something he thought he might be able to understand and possibly even control. His rage, however, seemed to be too big for him to handle, and he was terrified of facing the pain that was behind it.

Since he was young and the alcoholism was not chronic, Joe was able to commit to his recovery program early in treatment. Being away from both his family and alcohol, he was free to begin facing his emotions in a safe environment. After a couple of months in recovery, he began to approach the topic of his rage.

Like most people, Joe was afraid of his anger at first. Sitting in my office, he seemed to be trying everything he knew to avoid expressing his feelings. He just couldn't seem to get into it. He kept talking, trying not to face the anger and pain he knew was there inside.

"I'm just not angry," he explained, trying not to look at me. "Now that I've got a handle on my drinking, I want to get out in the world and live a normal life."

"What about your parents?" I asked, knowing he hadn't dealt with his feelings toward them.

"I never want to see them again," he replied in a voice too calm for such a statement. "Oh, maybe I'll see my dad. I need his help to get a car and a job." He grew quiet, and I knew by the look in his eyes that his thoughts had returned to Mom.

"Why don't you just sit back and relax for a minute, Joe? Close your eyes and think of all the reasons you don't want to see your mother ever again." He followed my suggestion, and I lowered my voice a little to see if I could get him a little closer to his feelings.

Joe became immediately anxious, so I asked what he was thinking. He recounted memories of his mother walking around in her underwear in front of him and sometimes allowing him to see her nude.

"That confused me. I was attracted to her, but I knew it was wrong. She kept doing it over and over for all those years. I really hate her for that."

His rage was beginning to surface. Usually at this point he would have suppressed his emotions and found some distraction, like drinking.

"See if you can let some of that out," I said. "You don't need to carry that pain, confusion and anger around anymore. Feel the anger in your body. Let it fill up your entire body and expand. If someone were to give full expression to what you're feeling, what would that look like?"

"Like a volcano erupting," he replied.

"Picture the volcano in front of you." I waited until he indicated that the image was clear. "Now go into the volcano and imagine yourself erupting with all of that same heat, force and power." He was still for a moment. And then the tears started.

"What are the tears saying?" I asked.

"I don't know. I guess I don't want to hurt her," he said when he was able to speak. "But she was wrong for what she did." I could see the presence of his anger right there with his compassion for his mother. This created a lot of internal conflict in Joe's mind and body.

"Picture her there in front of you, and say everything you never have said but needed to."

I listened then as his anger poured out, mixed with bitter tears. He yelled for a while, then got quieter as he said, "I know you and Dad were having a hard time. But that didn't give you any right to bring yourself to me like that." He finally began to calm down and breathe a little more deeply.

I was relieved to see Joe doing this work. I knew that if his rage had stayed buried within him, he could have hurt himself or someone else or both. He had contemplated suicide many times. In extreme anger episodes he had threatened both his parents' lives. Seeing this emotional release and the subsequent ones over the next few months was like witnessing the removal of a malignant tumor.

As he went through the emotional healing process, Joe learned to express his anger in healthy ways and to establish boundaries for his protection in intimate relationships.

FEELINGS ARE JUST LIKE VEGETABLES

Vegetables and feelings are best when they are fresh. As a matter of fact, they are downright good for us when they are fresh but toxic if left ignored for too long.

One of the freshest ways to express pain is with simple phrases like "Ouch!" Other simple and to-the-point ways of expressing basic feelings are:

"That hurts!"
"I'm hurting."
"I'm scared."
"I'm angry."
"I'm happy."
"I love you."
"Great!"
"Fantastic!"

These simple, current expressions of emotions are healthy and productive. They let the listener know exactly what is going on. These are statements we can make to let our feelings out while they are still fresh. Chapter 13 provides further detail about expressing feelings in healthy communication processes.

We all know what happens when we leave vegetables too long without using them. They become bad for us. It's the same with feelings. The longer we leave our feelings inside without expressing them, the more unpleasant they become. When old buried feelings come out, they tend to make our bodies shake and sweat, and our eyes and noses tend to run.

Buried feelings, like buried vegetables, don't just lie there. They get hot and generate energy, which has to come out one way or another. If we keep them inside, they might burn holes in our stomachs (ulcers). There is some evidence that cancer, a kind of over-burning of cells, is connected to suppressed anger (Speca et al. 2000).

When vegetables go bad, we need to uncover them and use them in compost where they will do some good. When our buried feelings start to cause problems, they need to come out. It's the only way. We can't pour something down there to kill them (like alcohol or some other chemical). That just causes new problems. We can't just work a little harder, exercise a little more or read a book about self-control. These are only temporary solutions.

If we do get caught up in trying these many and creative ways of avoiding our feelings, they just get hotter and hotter in there and cause all kinds of problems.

I CAN'T STAND TO BE ALONE

Much of what we do each day is a distraction from our feelings. Other people are the greatest distraction of all if we choose to use them in that way. This is one of the "great escapes" of codependency. Fear of being alone is the fear of feelings.

What would happen if all your going, doing and thinking just stopped? You would start to feel. Feelings. That's all that would be left. Take away the thinking and doing, and the feelings rise to the surface. After all, each of us is made up of thinking, doing and feeling.

Usually we wait until life grabs us by the collar or the throat and throws us to the ground before we really start to face our feelings. Even then, we may only face them until we can distract ourselves again. Why is that?

Perhaps it is because we have all been hurt, and we don't really want to face that. None of us had a perfect childhood. The rest of our lives have also had some rough spots, so we've been hurt some more. We may also feel fear, shame and guilt about our behavior and ourselves.

So what do you do? You can't sit around in self-pity all the time. You can't blame your parents for all your problems. Or even if you do, where's that going to get you? They are not likely to come and make it all better at this point.

Most of the time, you just keep on trucking. You do what you know how to do. That's just it. You don't do what you don't know how to do.

If you don't know how to be alone with your feelings, you will keep burying them until they get too hot and smelly and you are forced to deal with them because of some kind of illness or crisis. This is how we become "crisis junkies." We need the crises for the emotional release they always bring.

Then, as soon as the crisis is over, we will bury our feelings away again, not realizing they will be even more toxic next time they come up. As long as we are alive, our feelings will not die. Our challenge is to bring them to life in such a way that they heal, energize and inspire us to greater levels of health and happiness.

AFFIRMATIONS

- *I experience my feelings (and my vegetables) while they are fresh. They are good for me!*
- *My anger is part of who I am.*
- *By claiming and experiencing my anger, I am adding to my inner strength and self-esteem.*
- *I choose to find ways to embrace and give full expression to my anger in healthy ways.*

4

Breaking Free from the Passivity Prison

To be passive means to not be active. If we are passive, we let things happen instead of making things happen. If we are passive, we don't do, we are done to. We don't act, we react. This leads to the feeling of being a victim of the people and circumstances around us. Nobody likes to be a victim.

As infants we were all passive. We had no choice. We were just not capable of very much action. We could cry, soil our diapers, rattle our rattle, make gurgling noises and smile. That's about it. We were passive recipients of what the world offered us, like it or not.

When we were hurt or neglected as innocent children, there wasn't much we could do about it. We could cry, but sometimes we were even punished for that. We just couldn't pack up our diapers and toys and go looking for a functional family. This is the first experience any of us had of being a victim. Children are victims of an imperfect world that sometimes has sharp and cruel edges. This is nobody's fault; it's just the way it is.

As adults, we are no longer victims except in extreme cases of physical restriction and assault. Many adults feel like victims, however.

I'M HERE, YOU'RE HERE . . . .
WHY CAN'T I REACH YOU?

Paul was the kind of guy who looked as if he had it all together. Handsome, slim and a good dresser, he had a ready smile and a handshake when we met. He was a master at making a good impression and helping others to feel at ease. You can imagine my surprise when he said to me, "I don't know who I am. I look inside here and I don't find anything."

He had heard me speak on codependency a couple of weeks prior to our meeting, and this was his first experience with counseling or therapy of any kind.

"My son hates me. I can't seem to get close to him, even though I want that more than anything else in the world. He and my wife are close and I feel cut off from both of them. I know I'm supposed to express my feelings, but I don't seem to have any. I don't know what to do, so I don't do anything."

It was only after our seventh session that Paul began to talk about what really bothered him the most.

"She seems to love him more than she loves me. They are constantly together, and I don't think it's good for my son either. I tried talking with her about it once or twice, but it didn't go anywhere." Paul's feelings were coming a little closer to the surface as he spoke. The totally in control expression had faded into a look of sadness and fear.

"I don't know how to reach either one of them," he concluded, as he stared out my office window. "Sometimes I get really angry inside when I see them laughing and having fun together. And it hurts a lot when she turns me down again and again when I ask if we can make love. I don't know how much longer I can stand this. I have to do something."

But Paul did not do anything. He was paralyzed in his passivity "prison," locked away for his crime of not knowing how to communicate. Without intending to, he had suppressed his love and capacity for joy along with his anger, fear and pain. His unexpressed emotions made up the bars and walls of his prison.

It's as if Paul pushed in on the anger circle (see Figure 2.2) from the outside, and in the process closed off his fear, his pain and even his love. This is why he was sitting in my office saying he had no feelings at all. Since he was not aware of his feelings, he had no sense of who he was as a person. In some ways, our feelings are who we are inside. When Paul denied his feelings, he denied himself as a person.

THE OPPOSITE OF PASSIVE
IS ACTIVE NOT AGGRESSIVE

The only way Paul had ever broken out of his passivity was in an explosion of anger. As a young man in his early twenties, he had gotten into some screaming matches with his girlfriend that scared him. He didn't know he could get that angry. He even found himself wanting to hit her once. After a painful breakup, Paul made a strong decision to never get angry again. His anger had hurt someone he cared for, so he could not accept it as a means of breaking free from his passivity.

Action. That's what Paul needed. He only needed to decide on one small step and then to take it. There are many ways out of the passivity prison, and they all involve taking some form of direct positive action.

Paul signed up for a workshop on communication skills. He was watching his son grow up and his chance at building a relationship was slipping away. He was determined that his son would not end up hating him the way he had always hated his own father. He knew that the problem was his, and he was determined to do something about it.

THERE'S NOTHING WRONG WITH POWER

Paul did not like himself. He didn't feel that he had any power. He couldn't make decisions or take action unless he knew it was approved and recommended by someone else. The few eruptions of anger he had experienced made him feel powerful in the moment, but he hated the results of his aggression.

Paul was kneeling on a cushioned mat, looking at the dark blue pillow in front of him as if it held some hidden mystery that frightened and fascinated him. His body was rigid with the restraint and tension that had prevented him from taking initiative all his life.

With fists clenched, he raised his arms straight over his head and came down hard on the pillow. He was using the anger release technique I call the "power position," as described in chapter 12. I had given him some phrases to use, but he chose to remain silent. I encouraged him to hit the pillow again. He was starting to shake a little now, and I knew some of his pent-up emotions were breaking through.

Thunk! A pause, with breath sucked between clenched teeth. And then, *thunk! thunk! thunk!* with more energy and force this time. Paul was starting to sob now, but he wasn't fully letting go yet. A few tears fell.

"Can you feel your strength?" I asked.

"Yes," he whispered, "but it's scary."

"You aren't hurting anyone here, Paul. You're breaking out of the fear and self-hatred that have kept you locked away from those you love. Your anger is your ally, your strength. Get angry at the feeling of being stuck and cut off from others. Get angry at the fear that keeps you from taking initiative and making decisions. It's time for you to help yourself."

This time his blows to the pillow were much stronger than before. Then, reaching a point of exhaustion, he stopped. He started to sob, and I could tell he was fighting it. I encouraged him to relax and let the feelings come out, but he sucked them back as soon as he could.

When I suggested that he give the pillow another shot or two, he replied with a deep breath, "That's enough for now. It's amazing I was even able to feel that much."

Back in his chair, facing the empty chair across from him where he was picturing his father, Paul was different. He told his father that he was giving him back his passivity and rigid control over his emotions. He made the decision to give up his father as a role model, once and for all. I could tell he meant what he was saying. His passive father had never done what he was doing. He was leaving behind his primary male role model. The very act of going through these exercises was a tremendous break with his past programming and what he had been taught that a "man is supposed to be."

Paul still had a lot of work to do in changing a lifetime of behavior patterns in relationships. But he had done the groundwork of releasing his past and claiming his power. He was able to tell his son, face to face, how much he loved him and how sorry he was for being such a non-participant in his life. In couples counseling, he began the process of healing his marriage. He had broken through the emotional barriers closing him off from his family.

YOU MAKE THE DECISION AND I'LL SHOOT IT DOWN

"Where do you want to eat tonight, Honey?" It seems like an innocent enough question.

"Oh, I don't know, why don't you decide?"

"Okay. I've been thinking about Mexican food all day. Let's try that new restaurant out by the mall."

The first shot is about to be fired. "No, I don't think I want all that greasy food in my stomach. The last time I ate Mexican food I tasted it for hours afterward." Gotcha.

Slightly wounded but willing to push onward, Keith makes another suggestion. "Well, there's always Cassaway's downtown. We could get one of their spinach salads."

Unaware of what she's doing, Jill takes a bead on Keith's new suggestion. She has it in her sights, and, "I'm tired of Cassaway's. Besides downtown is depressing now that all those businesses have closed." Another direct hit.

Wounded, and beginning to consider a counter-offensive, Keith is not really conscious of what is going on. "Well, if we don't go downtown and patronize their restaurants, we are just adding to the problem you're complaining about." Angry, but not sure why, Keith is losing his appetite.

"I'm not complaining. I was just making an observation." ("Who, me? I didn't fire that shot!") Jill is covering herself well.

Unwilling to be an open target again, Keith takes a new tactic. "Well, I'm going to Mario's for lasagna. If you want to come along, that's fine. I'm tired of arguing." Finally someone is taking some action.

In the above example, Jill is being passive-aggressive, which requires that she take no direct action but is free to indirectly attack Keith for the action he takes or proposes to take. If Keith had continued with his counter-offensive, both would have been caught up in a destructive battle in which neither knew what was really going on. The resolution occurred because action was taken. The opposite of passive is active, not aggressive.

Keith's action was a good example of anger expressed in a healthy manner. He decided not to counter-attack, even though he was getting angry. To be aggressive (or passive-aggressive) would have been an unhealthy expression of anger.

No one can be totally passive on a continual basis. The activity of emotion, particularly anger, has to go somewhere. Many people are passive-aggressive and have no idea of what they're doing. When we are passive-aggressive, we are being dishonest with others and ourselves.

Anger does not have to result in aggression of any kind. It can be channeled into appropriate healthy action. This is the solution to passivity.

AFFIRMATIONS

- *My emotions are who I am.*
- *I accept my emotions and myself.*
- *When I have strong emotions, I take healthy action.*
- *The power I need to make my life work comes from inside me.*
- *My feelings are an essential part of my personal power.*
- *I now make decisions naturally and easily.*
- *Taking initiative is a natural and spontaneous action for me.*

5

Rage: Anger's Nasty Cousin

A small but fiery woman, Cora had a way of letting you know that she meant what she said. She had not made much progress in dealing with her depression, and she was almost constantly angry. The standard anger release exercises I had used with her just hadn't worked. She was just as angry after doing anger work as she had been before starting. I felt stumped.

The only thing that let me know we might be getting somewhere was that she kept coming back to her sessions. I wasn't prepared for what she was about to say.

"I just feel like if I could hold my gun right up to his head and pull the trigger, it would be better than sex." I knew she meant it. She was talking about a man she had hated for years, and she carried a loaded revolver with her at all times. The man was a brother-in-law involved in a major long-term dispute over her father's estate, and if I allowed her to she would rant and rave about him throughout most of her sessions.

I asked Cora how close she thought she was to taking any kind of violent action. She reassured me that it was only a fantasy and that she had too many good reasons not to go through with it. Her statement about the gun did tell me something about the depth of her rage, however. She had my attention.

This is the kind of patient a therapist really worries about, and with good reason. She was as potentially suicidal as homicidal, and she carried a loaded weapon. After every session, I got a verbal commitment from her not to harm or kill herself or anyone else and to call me any hour, day or night, if things got really bad.

Cora was seeing a psychiatrist concurrently with her sessions with me and was on appropriate medications to help her control her emotions. She also attended a support group called Emotions Anonymous, in which she had established some healthy relationships. I still found her progress to be disturbingly slow and sometimes nonexistent. As a therapist, I was really stretching to come up with a way to help this woman.

HEALING ON HORSEBACK

"That's the happiest I've ever been in my life." Cora's words grabbed my attention like a passing freight train. She was in the process of telling me about her past, and I had not heard much from her about happiness in any part of her life. Now she was describing the ten or so years she had spent riding and training horses and competing in barrel racing.

"It's the only thing I've ever been good at," she said matter-of-factly.

"Why did you quit riding?" I asked.

"Oh, I don't know. Jerry was jealous of all the cowboys. Then Sabrina, my favorite mare, died. I just never got back into it."

It was apparent as I listened to her that she had allowed the best experience of her life to be sabotaged by unhealthy relationships and her inability to deal with grief and loss.

"We've got to get you on a horse!" I couldn't believe I was saying that, but it was the first real breakthrough possibility I had come up with to help Cora out of her rage and depression. She immediately started giving reasons why she could not get a horse, blaming it on her husband and her circumstances.

"If I told you where you could go tomorrow morning and ride a green-broke gelding, would you do it?" I knew a woman who needed her young horse trained but didn't have the funds to pay for it.

"Yes!" This was the first real enthusiasm I had ever seen in Cora. She was ready for some action.

Soon after, Cora started riding Patrick every day. Her sessions with me went to every other week. Her depression lifted, and I saw very little sign of the rage. I didn't really understand the positive transformation until one day she told me what happened.

The day had been one of those that used to drive Cora to sleep for twelve to fourteen hours and wake up raging at her husband and daughter. Instead of staying home in her misery, she went to the stables. Although she always trained with a saddle, on this particular day she got on Patrick bareback.

"I love the smell of horses. Something inside me just relaxes when I get around them, especially Patrick. He seems to know what I'm feeling. He likes to blow on me with his big nostrils, and he actually licks my hand. This time, when I got on him bareback, he looked back at me over his shoulder without moving. The look of plain old horse love just did it to me. I leaned over and put my arms around his big brown neck and nuzzled my face in his mane. Suddenly something inside me let go, and I started crying. I cried for all the years of hurting when there had been no one there for me. I cried for all the times I had hurt others. Then I cried for no particular reason. I just cried and cried. I must have kept that up for a good forty-five minutes. Patrick never moved. I have never known a horse to be so still with someone on their back, especially a young untrained gelding. It was like he knew what was happening, and he was willing to do his part." Cora was smiling with an unfamiliar openness and relaxation. She had found a depth of healing that no amount of therapy could have created.

Cora soon came to counseling on an as-needed basis and then tapered off entirely. She has several horses of her own now and rides regularly.

This story reminds me of a lesson I keep learning over and over. Every one of us is a one-of-a-kind individual. Methods and techniques are great, and every therapist needs to have plenty of them. There are times, however, when nothing seems to work and we each just have to figure out what works best for us and do it, like Cora did. She got on the back of a big friendly horse that had just what she needed—a quiet stillness and lots of unconditional love.

LETTING RAGE OUT OF THE CAGE

Rage is what gives anger a bad name. It's the "nasty cousin" of anger that is a mixture of old unresolved pain, fear and anger. If you collapse the lines in the top diagram of Figure 5.1 between the pain, the fear and the protective layer where anger comes in, mix all that up and leave it there for a long time, it comes out looking more like the bottom diagram in Figure 5.1. In this diagram you can see that pain, fear and anger are all mixed up together with rage. It's like the old

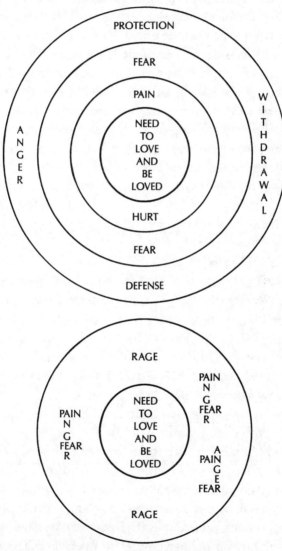

Figure 5.1. Anger into Rage

vegetables that were left too long in the refrigerator. It looks bad, smells bad and in some cases is poisonous.

Rage causes problems when it is left inside, and it causes problems when it is released. Rage is an emotional illness that can lead to serious depression, abusive behavior and even suicidal and homicidal tendencies. It cannot be ignored. It is often a matter of life and death.

Cora hated her rage. This made it stronger. She also hated some other people, which made her rage at herself because she felt guilty for hating anyone. This is why the standard rage-release exercises didn't work for her. The more she raged, the more she raged at herself, keeping her stuck. Patrick the horse gave her just what she needed—to grieve in the presence of total acceptance.

Some people, however, need to get mad—really mad.

RAGE FROM BOUNDARY VIOLATIONS

A crime that horrifies each of us is incest or sexual molestation of any kind. As a therapist, I am amazed at how often my clients are victims of some kind of sexual abuse. In my work with these individuals, I have often found anger work to be an important component in their healing process.

When Troy's father had first started molesting him, he didn't know how to respond. He knew he didn't like it, but he also knew he was supposed to do what his father wanted him to do. The situation was further complicated by the fact that he wanted his father's attention. It wasn't until years later in therapy that Troy realized fathers are not supposed to do that to their sons.

He had been raging for several years and didn't know why. He had lost many jobs and destroyed two marriages with his rage. He had never made a connection between his problems and what his father had done to him. In the therapeutic process, he started putting the pieces together and realized exactly why he had always been so angry.

As the awareness of the abuse and how wrong it was began to dawn on him, his rage finally had a legitimate reason for being there. It took no coaxing to get Troy to let go in the anger release work. His rage burst out of its cage with such energy and exertion that it took him quite a while to recover after each session. The crying started after about two or three good rage releases.

The anger work took Troy straight into the heart of the pain he had been carrying so many years. Until he got past his rage, however, he could not get near the vulnerable little boy who had been cringing inside in fear and shame. His healthy expression of anger showed his inner child that what happened was wrong and that it wasn't his fault. At last he was able to stand up for himself, without shame and without bringing harm to anyone. He claimed his power over his body and his right to be treated with respect.

When a child's tender, sensitive body is violated, particularly by a parent or primary caregiver, the emotional wound inflicted is deep. Recovery is involved and complex, and it cannot be rushed. Rage and anger work may be a necessary part of the process, and it may not be indicated at all. It can in some cases facilitate a major breakthrough which would otherwise have taken months or even years of less intensive therapy. Regardless of its significance in facilitating movement, rage and anger work is at the most only a part of the overall therapeutic process. In Troy's case, it was the beginning of a long, involved recovery from childhood trauma.

After his initial emotional release work, Troy was overcome with guilt and shame for a while. I had seen this happen many times before. The intensity of his rage and hatred for his father was more than he could live with at that time, and he didn't want to face the truth of what had happened. He questioned the validity of his memories, which gave him a chance to keep his father "good" in his mind. Then he retreated into a familiar emotional position of self-loathing and guilt. He was miserable, but he was familiar with this particular kind of misery.

Familiar misery is only comfortable for a short period of time if the person has known something better. Troy had a taste of the empowerment of claiming his worth and value with all of his physical and emotional strength during anger work, and he liked it.

Too smart to stay stuck in his familiar misery for the rest of his life, Troy did some more anger work after a few days. Each time he did this, he moved further out of the rage and more into healthy anger and empowerment. His statements while hitting the pillow changed from "Stop it!" and "Get off me!" to "It was wrong!" and finally, "I'm a good person!" and "My body is good." When I see sexual abuse victims striking out with all their physical and emotional strength while making positive statements about themselves, I know significant progress is being made. What starts as rage and hatred transforms into love of self and enforcement of appropriate emotional boundaries for self-protection.

WHEN RAGE BECOMES ADDICTIVE

The powerful rush of adrenaline that often accompanies anger feels good. It actually gives a person greater physical strength temporarily while the adrenaline is being released (as with Joyce and the Chevy in chapter 2). After the release of anger, there is often a sense of euphoria and general well-being. If there has been a significant physical exertion during the expression of anger, there may also be endorphins released into the bloodstream, creating an even greater feeling of pleasure. All of this adds up to one point: We can get addicted to explosive releases of anger and rage. It feels bad to store up feelings. We get tense, irritable and uneasy. We may even develop physical pain from the tension, and possibly develop stress-related illnesses. The relief from tension experienced during aggressive behavior actually creates good feelings on a physical level, although we may be in great pain emotionally. That's the nature of addiction. When pleasant feelings become associated with unhealthy and destructive behavior, we get addicted to that behavior, as in the cases of Joe and Cora.

The diagram of the addictive cycle in Figure 5.2 helps to illustrate how the pattern of suppression and explosion develops. The cycle begins when our needs for love, nurturance, support and security go unmet in childhood. This includes experiences of neglect, abandonment, rejection and the many types of direct abuse. Part of being born as a vulnerable child in an imperfect world means having experiences that are painful and frightening. As illustrated in Figure 5.2, one of the ways we protect ourselves from more pain is through the use of anger.

If our parents were not educated about the healthy value of anger, they may have punished or rejected us when we displayed this emotion. If you follow the cycle illustrated in Figure 5.2, you will see how this leads to anger suppression and shame. Unfortunately, we continue to be hurt in various ways, and many of our needs continue to go unmet. This causes a buildup of anger and frustration, leading to a breaking point in a situation we feel is "safe" to release our anger. The problem is that we tend to feel the safest (and the most angry) in our homes with those we love. This is also where we tend to find the "last straw" that sends us "over the edge."

That's when the explosion occurs, followed by the rush of power and energy. At this point in the cycle, we may be

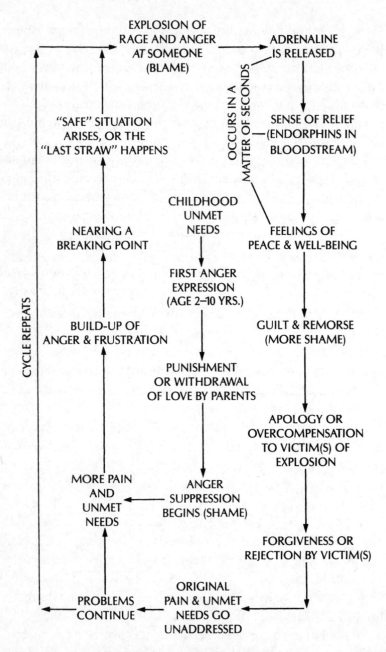

Figure 5.2. Addictive Cycle

verbally, emotionally or physically abusive. This usually leads to an apology or an attempt to "make it up to" the person or persons we have hurt. Some people don't do this part; they just retreat into tremendous shame and guilt and don't say a word about what has happened. Some powerful denial and blocking can occur at this point if the person is incapable of processing what has actually happened.

When apology or compensation does occur, the victim(s) may or may not forgive the abuser. It really does not matter. If the shame goes unhealed, the forgiveness will not be accepted. What matters is whether or not the person in the addictive cycle takes responsibility in the present, and takes care of unfinished business from the past. If they do, they've broken the cycle. If not, they will repeat the cycle and there will be more pain and suffering for all concerned. The following chapters are designed to provide as many healthy ways as possible to break this cycle of rage and anger addiction.

_____

AFFIRMATIONS

- *The best thing I can do for the world is to take care of myself.*
- *My emotions are my responsibility.*
- *Expressing my feelings is as important for my health as eating, sleeping and breathing.*

_____

6

Becoming Intimate with Anger

Have you ever been afraid of really loving someone? Have you been afraid of letting someone
really love you? Most of us have known this
fear. To love and to be loved is what we want more than anything, so why would we be so afraid of having the deep, intimate experience of loving and being loved?

Why is it that domestic violence is considered by police to
be the most dangerous situation they can walk into? Why do
we feel the most fear and anger with those we love the most?
These are important questions. Let's consider some possible
answers.

As adults, we fall in love. This experience of loving at some
point reminds us of how we were hurt in past experiences of

loving. Of course, we are afraid of being hurt, no matter how big, strong or healthy we may happen to be. So we try to protect ourselves. This is human nature.

It follows that the more we love, the more potential we have to be hurt, afraid and angry. Fortunately the love can grow and mature in such a way that the pain and fear are minimized and we no longer need anger for protection from those we love. This happens as our skill, strength, knowledge and awareness expand, allowing the more vulnerable inner core of love to grow and expand into the world around us. You can imagine this by picturing the walls of protection, fear and pain breaking down, allowing the inner circle of love in Figure 6.1 to expand and blend with the outer circle of skill, strength, knowledge and awareness. So how does this happen in real life?

Figure 6.1. Outer Circle

THE FIRST STEP TO TRUE INTIMACY

The first step to true intimacy is to know, understand and become intimate with yourself. Your self is what you bring into a relationship. If you don't know this self or you feel ashamed of some part of it, you will not be able or willing to share those aspects with your loved one. If there are wounds that have not healed, you will automatically hide and protect those wounded parts. You will not offer yourself fully to another, as is required for true intimacy, unless you feel good about the self you are offering.

This simply means that each of us must make a journey into ourselves to learn about our own defense mechanisms, to manage our fear and to heal our pain. Only then can we reach the healing core of love that is the heart of who we are. Only then will we be willing to allow someone else to really know and love us for all that we are.

In Figure 6.1 you'll notice a new ring has been added to the concentric circles. We face the world with our knowledge, skill, strength and awareness.

The first part of ourselves we offer to others is what we consider to be our best self. We smile, shake hands or hug, and act as if everything is just fine, whether it is or not. We show our social skills, demonstrate our knowledge and awareness in our conversation and try to give the impression of being a healthy, together person. This is the realm in which we operate at work or with people we don't know very well. This is the part of ourselves we use to "make a good impression" on someone we like. This may even be all we really know of ourselves.

In school and throughout our lives, we have gained knowledge, skill, strength and awareness about the world around us. Most of us never had a course on how to experience, understand and express our emotions, although it would have been a good idea. No one told us that our anger was okay or that it is normal to feel hurt and afraid. It's time now to begin to learn inner strength, self-knowledge, self-awareness and skills for dealing with our emotions. In other words, it's time to learn to accept, experience and express all of our emotions in healthy ways, regardless of what they may be.

WHAT ARE YOUR FAVORITE DEFENSES?

As indicated in the diagrams of concentric circles, we tend to protect and defend ourselves by withdrawing, getting angry or some combination of the two. A good first step to take on the journey within is to identify your own defense mechanisms.

Maybe you never get angry. On the other hand, you may feel angry all the time. Do you know how to take a break in a relationship to give yourself time to think and calm down? Are you always pulling away until you explode in anger? Don't judge yourself at this point, just figure out how you protect yourself.

Next ask yourself what you are afraid of when you are using these defense methods. We are usually afraid of being hurt, either through direct abuse or some form of rejection or abandonment. Notice that the two basic types of protection correspond to the two basic types of fear. We protect ourselves through anger and withdrawal, and we are afraid of being abused (unhealthy expressions of anger directed at us) or rejected (withdrawal of love).

Next comes the hardest part. Facing your pain and experiencing it completely to a point of resolution is one of the most frightening and difficult parts of becoming intimate with yourself. Your pain falls into the same two basic categories as your fear and your defenses. Your deepest pain came when you were abused, abandoned or both.

BREAKING THROUGH
THE WALLS OF FEAR

Expressing anger in healthy, safe ways provides the strength needed to break through the walls of fear and resolve the pain, allowing the free, healthy expression of love.

Remember Paul, the man who couldn't connect with his wife and son? His story provides an excellent example of anger as an important part of breaking through the walls of fear, allowing more open expression of other emotions in intimate family relationships. After his anger work and parental release, Paul was able to connect meaningfully with his son and begin a new dimension of intimacy in his marriage.

James's journey within was a much more difficult one. At age thirty-seven, he had never been married and had only been romantically involved with one woman for a very short period of time. When I first saw him he was completely isolated from relationships of any kind. James was employed as a computer programmer. His work was his only involvement with the world around him. It would be accurate to say that he had absolutely no intimacy in his life at all.

Both of James's parents were dead, and he only communicated with one of his sisters. His father had been a rageaholic who had verbally abused everyone in the family. James had been very close to his mother, who took it upon herself to protect him from his father's abuse.

"I've always been afraid. I don't remember a time when I wasn't afraid." James had a blank look on his face as he talked. He was a nice-looking man, slim and well dressed.

"I just remember feeling like I was hiding behind my mother from my dad the whole time I was growing up. He was always yelling about something. Mom has always been my best friend. I don't know what I would have done without her." James started to cry at this point, and I could tell how much grief he had yet to face over his mother's death.

For weeks James showed only minimum progress in therapy. While doing family-of-origin work one afternoon, he agreed to try some anger work. He was reluctant, stating, "I hate anger. I'm afraid I'll be just like him." He was referring, of course, to his father. He was paralyzed by his fear, and yet the very emotion that could help him claim his power was detestable to him.

I told him to imagine himself as someone who had the power and ability to overcome his fears and accomplish his goals for intimacy and communication. I talked him through several visualizations, but after only a few minutes I could tell he wasn't engaged in the activity.

"What are you feeling?" I asked.

"I'm afraid," he replied. The exercise had taken him deeper into his fear, and he wasn't able to break through.

James had no feeling of power or control in his life. His fear controlled him. He couldn't imagine his way out. He was paralyzed. His determination to be the opposite of his father added to his paralysis. He had to get angry to break free from his internal prison.

The first sign that he was getting ready came when he started to smile and laugh more. The more he enjoyed his life, the more likely he was to claim his power to get well and overcome his fear. I asked if he was ready to take some action on his own behalf.

"I'm ready to do something! I'm sick of being scared all the time. Also, I've met someone I would like to get closer to." He was showing more emotional energy and interest in intimacy than he had before.

I then suggested he go inside himself, find that scared little boy and offer him some of the strength he was feeling. I guided him through a visualization designed to allow him to embrace his frightened inner child, offering self-nurturing to replace the lost love and support of his mother. He connected well with the activity and felt good about the session. I had no idea what was coming next.

James finally got angry. He went into a rage that lasted a week.

He didn't hurt anyone, but he griped, cursed and complained at anyone who was anything less than perfect. On a Friday afternoon at the end of a long day, he spewed complaints about the imperfections of the world. He had some legitimate concerns, but I gradually talked him down and he became quiet. No sooner did he calm down than he began to sob deeply.

As a therapist, I have witnessed a lot of crying. I had never seen anything like I saw James go through that day. He cried nonstop for over an hour. Deep, body-shaking sobs gripped and shook him. I didn't know anyone could cry that deeply for that long. Afterward, he was exhausted for a couple of days.

Then, slowly, a new James began to emerge. He had broken through the wall of fear, grieved the pain and reconnected with his love. Direct anger release work was ineffective with him, as it only took him closer to his fear of becoming his father. When his anger did come out, he didn't like it.

He used his skill, strength and knowledge to make the journey into himself. Now he was ready to start learning how to risk and reach out in relationships with others. His true freedom emerged as he began taking effective action toward his goals.

James called a couple of years later and reported that he was happily married with two children.

NO ANGER, NO
BOUNDARIES, NO INTIMACY

Anger is an important part of a healthy boundary system. It provides the firm and powerful feeling needed to create an experience of safety and comfort within. Without skills for expressing anger in healthy ways, effective boundaries are impossible. Without effective boundaries and the accompanying feeling of security, vulnerability is too frightening and intimacy is out of the question.

When expressed in healthy ways, anger may not even look like anger. If anger were always aggressive, as we often expect, it would not be at all helpful in creating intimacy. Here are some points to consider about anger, when it is expressed in healthy ways:

- Healthy, current anger involves no blame or accusing.
- When expressed in appropriate ways, anger is nothing more than focused and directed emotional energy.
- When focused and directed, emotional energy gives emphasis, strength and clarity to expression.
- Healthy anger does not attack or hurt anyone.
- Healthy anger is an expression of love.
- As an expression of love, healthy anger gives strength to personal boundaries.
- Without the empowerment of healthy anger, boundaries are too soft, and in some cases nonexistent.
- When expressed appropriately, anger gives us the security we need to risk the vulnerability of true intimacy.

BUILDING HEALTHY BOUNDARIES

When we are clear and focused within ourselves, boundaries automatically emerge and begin to move into place. In other words, boundaries are to some extent established subconsciously, as a result of mature self-love. (This will be explored further in chapter 15.) Another dimension of boundaries requires our consciously focused attention and effort. We will look at these two levels in terms of our commitment to ourselves and to our relationships.

In Figure 6.2 you will see a graphic representation of commitment priorities in relationships, which seem to be necessary for stability, clarity and intimacy. The inner circle represents commitment to self; the next ring represents the role we play in the relationship; and the outer ring represents our commitment to the relationship itself. You will notice there is no mention of commitment to the other person—that's their job.

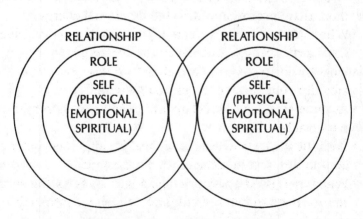

Figure 6.2. Commitment Priorities

1. Commitment to Self

Our first priority in a relationship with another is our commitment to ourselves. This is not selfish; it's merely practical.

Your best friend has just been in a car wreck and needs your help. You want to get there as fast as you can, but it's a few miles away and your car's gas tank is on empty. Do you ignore this and zoom off to the rescue? Of course not. You get some gas before making the trip. By the same token, we each need to take care of our own needs to some extent before we go about trying to give to others.

It's really very simple. You are the center of your universe. Everything you see, hear, feel and experience goes out in concentric spheres from your point of awareness there in the center of your world. This is not some weird idea; it's pure rational fact.

Yourself, your universe as you perceive it, is what you carry into any relationship you enter. All of your cumulative life experience, your "family baggage," your emotional and behavioral patterns are part of what you bring.

You are responsible for what you contribute to the relationship. The other person is responsible for his or her own contribution. This means simply that you have the job of maintaining your own physical, mental, emotional and spiritual health. That way you bring a healthy person into the relationship, which is a true gift to your partner.

Let's look at some of the inner dimensions to your relationship with yourself. Figure 6.3 gives some ideas for what our priorities within ourselves might be. The physical self is closer to the surface and more observable than any of the other aspects. We share our thoughts and ideas more easily and readily than we do our emotions, so the mental self would be next.

Our emotional self goes very deep into our being, and much of it is subconscious. Our emotions are more private than

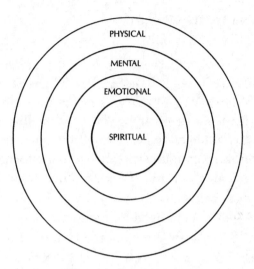

Figure 6.3. Your Self

many of our thoughts, so we may see them as closer to the core of our being. Within the emotional self we find the anger, fear, pain and love that was depicted in earlier diagrams.

You might say that the spiritual self or the spiritual aspects of love are at the heart of who we are. Our spiritual feelings, experiences and beliefs are deeper and more private than perhaps any other aspect of who we are. The spiritual dimension naturally expands to include the emotional, mental and physical self as focus and development occur at this deepest level of relationship.

This is our first work in creating a healthy relationship with another. It takes two basically healthy, growing people to make a healthy relationship.

2. Commitment to Role

We are each responsible for the role we play in our relationships. It is a mistake to make our role totally dependent on the behavior of the other. For example, "I would be a better husband if she would only . . ." The truth is that you are responsible for the kind of husband or wife you are, no matter what your spouse may or may not do. Your role is your creation and responsibility.

By taking charge of defining your role as husband, wife, lover, friend, mother, father, son, daughter, boss or employee, you are empowering yourself in the relationship and removing yourself from the victim position. The tricky part about this is that our basic training for these roles was in our family of origin and early childhood experience. This is one of the reasons that family-of-origin work is so important as a part of any couples or relationship counseling process.

Here are some ideas to help you clarify and take charge of the roles you play in your significant relationships:

1. Write down what you learned about the roles of wife and mother from your mother, and husband and father roles from your father. (Add any other roles you are interested in exploring, the source being your primary role model in that area.) This will give you an idea of your subconscious mind-set regarding these roles.
2. Write new definitions of these roles for yourself, using your own knowledge and goals as guidelines.
3. Next write about all the reasons you feel you cannot fulfill the ideal roles you have defined for yourself. Consider these to be some of your barriers to intimacy, and use the skills you gain in this book to overcome them.
4. Create affirmations in first-person, present tense to form new attitudes and beliefs about yourself and your ability to fulfill your own ideal role in your relationships. Use your negative and self-limiting beliefs from 3. above as a springboard for arriving at these new beliefs.

5. Plan specific behaviors that will help you to actualize your ideal role fulfillment.

This is a further extension of what you offer in your relationship. Your commitment is to bring into the relationship a healthy, growing individual who is further committed to being the best spouse, lover, parent or friend possible. All of this happens before even considering the influence of the other person.

3. Commitment to the Relationship

This is where we really begin to give consideration to the thoughts, feelings and needs of the other person. You will notice in Figure 6.2 that the outer ring marked "relationship" is the only part of the two circles that overlap. This is to indicate we each have individual responsibility for ourselves and our roles, and we share mutual responsibility for our relationships. When our commitment follows this priority, we bring a healthy person with well-defined functional roles into the relationship. Therefore, our contribution to the relationship is the best we have to offer, and we are responsible for our contribution.

There is a tremendous amount of material that could be covered under the heading of boundaries, and this covers only a small part of that subject matter. In chapter 16, "A Picture of Emotional Wellness," boundaries will be explored further, particularly in the discussion of Figure 16.4. The point here is that emotional, mental, physical and spiritual health automatically create a powerful basis for functional boundaries. In making your health your responsibility and your first priority of commitment in your relationship, you are taking an important step toward creating healthy boundaries.

With these steps taken, we are ready to invest all that we choose in our relationship, making healthy intimacy a very real possibility.

Imagine your relationship as a third entity in your marriage, friendship, etc. Together with your partner, invite a loving spirit (God, your higher power or the loving deity of your choice) into the relationship. Decide that your behavior toward each other is always going to be governed as if you were in the presence of a divine, loving being. Bring only the best of yourself to this sacred space of your relationship, and when bringing other aspects than your best, do so with the utmost respect and sensitivity. Treat your partner as an honored guest at all times, and together invite the honored guest of a loving spiritual presence into your relationship. This can become an ongoing meditation and/or prayer for the health and success of any relationship.

Without at some point claiming our anger and its sense of empowerment, we do not feel the strength and courage necessary to risk true intimacy, sharing our deepest feelings, thoughts and dreams. Without healthy anger, we certainly will not have healthy boundaries.

THE WONDERS OF TRUE INTIMACY

There is perhaps no deeper feeling of safety than the kind we knew with our mothers while in the warm, peaceful silence of the womb. Since the moment of birth, when we were separated physically from that warm security, we have been constantly seeking some way to re-create that experience of peaceful bliss with feelings of comfort and safety. This is one of the reasons that we want to be intimate as adults, no matter how frightening or unfamiliar it may feel. To be wrapped in the love of the one we trust, physically and emotionally open to giving and receiving, is the closest we come to re-creating that total bliss of the first few months of life.

To many the term "intimacy" means sexual involvement. One of the reasons sexual contact is so important is that it sometimes creates many of the same feelings of physical warmth that we felt in the womb. As we all know, however, sexual involvement without commitment and a feeling of safety leads to the opposite of comfort and security. This is why we need our priorities of commitment intact and need to have healthy boundaries before risking sexual or other types of intimate involvement.

True healthy intimacy does not come easily. The journey may be long and challenging with many pitfalls. We keep trying because it offers one of the highest levels of human experience possible. There is a miraculous healing expansion of love that spontaneously occurs when we open our hearts to one another. The rewards of intimacy are so great and enticing that we sometimes get them mixed up with a mystical or spiritual experience. We can even get caught up in a process of idolizing our loved one, expecting them to solve all our problems and make our lives forever wonderful. This leads to the heartbreak of codependency and love addiction, and ultimately to disillusionment and isolation.

The wonders of true intimacy with another can only be experienced when we have established a deep level of intimacy with ourselves, claiming and expressing all of our emotions openly and honestly.

AFFIRMATIONS

- *I am developing skills for maintaining my safety while being vulnerable in relationships.*
- *The more I care for myself, the more I have to offer to others.*
- *Intimacy begins with the journey into myself.*
- *The journey into myself is as vast and unlimited as the journey into the world around me.*
- *The more I trust myself, the more I can trust those around me.*
- *The more intimately I know myself, the more intimate I can be with others.*

7

Anger Among
Our Children

Every one of us began this life mentally, emotionally, physically and vertically challenged. We had needs, feelings and desires yet could only wave our arms and legs and wail to express ourselves. We couldn't walk or manipulate objects to approach what we liked, escape what we feared or fend for ourselves. People talked about us in our presence as if we weren't there. At times we were handled and moved from place to place like a piece of luggage. There was nothing we could do about any of this.

In some cases, we were struck cruelly, and touched in our most vulnerable places. At times we were left alone, abandoned and neglected. Some of us were never acknowledged as unique individual beings with a heart and mind of our own. When this happened we felt lost, alone and confused. Some of us even wondered if our birth was a mistake, and if it was really okay for us to be here.

We were children.

Every human child experiences some version of the above treatment, regardless of how loving, healthy, educated or wonderful our parents may have been. Childhood by its very nature includes some version of pain from the unavoidable neglect and abuse of being a vulnerable, precious, powerful and fragile being in a world that is at times cold, blind, harsh and cruel.

This alone is enough to make children good and angry, but it doesn't stop there. Most schools provide no comprehensive and systematically applied educational programs for children on:

- Emotions and how to understand, manage and deal with them
- Basic social skills necessary for survival and building friendships at school, at play and later in the work world
- The basics of building, strengthening and maintaining healthy and intimate love relationships
- Healthy family communication and parenting skills
- Sexuality and what it means to be a healthy sexual being
- Discovering a unique purpose in life and developing a plan for its fulfillment

Perhaps more importantly, most formal education programs provide little comprehensive and systematically applied educational programs for parents on how to provide for these needs in their children.

THE VICIOUSNESS OF NEGLECT

Neglect can seem so benign. The woman laughing on the telephone with her friend doesn't seem vicious. The man sitting at his desk or in a meeting doesn't look vicious. Yet when we see the hollow, empty look slowly growing in the eyes of the son or daughter who feels ignored, we begin to understand the damage that is done by neglect.

In the cases of school violence in recent U.S. history, we have learned some things about the children who perpetrated the violence and angry acts on their classmates and teachers. They were not talking openly to their parents. Like the boys in the classic novel *The Lord of the Flies* (Golding 1959), these children were left to their own devices and unmonitored by loving, interested and concerned adults.

This kind of neglect is all too common, and we need to be aware of it if we are to help children. The most insidious and challenging thing about neglect is that the neglectful parent may actually appear to be hardworking, loving and concerned.

All of the "school shooters" who made the news in the United States in the first part of the twenty-first century can be seen as "outcasts" and "misfits" in their peer relationships. We are learning that we can't afford to cast anyone out anymore. We are learning that we have to find a place for children to fit in, however unique, different or limited they may be.

We have learned the hard way that if we neglect these lost and confused children, they may temporarily turn into little monsters and start killing everyone in sight.

Suicide has been recognized as a leading cause of death among adolescents (American Foundation for Suicide Prevention 1996, *www.afsp.org*). Because it usually happens one tragic death at a time, suicide does not create the sensationalism that makes world news headlines like school violence has. Yet according to one research group, another young person commits suicide every hour and forty-five minutes (*www.suicide.com* 2001).

The neglected child seems to be speaking through this horrifying outbreak of violence, saying, "We can't stand it anymore! What will it take for you to recognize us and see how mixed up we are? We've been killing ourselves for years, and you haven't seemed to notice. We've been forming gangs and doing drugs and murdering each other in the streets, and yet our problems are not being addressed. Now that we are murdering each other in your upper-middle-class schools— now maybe you will recognize that we are in trouble and do something to help us!"

We noticed. And fortunately a lot of wise and good people responded, and there are more violence prevention programs in schools today than ever before.

But the neglect continues. Parents are still human beings, and many parents are still uneducated and unaware of their children's basic emotional needs. So what will be next? What will be the next desperate cry of the neglected child? Will we hear it in time? We have to pay very close attention if we are to solve the problem of neglect. The antidote for neglect is loving attention. And as we pay attention enough to see what's going on, we must educate ourselves on what to do about it.

IT'S NEVER ABOUT THE CHILD

A savvy author and horse trainer named Wyatt Webb has a pat response when someone tells him about a problem with a horse. He says, "It's not about the horse," which is also the title of his book (Webb 2002).

When families bring their children to me for therapy, I sometimes feel like saying, "It's not about the child," but that would neither be wise nor kind. The fact is that my thirty-plus years of experience as a professional tell me that when a child is having a problem, the solution is almost always in the system of which the child is a part. With some rare exceptions, I will not see a child for therapy unless the parents are also willing to be involved. It's not that the child has no problems; it's that the child does not have the solution. The healing must occur in the system—family, school or cultural.

In general it is safe to say that solving the problem of anger among our children is our responsibility as adults. Labeling, diagnosing and medicating children as a solution can do much more harm than good, and does nothing to address the origin of the difficulty. Children are innocent victims of the systems into which they are born. You and I as adults are operating those systems, and we must do everything in our power to better care for and prepare our children for the world they are growing into.

CHILDREN LIVE OUT THEIR PARENTS' UNTOLD STORIES

Bruce had always been close to his mother. From all appearances, their family was happy and healthy. His parents' marriage was okay, and he and his sister were nice kids. Bruce was absolutely brilliant. He made excellent grades in school, with very little effort. The same was true for his sister.

I was first consulted because of Bruce's panic attacks. For no apparent reason, he would occasionally begin to tremble and curl up in a little ball, whimpering softly. He was not generally afraid, and though not known to be an athlete or fighter, he had never shied away from a challenge or new situation.

He couldn't tell me what caused his panic. As bright as this handsome, fit fifteen-year-old was, he had no clue as to what was causing these embarrassing and frightening attacks. I saw him sometimes individually, but focused the therapy mostly on his entire family.

Bruce's parents seemed to be healthy, moderately happy people. Dad was quiet, passive and relaxed. Mom, whose name was Margaret, was more expressive, although she also appeared content, calm and pleasant on the surface. Soon, however, a deeper picture began to emerge. As Margaret began to tell her story, it became apparent that she needed some individual sessions.

In her private sessions, Margaret talked openly about her background, and expressed that she was ready to do some emotional healing of her own. Over the next few months, her story began to unfold. Though her childhood was relatively normal in some ways, her parents' particular choice of discipline was extreme. If she did something that they felt was wrong, which sometimes amounted to nothing more than crying when they wanted her to stop, they would lock her in the cellar.

As far as she could remember, it seemed to Margaret that this happened hundreds of times throughout her childhood until she was around eleven or twelve. She never told her friends about this, because at first she thought it was normal. Later she kept it to herself because she was ashamed. The terror she felt in the darkness of the cellar was so deeply buried in her subconscious mind that she couldn't really have talked about it if she wanted to.

"I just learned to go on about my business as if nothing had happened. I didn't realize how wrong their behavior was until I became an adult and read a book about child abuse. I still didn't talk about it. I didn't know how." Margaret reported all of this with a pleasant smile on her face. She was still going on as if nothing had happened.

"As long as I was okay and didn't have any problems, they would leave me alone and wouldn't put me down there. So I just learned to be okay no matter what." Margaret had told her husband about the cellar experiences in her childhood, but other than him, I was the only person privy to her story.

"It's funny," Margaret commented toward the end of one of her sessions, "sometimes when I see Bruce in one of his panic attacks, he looks like I felt and probably appeared in that cellar. I used to be so scared down there. I would just curl up and hold my knees and rock for hours until they came to get me. I was always so glad to see my parents, and they were so nice to me. I always thought I must have done something wrong to deserve the punishment."

I worked with this family on and off for several years, during which time Margaret made significant progress. Bruce, however, seemed disconnected from therapy. His panic attacks eventually started to subside—and that's when the anger began.

"I just get so angry I feel like I could kill someone. I would never hurt a soul, so why do I have these thoughts and feelings?" Bruce was starting to open up to me, and coming in more frequently for individual sessions. "My whole body just fills up with rage, and I have no idea where it's coming from."

Bruce had strange, bizarre and complex dreams. That was one way his emotions were trying to work their way out through his system. The dreams were often violent, but also contained themes of terror and entrapment.

When interviews with Bruce and his parents revealed no major traumatic events in his past, it began to dawn on me that he had been subconsciously picking up his mother's unresolved trauma. I asked him how he felt about his mother.

"I would do anything for her. She has always been there for me. She's the best mother in the world." Bruce was crying as he talked. I waited a few minutes and asked, "What are the tears saying?" He was quiet a little while longer, then, "She seems real scared sometimes, but I think I'm the only one who notices. Sometimes she holds me so tight it seems like she's hanging on for dear life. I just wish I could take all of that fear away from her." Apparently he had been doing just that, without fully realizing it.

I thought at this point about how much information can be transferred from parent to child through close physical contact, particularly during emotional trauma. I was strongly considering that Bruce had unconsciously taken on some of his mother's fear and panic—that it had been stored in his body and was now trying to make its way out via the panic attacks and more recently via the anger.

Gradually, as Margaret continued to work through the trauma of her memories, she got in touch with and began to release her anger toward her parents for what they had done to her. A few months later, Bruce's symptoms subsided and then disappeared. His mother's story had been told, and he no longer needed to "tell" it for her.

Carl Jung said, "Children live out the unlived lives of their parents" (Jung 1989). It does not seem so great a stretch to assume that children would also live out their parents' untold stories in an attempt to resolve their unresolved trauma for them.

Communication studies suggest that 93 percent of communication is nonverbal (Mehrabian 1981). Margaret never spoke her stories of being locked in the cellar out loud to her son, but her body language told the stories over and over to him throughout his childhood. Through his dreams, panic attacks and anger eruptions, Bruce was trying to work out his mother's pain, fear and anger for her. His anger seemed to specifically stem from his mother's unexpressed rage toward her parents for what they had done to her. As Margaret's story was told and her emotions released, Bruce's job came to an end.

Could it be that your children are living out your untold stories? Most parents attempt to protect their children by keeping their most painful, traumatic and shameful stories a secret. This just doesn't seem to work. The stories are already being told nonverbally, whether we like it or not. We need to tell our stories verbally, so that our children can understand why they have the dreams and emotions they do, and further, so that they can let them go and resume their lives.

I have also seen children acting out their parents' unexpressed emotions. Children will pick up and carry unclaimed and unexpressed anger, sorrow and fear for their parents, sometimes much to their detriment.

ANGER IN A NEUROLOGICAL TIC

Matthew made funny little noises from time to time, and jerked his head to the side. Sometimes he made a grunting sound in his throat.

A very warm and loving child of seven, Matthew seemed exceptional in many ways, until he showed his symptoms. He had a total of about six different tics when he, his father and his sister first came to my office. The problem was getting worse over time, and it was coming to the attention of his teachers and classmates at school. So far, his grades were not suffering and his social behavior appeared normal.

Matthew's father, David, was angry, and he knew it. He had seen me several times in an effort to deal with his anger and address his marital problems, months before he brought Matthew in. David and his wife had been fighting intensely for over a year. His wife was more explosive than he was, and usually initiated the conflict. But David was becoming increasingly more intense in his defensive reaction. They had avoided any physical violence, but Matthew had witnessed many vicious screaming matches.

This was David's second marriage. His first wife was a

workaholic and an alcoholic, and after fifteen years of marriage, they divorced. They had tried to have children for half of their marriage, before Matthew was born. David quickly became his son's primary caregiver, because of his wife's emotional and physical absence.

David had experienced no problems with his anger during his first marriage, but was becoming more and more angry with his current wife after only two years of being with her. His concern now, however, was his son's tics. The symptoms had only started about eight weeks before the first family session.

Matthew quickly took advantage of the opportunity to play with the toys I provided, and to draw pictures on a flip chart with colored markers.

"Are you worried about your tics, Matthew?" I asked after some casual conversation with his dad and sister.

After a pause, he responded, "A little bit. Sometimes it's kind of embarrassing. The kids at school are starting to make fun of me. But it's okay. I can take it." I could see the struggle in his face as he talked. Several tics erupted in succession over the next few seconds.

"Is there anything you like about your tics, or do you wish they would go away?" I inquired further.

Matthew was quiet for a moment as he continued to work on his picture of his family, and then said in a serious tone, "I need them. It's like I have to do them, and then I feel better." I could tell he was revealing a precious secret.

Through play therapy and Matthew's drawings, I learned fairly soon that he saw himself as his father's protector. It was also clear that he loved his stepmother. The stress he was under when she and his father fought was tremendous. He seemed to place himself in the middle, as if somehow he could absorb the tension and ease their conflict.

David watched in awe as his son's story emerged. He had

no idea how deeply affected Matthew had been by his and his wife's conflict.

"Will you teach me how to do those tics, Matthew?" He looked at me skeptically when I asked this of him. "I just want to understand you better," I continued, "and I figure if I can learn how to do the tics, then I will know a little more about what's going on inside you."

"Okay," he said quietly as he put down his marker and sat on the couch next to his dad.

In a very sweet and cooperative way, as if he were even proud at times, Matthew proceeded to show me every one of his tics. He explained that some of them he couldn't do that well, however, because they just seemed to happen on their own.

"Just do the best you can," I responded. "I would like you to learn how to do them by your choice, so that you can use them when you need to, and control them when you don't really want them to come out. Does that sound good to you?"

"I guess so." Matthew was clearly doubtful about my approach, and seemed a little nervous.

"You can keep your tics as long as you like, by the way. No one is going to take them away from you. I just want you to have choices, so that you don't get embarrassed and made fun of." As I spoke, I saw Matthew's face relaxing. It was clear he didn't want to give up the tics entirely.

David and Matthew came for sessions twice a week after school for about three months. I also met individually with David during that time. He and I agreed that we would try the family therapy and behavioral rehearsal approach to dealing with Matthew's tics before considering medication or a neurological consultation.

"He's getting much better," David reported in his first individual session after the one in which Matthew "taught" me his tics.

"He's still doing it, but only about half as much." David

seemed pleased and encouraged as he spoke. Then his face changed.

"I can't stand the thought that he is carrying this tension because of my wife and me fighting. He's the most important thing in the world to me, and I will do whatever it takes to make sure he's okay. Even if it means divorcing again." David's voice was quiet and determined. He looked down as he spoke.

"We don't have to decide that right now," I said. "Let's keep doing what we're doing, since we're getting results. It is important that the fighting stop though, David, for Matthew's sake and for the sake of your marriage." He was looking at me now, and I knew he was with me in my thinking.

"You're right. I think Matthew needs that as much as he needs the therapy," David said with conviction.

In subsequent sessions, something new started to happen. Matthew's tics continued to subside, and he used the safe environment of family therapy to express his feelings about the conflict between his dad and stepmom.

"I hate it when you fight!" Matthew yelled as he pounded the pillow I had given him. His dad was in the room, watching with a sober look on his face.

"Can I talk to you alone for a minute?" Matthew asked me.

"Sure," I said. David was already on his way toward the door of my office.

In that session and in several following, Matthew invented new forms of anger release that I found quite impressive. They work better for a seven-year-old than they would for an adult, for reasons that will become obvious.

His favorite way to express his anger was by throwing himself bodily into the large overstuffed chair in my office. He didn't hurt himself, and the chair provided a nice soft landing. Sometimes he would do that ten or more times in a row before resting. It was an impressive display of energy, demonstrating just how strong his anger was.

"I feel better," he said, panting. After a few minutes, he added, "They're not fighting as much. I hate it when they fight."

"I know," I said. "They don't like it either, and that's why they're learning how to stop it." The look of calm on Matthew's face was heartwarming to me.

He only needed a few more anger release sessions before the tics were gone entirely. David and his wife were getting marriage counseling and also doing some individual work to address their own issues. This case showed me once again how powerful family therapy is for bringing about resolution of children's emotional issues.

Matthew's tics could be seen as tiny, unconsciously controlled explosions in his physical, neurological system. The anger release gave him larger, more expressive ways to explode, and more opportunity to show and talk about what was going on inside. Once he understood that the tics were his and no one could take them away, and that there were other ways to deal with his stress, he apparently no longer needed them. This approach is based on the theory that every malady or symptom has a story behind it, an emotion or need that is being expressed through the problem.

WHAT CAN WE DO FOR THE CHILDREN?

If we can agree that "It's never about the child," then we have to take responsibility as adults for the systems we create and participate in. We have choices and freedom to affect these systems, whereas our children are helplessly subject to their influence.

So what are the systems of which we are a part, that oppress, control, neglect and, at times, abuse our children?

Here's an overview to consider:

- **Our own internal system**—Countless times, I have helped
parents understand that their issues with their children's
anger could only be resolved when they dealt with their
own issues. Each of us is responsible for doing our own
inner work and self-exploration to ensure that we are not
projecting our "untold stories" or "unlived lives" onto our
children. We have to claim, nurture and care for the beautiful, innocent, creative, playful, wounded and frightened
children within our own souls if we are to nurture and care
for the children around us.

- **Our current family systems**—The most important fact to
remember is that marriage is the foundation of the
family. Excessive focus on children at the expense of, or
as an escape from, the marriage does great harm to the
marriage and the children alike. Parents need to study
and understand the following concepts to provide their
children with the best possible system in which to
thrive and grow:
  - The marriage is the foundation of the family
  - Children live out the untold stories and unlived lives
  of their parents
  - Psychological projection—how parents can sometimes project their own unresolved issues onto their
  children (as reflected in the next two concepts)
  - The concept of the "golden child"—the one who is
  favored and "can do no wrong" in the parents' eyes
  - The concept of the "problem child"—the one who
  always seems to be in trouble, or the cause of problems. This child can become a kind of "dumping
  ground" for the parents' or the entire family's pain,
  fear and anger, and is often the "identified patient"
  when the family seeks help.

- The idea that the best gift a parent can give a child is a healthy parent and a healthy marriage
- **Our extended family systems**—We must understand the impact of relationships with grandparents, aunts, uncles, cousins, etc. These influences can be powerful and lasting, in either a positive or negative way. It is the parents' job to ensure that the extended family system is safe for their children, and the primary authority must stay with the parents, for the benefit of the child.
- **Community systems**—We are responsible for the influence of close friends, schools, church groups and any other collection of people to whom our children have regular exposure. The bottom line here is that parents and responsible adults must do their best to see that these systems are healthy, so that the child can learn, grow and thrive within them.
- **Cultural systems**—Many of us feel like helpless or angry victims of the cultural influences around us. We can and must do everything in our power to help our children deal with the culture of which they are a part. Here are some suggestions:
  - **Stay in touch with your child.** Talk to them about their music, movies and video games. Show an interest in the friends they choose, the clothes and hairstyles they wear. Learn about the culture they are entering, letting them be your guide. Let them teach you about their world so that you can help them with the emotional adjustments they will have to make along the way.
  - **Get involved.** Use school committees, local politics and/or community action processes to express your opinions and exert an influence. Vote. Express your feelings about what's going on. Ask others what they are doing, and what you can do to have a positive influence on cultural changes. Go to *www.schoolsuccessinfo.org* for more ideas.

▪ **Look for positive, uplifting aspects of cultural developments.** Share these insights with your children, so they will learn to seek what's good and what's working rather than be consumed by the prevailing fear, anger and negativity that is programmed by so much of popular media. A couple of great resources for this are *www.wisdommedia.com* and *www.globalideabank.org.*

WHAT DO WE DO ABOUT THE VIOLENT ADOLESCENTS?

Angry children need love. The older and angrier they get, the harder they are to love, and the more frightening they can become. If you have an angry teenager in your home, extended family, your child's school or your community, here are some ideas that may help:

• Do everything in your power to get to know them.
• Find out what they like to do and do it with them. That's a stretch in some cases, but do the best you can. They will notice the effort. Stay true to yourself—if they see you trying to become like them, they'll lose respect for you.
• Ask them to tell you about the things they're interested in. You may have to prove that you're really interested before they will open up, but if you're sincere and persistent, they will start talking.
• Be a steady, loving presence in their lives. You may have to forego some of your other activities, but if you have an adolescent who is possibly moving toward violence or suicide, it's worth it.
• Get in touch with your own healthy anger, so that you have the personal power and confidence to deal with the energy of adolescent anger.

- Work to master humor and love. Find as many ways as possible to have fun with the adolescent and show your love. Make sure that you are pursuing the relationship for them, and not to fulfill some unmet needs from your own past.
- Consult with other adults and parents who are good with teenagers. Watch how they interact with kids and learn from their example.
- Pray. You're going to need all the help you can get, and you need to know you are not alone in your mission to bring love to this unhappy child.

EMBRACING THE OUTCASTS AND MISFITS

This is simply impossible if you have outcasts and misfits in your own subconscious body/mind. So the first order of business here is to make sure you have found, embraced and made a place for the children within you that represent remnants of memories that you have yet to resolve. These are the inner children that symbolize your pain, shame and self-doubt.

Rest assured that the outcast child who you approach in the outer world will not accept your embrace if they see unresolved fear and anger in your eyes or actions.

We know that the outcasts and misfits are the children most likely to become violent, so it only follows that we must pull them into the arms of love and/or acceptance, and find a place where they fit. If our system doesn't have a place where a child fits, there's something wrong with the system, not the child.

Look around you in your family and your community. Do you see the outcasts and misfits? The ones who seem to have no friends, or who only hang out with others like them? Look for the ones who don't act "right," are too this or too that or not enough of the other. Especially look for the ones who are not talking about their feelings, and seem to carry a lot of depression and/or anger.

Genius often hides in such places. If you are wise, healthy and dedicated enough to win an inroad to the heart and mind of one of these "personas non grata," you may discover a hidden treasure. The movie *Good Will Hunting* depicts such a case, where an angry, violent misfit is also a gifted genius. The movie *The Breakfast Club* also shows us the beauty in the shadow of the misfit.

Kindness and compassion will sometimes be greeted with doubt, fear and even anger at first. If you really mean it, and have the courage to do so, you can penetrate that outer shell and touch the tender heart within. You may be saving someone's life.

Consider the outcasts and misfits in your world to be unexplored territories of your own soul, undiscovered treasures waiting for you. The rewards will be as great for you as for those you help.

When we look deep enough into any living being, we find the face of God.

Teach this to your children, like Max did in the following example.

Max had come to me for almost four years to heal from a very painful childhood and to learn to manage his anger toward his wife. He was making excellent progress, and was tapering off in his sessions.

Max's son Derek was six years old and the apple of his dad's eye. Max was determined to give Derek the healthy guidance, love and positive role-modeling he had never received as a child.

Smiling ear to ear, Max told me of some of his recent successes with his wife and son. "I have always been afraid I would end up homeless and living under a bridge. So, I decided to confront this fear a little more directly. After church Sunday, Derek and I took about forty hamburgers to the homeless people living under the overpass downtown. Derek loved it! Now he wants to feed all of the homeless people in the city. Those people were so grateful."

Max was quiet for a moment, as he wiped his eyes and regained his composure. He had given a great gift to some outcasts and misfits, to his son and to himself.

METHODS FOR HELPING CHILDREN DEAL WITH THEIR ANGER

What to say

When your child is in the middle of expressing anger, your verbal response is extremely important. Though it remains true that your nonverbal signals will speak more loudly than your words, we must not underestimate the power of the spoken word, particularly during intense emotional experiences.

- For a very young child, or if the anger is being expressed mostly in nonverbal ways, say something to the effect of, "Wow! I can see that you are really angry right now. I'm sure you have good reasons to be angry. Your anger seems really strong to me. I want you to know that it's okay with me for you to be angry, and I want to help you deal with it so that nobody gets hurt—including you." In these and other words, communicate the idea that "There's nothing wrong with feeling anger; the important thing is what you do with it."
- Practice reflective listening. Repeat back to the child in a nonjudgmental, soothing tone what you hear her

saying. This provides a comforting effect and lets the child know she's being heard. Start with phrases like, "So what I hear you saying is ..." or "So you're saying..." Stick with their words and references, using as little interpretation and as few of your own words as possible.

- Express empathy and understanding. This is simply a matter of imagining yourself in the child's position, and attempting to see things from his viewpoint. Use phrases like, "When I put myself in your shoes, I can see why you would feel that way," or "From where you stand, it looks like ..." or "I think I see what you mean" or "That makes sense to me."

- Avoid teaching, correcting or instructing while your child is angry. Only when the child starts to calm down and relax, you may want to share some of your own similar struggles or experiences. The goal is to help them deal with and understand their anger. Discipline needs to be kept separate from this kind of communication, and administered when both you and the child are calm. That way, the child gets the clear message that it is not their emotion that is being disciplined; it is their behavior.

What to do

If your child is small enough, you might want to try holding her during her anger episode. This has been found to be highly effective in many cases. It provides loving, powerful and safe boundaries when the child is feeling out of control. The nonverbal message is, "I'm here. I'm not going to leave you. I'm not going to hurt you, and I won't let you hurt yourself or anyone else. I'm going to hold you until you feel safe again." Here are some recommendations to make this procedure safe and successful:

- If you are extremely afraid or angry yourself, do not try this technique. Your emotions will feed the anger and fear of your child and make the situation worse.
- If you feel comfortable doing so, hold the child from behind, ideally with him sitting in your lap. Protect your face in case he tosses his head back toward you. The goal is for no one to get hurt.
- There needs to be both love and power in your embrace. Strong but not too strong, relaxed but not too relaxed. This lets the child know you are in charge, that you love her and can and will protect her.
- Be ready and willing to devote some time to this. If you don't complete the process, you may do more harm than good. Hold the child, and wait until he calms down and relaxes. Often he might cry or even fall asleep as the anger subsides.

Through this gesture you are communicating love, acceptance, safety, protection and power all at the same time.

What to have the child do

In some cases, the child may need to release anger physically. This can be accomplished in a number of ways:

- Supervised play with toys, or play therapy in a professional setting, can be very effective in helping children release anger. The violence that occurs between the toy characters is nondestructive and can be very informative to the therapist and/or the parent who is observing. This can also include drawing pictures, or throwing clay against a wall or board where no harm can be done.
- Hitting pillows or a mattress with a harmless object such as a nerf bat or bataca bat. This can be done in a playful

manner, and the child will still receive benefit. In therapy, I often call it "the anger game," so that children feel safe in approaching the activity.

• Children may sometimes benefit from the "temper tantrum technique" described in chapter 12. Parents should use their own judgment as to when it is necessary to contract for the services of a professional for this type of exercise.

• One of the best parents I know told me that he had his daughters use the "Name it, claim it, aim it" technique for dealing with anger. In other words he taught them to put a name on their feeling, take responsibility for it and direct it into some kind of release or constructive activity. An example might go something like, "I'm angry and sad, Daddy" (naming and claiming it), "and I want you to help me talk to Bobby about taking my things" (aiming it). This is an excellent approach, and I highly recommend that parents use this and any other guidelines they run across that help them teach their children to manage and express their emotions in healthy ways.

AFFIRMATIONS TO BLESS
THE CHILDREN

Here are some thoughts and affirmations for all of us who love children and want to see them soar and become who they were born to be:

- *Children come through their parents, not from them.*
- *Children come from God, the Creator.*
- *Children are parents' responsibility, not their property.*
- *Children's intentions are always good at the core.*
- *Children are far more innocent and vulnerable than we may realize.*
- *Children are far more wise and powerful than we may realize.*
- *Children need our guidance and teaching.*
- *Children can provide us with great guidance and teaching.*
- *Children reflect the adults they grow up around.*
- *Children reflect the unique individual spirit that sets them apart from all other beings.*
- *Children's safety, care and education are our collective responsibility.*
- *Children represent our freedom to contribute to the future in positive ways.*
- *Children are the parents, leaders and elders of tomorrow.*

8

Protecting the Child Within

So who is it that protects the child within?

You naturally developed an "inner parent" as you matured, and your role models for this development were your own parents and parent figures. This is exactly why it is so important that you consciously develop your self-parenting skills, so that you are in charge rather than being unconsciously driven by the patterns of your past. You can learn to be the parent to yourself that you always wanted.

You can see in the first diagram of Figure 8.1 that the words "Power" and "Authority" go in the realm of the inner parent.

These are words that go with the expression of love and nurturing as well as mature, healthy anger. The inner child is
associated with the more vulnerable emotions of fear, pain
and the need for love, represented by the inner three circles
in Figure 8.1. All of the emotions of the inner child can be
expressed in mature adult ways. The point here is to identify
the protective nature of anger and its rightful place in the
realm of the inner parent. You can also see that the relationship between the inner child and the inner parent goes right
through the adult self. Our behavior as adults is thus a reflection of our internal relationship with ourselves.

The second diagram in Figure 8.1 shows another perspective on the parent, adult and child. The adult is on the outer
layer, because that is what we greet the world with. The inner
parent comes next, because it is the protector or buffer
between the world and the inner child. The inner child is the
deepest aspect of our being, where our emotional and spiritual self resides. All of this is communicated with the world
through the adult as the diagram indicates. Anything coming
from the inner child will be filtered through the inner parent
and the adult before reaching the world outside. If as adults
we lose control, the childlike emotion explodes through the
inner parent and supersedes the adult. This is when we might
say the child has "taken over."

This is analogous to the diagram in Figure 6.1. The adult is
the outer ring of the realm of skill, strength, knowledge and
awareness. The parent is next, the ring of protection that con-
tains anger and withdrawal. The child is represented by all
three of the inner circles, containing the vulnerable feelings of
fear, pain and the need for love, which includes the capacity
for joy.

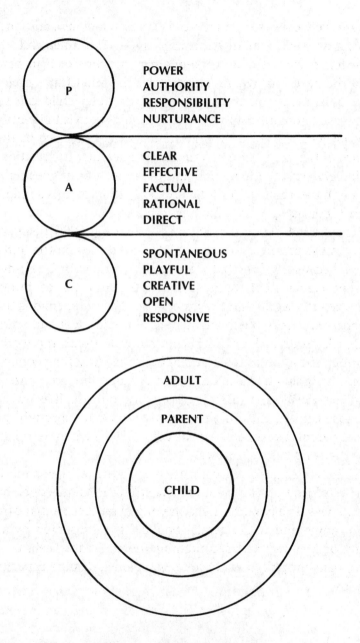

Figure 8.1. Two Views of P-A-C

THE SOFT, VULNERABLE INNER CHILD

Many of us, particularly men, cringe at the thought of being soft and vulnerable. That's one reason there is so much effort put into creating that tough, hard exterior—just to make sure no one suspects there are fear, pain and a need for love underneath. It's a sure bet that the tougher and meaner the exterior, the deeper the wounds of the inner child.

We all entered the world wide open, totally vulnerable. Subconsciously each of us remembers the great love and the great pain in that stage of our existence. This is why it is safe to say that within each of us is a soft, vulnerable child, however deeply it may be buried in the subconscious mind.

Most of us have seen the tattoo on the muscular, hairy arm of a tough-looking man that says simply, "Mother." To me this is the man's connection with his own inner softness, which was experienced most profoundly when he was a child with his mother. I have worked with many big, strong, angry men, some of whom were abusers. Within each of them I discovered a frightened, wounded child, vulnerable and in great need of love.

I have talked about a certain type of man to make the point of the universal existence of inner softness, because the vulnerability of many others is easy to see. Some of us, male and female, show our inner feelings whether we like it or not. We may have never learned to hide them. This can be both a blessing and a curse, depending on what the feelings are and when and where we show them.

To be vulnerable does not mean to be weak. We can learn to share our deep, intimate feelings in a very open manner while exercising sophisticated skills for taking care of ourselves. The fact is that we are all emotionally vulnerable at our core. That's not a problem. It is in fact a blessing. By sharing our vulnerability with each other, we provide the opportunity to lay down the defenses we have always used to protect and distance ourselves. To approach someone with our heart and both hands open and exposed indicates there is no threat. We can trust. It is safe.

I invite you to make the journey into yourself and see if you can find your own inner child, the most vulnerable aspect of your being. The rewards for the discovery are virtually without limit. To fully experience your emotions is to be completely involved in life. To deny your inner emotional self is to live a halfway existence of boredom, fear and internal conflict.

THE CHILD OF THE PAST, PRESENT AND FUTURE

When we talk about the inner child, we're referring to an image of your child self. This image may be one that you access by looking at a photograph of yourself as a child, or simply by closing your eyes and picturing yourself as a child. The child can be of any age; however, it is useful to be able to visualize yourself at different ages in order to access different memories and emotions. Let's look at some of the different aspects of the child within:

• **The inner child of the past.** This is an image of yourself that matches with a certain time in your own past. This child can help you find and access memories and feelings that will help with your healing. S/he may appear sad, lonely, lost, afraid or deeply hurt. In some cases, to give you information about your emotional state, your brain might give you a surprising image that is confusing at first. Years ago, when I was doing some of my own healing work, I saw an image of myself as a child that was both surprising and very helpful. I saw myself at the age of about four or five years, walking around looking kind of lost under a glass floor in my family's home. This image of my child self represented the part of me that never felt seen, heard or recognized. This spontaneous image was very helpful to me in my healing and self-understanding. Trust your mind to provide you with the images of your child self that will inform you about the inner work you need to do.

- **The inner child of the present.** While the inner child of the past helps you with your healing, the inner child of the present helps you with your self-care on a current and ongoing basis. In order to get clear readings from the present child, the child of the past must have some degree of healing already accomplished. In other words, you won't get accurate readings about your present emotional state from the child image until the inner child of the past is relatively nourished and healed. The work you have to do with the past child will fade over time, and the relationship with your inner child of the present will grow stronger, deeper and more enjoyable. Use this aspect of the child within by checking in on a regular basis to see how you're doing emotionally. Just close your eyes and picture yourself as a child. Depending on your inner clarity and where you are on your healing journey, this image will tell you something about how you are faring emotionally, right now.

- **The inner child of the future.** Some of the images of your inner child can be a kind of bellwether for you, indicating future possibilities for your development and self-expression. Here are some images to consider about your inner child of the future:

  - **The divine child.** Carl Jung refers to the divine child as one of the archetypes in some of his writings (Jung and Kerenyi 1969). One of the definitions of the word "divine" is simply "from God." If you believe we come from God, or the Creator of the universe, then you can accept this idea. The divine child is radiant, pure, innocent, open and vulnerable. The divine child remembers where s/he came from, and never loses the connection. This is an image of our inner spiritual nature. This reconnection with the divine is the reward for your inner journey of healing, and can be seen as a doorway to a deeper and more fulfilling connection with your Creator.

- **The magical child.** This image of the child suggests a wellspring of energy. From this wellspring emerge your humor, spontaneity, creativity, joy and capacity for unconditional love. This is in some ways just another way of looking at the divine child, as these qualities, too, are the reward for your journey of self-discovery and healing. The magical child also provides a doorway to wisdom and undeveloped powers, suggesting a connection between the child and the wise elder that also lives inside each of us.

- **The playful child.** Think of exuberance, light, energy and unabashed self-expression. This image can be seen as the magical child in action, bringing varieties of physical playfulness into everyday behavior. Since most of you had some opportunity to play as a child, accessing this part of yourself is a matter of remembering. For others of you who never had the safety in your home to play, you may have to learn how to play for the first time. Children and animals are your best teachers. Also, some adults may actually be able to help you!

- **The integrated child.** As you heal, grow, expand and develop into the magnificent, brilliant being you were meant to be, all of the wonderful aspects of the child become diffuse throughout your mind, body and self-expression. In other words, the wonderful child aspects and qualities we are discussing here are available to you as an adult at any given moment on any given day in any given situation.

So how does this relate to anger? Simple. The child is vulnerable in her/his beautiful, exuberant and creative expression, and therefore must have the protection of mature, healthy anger. In the integrated adult context, it could also be said that in order to be creative, spontaneous, playful, open and emotionally expressive, you definitely need to know how to take care of yourself.

I JUST CAN'T FEEL ANYTHING

Lora first approached me following a brief talk I had given on anger management. She was an attractive woman in her late thirties who presented herself in a pleasant, confident manner.

"I think my childhood was fine. My parents loved me, and I always had everything I needed. I just can't seem to feel close to my family, and they notice it too. I really have no idea what I feel. Do you think I need to come see you?" she asked with a pleasant smile.

"What do you think you need to do?" I turned her question back to her. She smiled again, and said, "Yes." She took one of my cards and said she would give me a call to set up an appointment.

During her therapy sessions in the coming weeks, Lora talked openly about her childhood experiences. She described a family in which everything was normal, acceptable and bordering on perfect. As I inquired further, I learned more about this woman and why she was so disconnected from her emotions.

"Did your parents hold you, touch you or spend one-on-one time with you?" I asked.

"I'm sure they did, I just can't remember anything like that happening. We weren't that kind of family. No one talked about how they felt, and no one ever had any problems . . . at least none that they talked about. We always knew what we were expected to do, and we did it." As she spoke, it occurred to me that Lora was doing exactly what her family had done. Her whole life had been a performance.

Lora went through all the motions without any of the emotions. Over the weeks, I came to understand that she had been neglected in many ways as a child, and was therefore neglecting herself as an adult in the same ways. Unfortunately, she was neglecting her children as well.

In about the fifth session, things began to change.

"There is one place where I feel my emotions, but I'm afraid to tell you about it. It's very embarrassing." I waited after she said this to give her a chance to continue.

"I think I'm hooked on the Internet." She giggled nervously, and then continued. "Well, it's not really the Internet. It's a guy. We've been e-mailing for a while now, and it's getting out of hand. I can't stop thinking about him. I've never laid eyes on him, but he's very real to me. I say things to him I've never said to anyone. It would destroy my husband or my children if they found out. It's just not like me."

Lora had found a way out of the empty, loveless prison of acceptable behavior that her parents had taught her. Without leaving her home, she was having an illicit liaison with someone she'd never met. The e-mail format gave her a sense of freedom to explore parts of herself that she would not dare to reveal with anyone in person.

"He wants to meet me, and I told him that will never happen. I would die first." Lora's consistent smile had faded.

There was a new look on her face, more energy and agitation in her eyes and in her movements.

"You finally found a way to break the rules, didn't you?" I commented.

"What do you mean?" she asked, pretending not to understand what I was saying.

I didn't answer, giving her some time to ponder my statement.

"It is definitely against the rules. It is also the most fun I've ever had!" She paused for a moment. "But I have to stop before I get caught and ruin my marriage and my family. I just don't think I *can* stop. I've been trying for weeks." She was showing some real emotion as she said this, squirming and fidgeting in her chair.

As we explored further, we discovered that Lora told her e-lover everything she felt. She expressed anger, fear and sorrow to him that she had never expressed to anyone. She was discovering herself through this surprising medium, and it became apparent to me that she couldn't quit until she had an alternative and acceptable way to be herself and express her true feelings.

"I feel really alive when I'm talking to him. It's weird, like he's real and right there in the room with me, but I know I'll never meet him. I'm even starting to dream about him. What do you think I need to do?" For the first time since she started therapy, Lora seemed open to doing some work on herself.

The experiential work I did with her to create a dialogue with her parents was fairly flat for her emotionally. Now that she was starting to come to life in her sessions, I decided to do some imagery work with her to see if that would give her more conscious access to her emotions.

As I guided Lora through the process of visualizing her inner child, I could see that her resistance was building.

"This isn't working for you, is it?" I asked.

"It's not that. It's just that I don't like what I see. She's ugly. She cries all of the time, and no one likes her. She is too needy. I don't have time for her. I don't even like her." Lora actually seemed to be feeling some anger.

"How did your parents feel about you when you looked or acted like her?" I asked.

Lora was quiet a moment before speaking. She was starting to get it. "They felt exactly what I'm feeling right now. I guess I'm just following their example."

"Between you the adult and this unacceptable child inside, who do you think it is that is in charge of the Internet affair?"

She looked a little scared for a moment, then angry when she almost shouted, "I am! I'm the one who sits down at the computer when everyone's out of the house or asleep. I'm the one who keeps going back and reading his e-mails and responding." I waited without saying anything.

"Well, I guess it's more like a child who can't stay out of the cookie jar, isn't it?" She was perking up some now, making some connections in her mind.

"She's trying to set you free. The little girl who has always been unacceptable also carries many of your emotions, so she's found an emotional outlet that feels good to her and gets you out of your prison of rigid rules and proper behavior." I could tell she was right with me as I spoke, and she started to get angry again.

"That's great!" She almost shouted, in uncharacteristic sarcasm. "So the only way I can find to express my emotions is in this weird, perverted electronic relationship with an imaginary lover! There's got to be a better way."

"Does your husband know how you really feel?"

"Nobody does, except you and this e-mail guy. Of course, he could be a woman or a child, for all I know." Lora was frustrated and angry. I could see that she was in the process of accessing emotions that had been buried all of her life.

"The little girl inside you is not going to take no for an answer. Let's see if we can find some other ways for you to be yourself in this world, without going against your morals and personal values."

In subsequent sessions, Lora started feeling some anger toward her parents for neglecting the natural emotional parts of her existence. She then made some very real connections with her little girl inside, and came up with some things she wanted to tell Bob, her husband.

It probably comes as no surprise that Lora's husband was very much like her parents. If she had not achieved some degree of resolution with her parents first, her communication with her husband would have been cloudy and most likely ineffective. When she became clear on the fact that she had to express her anger, fear and sorrow in order to access and express her love and joy, she was truly ready for some heartfelt communication with her family. As it turns out, however, her anger came first.

THE SOFT INNER EDGES OF ANGER

"He infuriates me! He seems like he's made of plastic, and all he cares about is how things appear. I feel like hitting him, just to get a reaction, or some kind of change in that frozen face of his!" Lora had just come in for an individual session after a difficult couples session with her husband.

I told Lora about a couple of options for anger release work, and she agreed to try one of the imagery techniques.

"If your anger took a form, what would it look like?" I asked. "Close your eyes and see if you can find an image that fully and completely gives form and expression to the depth and intensity of your anger."

"I see a long tube, with a laser beam coming out of both ends. It's like nuclear energy. White-hot power. And it's sort of floating and spinning in the air." Her breathing slowed down a little as she described the image.

"How do you feel about it?" I asked.

"Fine for now. I like the power of it. I just hope I don't hurt anyone. I really don't want to hurt Bob, or especially the children." She was softening a little more as each moment passed.

At the first part of the next session, Lora was bright and energetic. The change in her was noticeable, and I waited to hear what she would say.

"I changed the laser tube into a vitamin pill and swallowed it! I have felt so much more energy since I did that. Bob and I made love last night, and I think I scared him—but I think he also liked it." She was laughing with more freedom and abandon than I had previously seen in her at any point in the process.

"And you'll never believe what happened next! I dreamed about the little girl. We had the best time running and laughing and playing together. I can feel her right now, sitting here inside me. She's happy for the first time in my life." Tears of joy were slowly running down Lora's smiling face. "I think she likes it when I'm so powerful and expressive."

Lora had found the soft inner edges of anger, her precious little girl inside, almost completely on her own. Transforming the image of the laser tube into a vitamin pill and consuming it was her idea, and it was perfect. She had spontaneously completed her own process, by embracing her anger and incorporating the healthy energy into her system. Then her subconscious mind gave her the dream connecting her with her inner child, which showed her the direct relationship between her power and the freedom of her child self. Her process reflected the brilliance of the natural healing process at work.

The reward at the end of Lora's inner journey was a joyful, playful, expressive and exuberant child. Her process from that point forward was learning to communicate her emotions in a meaningful and mature manner, so that she could be heard and understood. The hard part was over. Once substantial emotional healing has been accomplished, skill development is fairly rapid and relatively easy for most people.

DIALOGUE BETWEEN TWO PARTS OF THE BRAIN

One day I would like to see scientists study what happens in the human brain when inner child imagery and emotional healing work is taking place. From my own study of the brain research associated with emotional intelligence (Goleman 1997; MacLean 1990) and my own cumulative clinical observations, I have concluded that this therapeutic process actually amounts to a conversation between two parts of the brain.

It's not complicated. Here's how it works when you imagine yourself as an adult relating to your inner child:

• Emotional memory is stored in the "emotional brain" or limbic system, sometimes referred to as the "neomammalian complex" (MacLean 1990). The image of your child symbolizes and personifies emotional memory.
• Rational memory is stored in the "left brain" or left hemisphere of the neocortex. The image of yourself as a current adult accesses and personifies much of this rational memory.
• Imagination and the creation of imagery utilizes the "right brain" or right hemisphere of the neocortex, which has the capacity to access and activate emotion. When you get an image in your mind, you are using your right brain.

• The image of the adult interacting with the child (as in Lora's dream) is actually a symbolic representation of a process involving connections between both hemispheres of the neocortex and with the limbic system.

My theory is that when this happens, new connections are actually formed between different parts of the brain, giving you more conscious (neocortex) access to and control of your emotions (limbic system). Another way of saying this is that your adult brain talks to your child brain and forms a cooperative and supportive relationship. This gives you energy, life and vitality as an adult and brings stability, reason and guidance to your child self.

Referring back to Figure 8.1, it would be similar to a dialogue between the inner parent and the inner child, sending powerful and dynamic energy and stability to and through the adult.

You are both child and adult, and when you combine these in a balanced and cooperative way, you activate the magic of your creative spirit and the brilliance of your inner wisdom. Each one of us is so much more than we have ever dreamed or realized. The inner child is your doorway to the discovery of your own brilliance.

SKILLS FOR CONNECTING WITH THE INNER CHILD

Once the basic healing work is done, the next challenge facing us is how to take care of ourselves day by day outside a therapeutic environment. This requires the same kind of strength that was needed to break through the wall of fear and face the pain. Without a continued dedication to self-love and inner focus, you will slip all too easily into old, unhealthy patterns.

Remember the story of Joyce, the woman who lifted the car off her son? The same kind of power and strength is available to you when you love and care for your vulnerable inner child. Of course, you won't have occasion to lift a car off your inner child, but you will need tremendous inner strength to express your innermost feelings openly and to take care of yourself on a continual basis.

Here are some suggestions for self-care and maintaining a connection with your inner child:

- **Create space and time in your daily schedule to talk to and listen to your inner child.** The key to this is imagery. Picture the child sitting beside you or in your lap, or jumping around the room. Just "checking in" with your child self will give you a reading on how you're doing emotionally. You may find her hiding in a corner, or he might be scared and trembling. You may find as you offer support and understanding to the child that the image will change, giving you feedback on how you're doing in your self-care. Explore and enjoy your self-discovery! (There are many books and tapes available to help you with this process, including information on parenting and your child's anger. You will find some of them listed under the headings "References" and "Products" in the back of this book.)
- **Take quiet, alone time on a regular basis.** Ideally, twenty minutes to an hour a day, find a private comfortable place where you can relax, meditate and/or pray without interruption. You can incorporate journaling and inspirational reading into this time as well. Always allow at least fifteen to twenty minutes of being still and silent. This opens your inner space to the child, and accesses your spiritual nature. It will also do wonders for the health of your body, mind and spirit. Make this quiet, alone time a top priority, and you will bring more of your authentic self to your

spouse, your children, your friends and your work.

- **Listen to your body.** When your body is showing signs of stress, that's your inner child saying, "Slow down. You're not Superman or Superwoman, and you're neglecting me." That's when you practice your skills for relaxing, playing, creating and simply "goofing off." If you ignore that voice, it will just get louder until you pay attention. An unhappy inner child may try to communicate through a headache, stomach problems, depression or even major illness. When we listen to the subtle messages, we don't need the "loud" messages of illness and catastrophe.

- **Systematically and consistently create opportunities to express your feelings openly in a safe environment.** Find a support group or a group of friends, and get together regularly for the purpose of keeping the door to your heart open. Twelve-step recovery groups, therapy groups, men's or women's groups, book study groups, and other forums often provide this venue.

- **Create opportunities for laughter and fun.** If you don't know how to play, then learn. Do a Web search on "laughter and humor" and you will find lots of information on the health benefits of laughter and humor and how to get more into your life. Check out the Web sites *www.livinglifefully.com, www.selfhealingexpressions.com* and *www.worldlaughtertour.com*. There are conferences and workshops on play and laughter going on all over the country year-round.

- **Be creative.** This accesses the magical child in you, and further allows you to become a vessel for the expression of the Creator that lives within you. Take dance lessons or art lessons, or learn to play a musical instrument. Get on the floor or in the dirt with a child and let them show you the creative world they live in. Join them there and feel yourself come alive.

- **Temporarily or permanently end all relationships in which you are being physically or sexually abused.** Seek help, and only consider reentering the relationship if the abuser has been through intensive therapy and you have personally seen significant progress. Even then, proceed cautiously—you have a precious child to protect.
- **Only risk and commit to relationships in which you are loved.** You deserve love, and without it you will not live fully and become the person you were born to be.
- **Embrace all that you are.** Do not reject any aspect of your being. If you have problems, get help. You can have the life you want—and it's up to you to create it.

Doing these things consistently after a lifetime of codependent and unhealthy relationships is no small task. You will need all of your energy and all of your physical, mental, emotional and spiritual power to make it. That's where your inner child comes in. S/he is a great source of love, creative energy and joy, and the more you care for the child within, the more energy you have to continue—so—it gets easier as you go!

DIALOGUES WITH THE INNER CHILD

To begin this process, remember how you looked at the age of three or four years and try to get a clear mental image of yourself at that age. A photograph may be helpful, if you have one.

The child within you lives in your heart, the emotional center of your body. It is helpful, however, to picture your child self outside your body in order to communicate more effectively with him. As we discussed above, there are several phases to the inner child relationship. The first is the healing of your wounded child of the past. The second stage, which lasts the rest of your life, is nurturing your inner child of the present. This child is not all that you are. You are an adult who has survived a lifetime of risks and hardships, growing and learning along the way. You have a brilliant mind, which you have used only partially because of the limitations of your parenting and the world you live in. There is much more to you than you know. There always will be. This is the miracle of life, love and learning. If you are fortunate enough to have already recognized your greatness, you probably know that you are still not through. The closer we come to knowing who we really are, the more we realize how much we have to learn.

As an adult and inner parent, try making the following statements to your inner child and see what happens:

"I've been the kind of parent to you that my parents were to me. I didn't know any better. Like them, I have abandoned and neglected you at times without meaning to. I've treated you as if you weren't even there because I really didn't know you were there. I thought that when I grew up, you just went away.

"I realize now that I have even been abusive to you at times. You are all of my feelings, and I have always thought some of those feelings were bad. So I tried to control you with substances (food, cigarettes, alcohol, drugs, medication, work, sex, love relationships), thinking I could make the feelings that I didn't like go away. It didn't work. The feelings just got worse. I realize now that I hurt you, and I'm sorry. I am ready to change now and take care of you. I accept you just as you are, no matter what you are feeling. Your feelings are my feelings, because you are who I am inside."

Now become the inner child. Sit on the floor, curl up on the couch or assume any childlike posture that seems to fit what you are feeling. As the inner child, you are only feelings. You don't think or analyze, you just feel. Try responding to your inner parent with:

"I'm glad you are finally recognizing me. I've been waiting for this for a long time. I like what you are saying. It makes me feel better. I'm not completely ready to trust you yet. I need to see some action. I need to be able to count on you throughout each day. I am completely dependent on you. If you don't love and care for me, no one will. You are all I have.

"When I am hurting or afraid, just hold me and tell me you love me. That's all I ask. Don't try to talk me out of my feelings, that's just who I am. Just love me and tell me that you'll protect me no matter what. I need to be told that you love me often, not just when things go wrong. When I am happy, I need you to smile and laugh and do fun things. I come out through your smile and laughter and playfulness. I also come out when you are loving and creative. I have a lot to offer you, if you will create a safe and healthy life for me. There is more joy and love in me than you have ever known, waiting to come out. Love and joy is who I am, and I am who you are. I'm counting on you. Please remember me."

If you're ready, you might respond with something like:

"You can count on me. I won't forget you. I will make mistakes, but I will learn to avoid repeating them. I accept you just as you are, no matter what you are feeling. Your feelings are my feelings. I love you unconditionally. You are who I am inside. In loving you, I love myself."

If you have difficulty with this exercise, write about your experience. This may help you figure out what you need to work on to get closer to the experience of self-love.

Your inner child may be too wounded or frightened for you to make a connection at this time. The concept may still seem foreign to you. If you like the words in this dialogue and you want to feel their depth and meaning, don't give up. Hang in there, and this will work for you. It has worked for me and many others, and I still use these methods both personally and professionally.

AFFIRMATIONS

- *I was born innocent and open.*
- *The innocent, open child I once was is still alive and awake inside me right now.*
- *My inner child is all of my emotions.*
- *I accept myself, no matter what I am feeling.*
- *All of my feelings are okay with me.*
- *I have the strength, skill and knowledge necessary to protect and care for my vulnerable inner child.*
- *I am an adult with a precious child inside.*
- *I have everything I need.*
- *I am whole and complete.*

9

The Role of Anger in the Grief Process

The only bad thing about grieving is getting stuck in it. As long as we are moving through it, the grief process is a healing experience in which we learn and grow in important ways. When we are stuck in the grief process, serious problems can result. Here are some indications that a person is stuck in grief:

- They have stopped talking about the loss, and they don't want anyone else to bring it up. The subject is taboo.
- They use statements like, "I've dealt with that already. It's over. I've put that behind me." They may or may not look sad, angry or depressed while saying this.

119

- There is a lack of joy and fulfillment in their life. They don't smile or laugh much.
- Substance abuse may be a problem.
- For some, major illness or a series of minor illnesses may begin to occur.
- They will begin to show general symptoms of depression, such as excessive sleeping, insomnia, weight loss or gain, or an extremely pessimistic attitude.
- Angry outbursts may begin to occur for no apparent reason.
- There could be an unwillingness to trust or risk in relationships.
- The person may lose their will to live and actually become suicidal.

As you can tell, these symptoms can be potentially life threatening. Learning how to grieve our losses effectively is an essential part of being an emotionally healthy person. Our life may depend on it.

TOO MUCH, TOO SOON

When Ray was only eleven, he was already being asked to save lives. His mother was a bedridden asthmatic, and he was given the responsibility to care for her.

"Dad loved sports. He lived, breathed, ate and drank athletics of all kinds. My brothers were big, strong star football players. I was small and liked to read. It seemed only natural that I would be the one to stay home with Mom." Ray had a way of talking off into space, as if he were watching his own private movie. It was a very sad movie, filled with pain and unresolved grief.

"I learned how to give CPR when I was twelve. I saved my mother's life three times. One time, the one that stands out the most, I was sure that I had lost her. All I could think about was that I had let Dad down. I wasn't athletic and that hurt him, and now I was about to fail at the one job I had been really good at—keeping his wife, my mother, alive.

"She was already blue when I got to her. I had only gone to the bathroom. I worked on her for forty-five minutes before the paramedics arrived. She just barely made it, and no one knew what I had been through but me. I couldn't talk about it. The fear, shame and guilt were just too strong. Finally they put her in the hospital. I still felt it was my responsibility to be with her. One night she seemed to be resting well so I decided to go home. I had spent six straight nights in a chair by her bed. She died thirty minutes after I left.

"No one blamed me. They didn't have to. I knew it was my fault. It seemed to me that I had been born to keep my mother alive, and now I had failed.

"As soon as I was old enough, I started riding fire trucks and ambulances and eventually became certified as a para-medic. I was determined to be the first to every emergency, to save as many lives as I could. It was the only way I knew to make up for what I had done to my mother and to my family."

Ray's face was dark with his own thoughts and visions. The movie he was watching was filled with death and dying. Through the negligence of the adults around him, he had just had too much, too soon in his young life.

At thirty-seven Ray looked like an unhealthy man of fifty-five. He was in the hospital for his fifth serious suicide attempt. He had been clinically dead from these attempts three times. The real clincher in his depression was the voca-tion he had chosen. He blamed himself for the deaths of all the car-wreck victims, burn victims and drowning victims he had been unable to save. The fact that he had been instru-mental in saving hundreds of lives made no difference to him—that was expected. This was the most serious case of unresolved grief I had ever seen in my professional career. The task of helping him to see his life realistically and forgive himself seemed gigantic to me. Like Ray, I had no choice but to try.

I wrote the following poem about a female client with serious depression and rage problems. She was a lot like Ray. One of her suicide attempts had left her in a coma for three days. She came to me to deal with her anger.

FAITH EATER

Dark and low she growls through life
Eating the ashes of her birth
Munching on morsels of meaning
Devouring all traces of worth

Eyes dark from cinders
Her vision burning with hate
She snarls at glimmers of goodness
Tearing and chewing at fate

From behind black eyes she mumbles her tale
Of frustrated struggles with death
She's come to me for sustenance
Ready to consume my breath

But I blow no winds of wisdom
I breathe no fragments of faith
Standing still in the ashes beside her
I see too clearly the wraith

Shocked, she shudders to notice
She's alone no more in her plight
Slowly we move through the wasteland
As I secretly search for the light

As her mind wanders, I see it
A spark, alive, within
This fire I kindle, now gently
Warming my heart, to begin

This poem captures some of the struggles that I have experienced and that other grief counselors go through in helping clients with unresolved grief and suicidal issues. Deep grief and self-loathing can at times be like a black hole, sucking all life, light and energy into it and giving nothing back. But there is always light in the depths of the darkness, however hard it may be to find.

STAGES OF THE GRIEF PROCESS

It is important that we understand what is involved in the grief process. We will all go through it, and many of us already have. A fact of life is that the longer we live, the more death we experience around us. Stages of the grief process include:

1. **Shock.** This is the body/mind's way of saving you from the devastating pain of the loss, at least initially. It is a blessing at best, but at worst can become a long-term numbness to feelings that resembles a sort of living death. It will pass naturally as long as the other components of the grief process are honored.
2. **Denial.** This is your mind's attempt to protect you from the reality of the loss. You may lie to yourself and think about the person as if s/he were still alive. A certain period of denial is normal, but if prolonged, it can keep you stuck and prevent resolution. There are many forms of denial, as varied as people are different from each other.
3. **Anger.** When you lose someone you love, it is natural to be angry for a period of time. You may be angry with the person for leaving you, angry with yourself for what you

did not do to save them (as in Ray's case) or angry with God for taking them away. You may just be angry at the unfairness and injustice of life.

4. **Guilt.** There seems to be a human tendency to blame ourselves when something happens to a loved one. In loving someone, you automatically take some degree of responsibility for her or his welfare. It is only natural to question yourself for a period of time after your loved ones die. This is a normal part of the grief process, but it is extremely important that you move through it and don't get stuck in this stage. Again, Ray's situation offers an example of what happens when someone gets stuck in the guilt stage of grieving.

5. **Pain and sorrow.** These feelings often exist throughout the entire grief process, and are the core feelings of grief. In the early stages, however, you are often distracted from your sorrow by denial, anger, guilt and the resulting confusion. Fear can also be a tremendous barrier to the experience of sorrow, triggering all of the defense mechanisms. To truly face and experience the pain and sorrow is necessary and healthy, however, and it moves you forward in the grief process. Working with love is the key for moving through this phase, because only love has the power to move us to the depths of our being where the greatest loss is registered.

6. **Release and resolution.** This stage of the grief process is accompanied by a sense of acceptance of the reality of the loss, a sense of "letting go." There may also be a degree of forgiveness that occurs in this phase. The denial, guilt and anger stages are over, and the pain and sorrow is not as intense as it was before. Many people ask, "How long does it take?" The answer is different according to the severity of the loss and the health of the individual who is grieving. Grieving moves in cycles, and

it may seem as if we are through for a substantial period of time. A birthday, anniversary or another loss can bring back many of the same feelings that were there when our loved one died. Any loss or low emotional period can bring back the feelings of loss, particularly if you have not reached resolution. When the release finally occurs, your entire body will feel it. I have watched many people go through emotional release in their grieving, and I am convinced that it is as much a physical, nonverbal process as it is verbal and conscious.

7. **Return to the willingness to love.** This is the final stage of the grieving process. Healing has occurred, and the grieving person is able to laugh again and to get involved in life. Fear can slow you down or even stop you at this point, because new love means the risk of new loss. By honoring and completing all aspects of the grief process, however, you will overcome your fear and move forward. This occurs through an appreciation for yourself and the life you are left to live. Nurturing your inner child is an excellent tool to use to help you through the entire grief process, and particularly as you move back into the world after a period of grieving. Part of the return to love also includes remembering the love you felt for the one you lost. The love lives on, and the anger, guilt, pain and sorrow fade away.

This final stage of the grief process is ultimately a spiritual one. It is a fact that all of us on this planet will die. You need to have some way of living, laughing and loving with this reality. That's where spirituality comes in. True security cannot be found in another person or in any external circumstances. You have to turn within, to your own concept of the infinite, to ultimately find peace and security in a life that is only temporary in its tangible form.

GRIEVING IS AN ACT OF LOVE

The greater the love you feel for someone or the greater the emotional investment in a given situation, the greater the sense of loss you feel when death, transition or tragedy occurs. The depth of grief you experience is directly proportional to the depth of love experienced, invested or needed. Grieving is actually an aspect of love, and healthy grieving is an act of love and remembering love.

The reason that anger, shock and denial interrupt and in some cases stop the grief process is that they take you away from love. That is what they are designed to do as protective mechanisms.

Here's the real clincher about love and the grief process—remembering, writing about and talking about love takes you directly into the pain. As this happens, however, all of the unconscious defense mechanisms designed to protect you from pain are activated. This is where the anger, shock and denial come in. The instinctual reaction of avoiding pain is natural. If you allow this to dominate, however, you will never complete a grieving process. We must be conscious of our instincts and act according to our wisdom.

Ultimately it is only by focusing on love that you will gain the strength and depth of emotion necessary for moving into your pain, releasing your sorrow and completing the grief process.

Ideas and Skills to Facilitate Your Own Grief Process

1. **Understand that grief comes in waves.** When the initial shock wears off, the first wave might feel overwhelming. Fortunately, each wave of grief eventually subsides, just as waves in the ocean do. You can comfort yourself

during each wave of sorrow with the awareness that "this too shall pass." The better you respond to the waves of grief, the more quickly they pass, and the sooner you will complete your grieving process.

The grief process lasts from a few months to several years, depending on the type of loss experienced. That means the waves will continue to come and go for that period of time. Fight them, and they will just get stronger. Learn to go with them and move through them effectively, and they will subside more quickly.

2. **Welcome a good cry.** Don't be afraid to cry. Some crying can be and even needs to be done alone, whereas aspects of the grief process require that you do at least part of your crying in the presence of trusted loved ones. You absolutely must know how to cry. Crying can actually be seen as a skill, in that some people know how to do it, some don't, and it can be taught. Here are some exercises to help you cry if you have difficulty doing so:

- Go into a dark or dimly lit room, where you will not be interrupted. Curl up on a bed or on the floor in a pile of pillows. Let your emotions and the sensations in your body be your guide; they will tell you what to do if you have the sensitivity to listen.

- Make a vocal sound that matches with the feelings of sorrow and pain in your stomach, heart and throat. This may come out as a wail, a whimper, a howl or a roar. It is essential that you let these sounds out, as they give you emotional release that otherwise is just not possible.

- Deep, long sobbing is the key to powerful emotional release. That's what you're going for in the effort to cry. Quietly leaking a few tears is better than nothing, but it won't get to the heart of the matter. When you experience deep loss, your body needs to sob deep and long

until you feel a release and a sense of relief. You may
need to do this several times during the grieving process. Sobbing occurs as a kind of rapid coughing or con-
vulsing rhythm in your belly, so the belly must be
relaxed for this to happen. Relaxing your stomach and
breathing deeply can often facilitate crying.

• Sometimes there is a powerful layer of anger or even
rage surrounding sorrow. Because of this, anger release
work may sometimes be necessary to allow crying to
start. I have seen literally hundreds of clients go into
crying after powerful anger release. Refer to chapter 12
for anger release methods. The verbal statements that
might go with anger release for grieving might be "No,
no, no . . ." or "Why did you leave me?"

3. **Take part in a grieving ritual.** Grieving rituals are
extremely important for those of us in cultures and socie-
ties that do not have them. Your own private grieving
ceremony will allow you to process your feelings and
move through your waves of grief on your own schedule,
requiring nothing of others. Here are some ideas for
rituals and ceremonies that may be useful to you,
beyond the funeral process that most families utilize:

▪ Go into a private space where you will not be interrupted.
▪ Put on some appropriate music that will remind you of
the person or that will connect with the feelings you
want to move through.
▪ Light candles to set a sacred space, and to create a quiet
and reverent mood.
▪ Take out photographs, videotapes, audiotapes, cards,
letters and memorabilia that contain or remind you of
your lost loved one or of the situation you are grieving.
Place these around you on the floor or on a table in front
of you.

- Talk out loud to the departed, or to anyone associated with your loss. You can also write letters (that you may or may not send to anyone still alive) expressing all of your feelings.
- Stay in this space until you feel some sense of release or resolution. Understand that you may need to do this several times during your grief process, or in some cases one such ritual will be sufficient.

Ceremonies and rituals that involve family and loved ones also affected can be very healing. Some examples include:

- Releasing balloons in a park or floating a candle down a stream or river.
- Storytelling ceremonies in which you and your group get together to swap memories of the departed. Be aware that if these stories focus on anger, guilt or denial, they can do more harm than good. While it is necessary to move through these aspects of grief, the purpose of such a gathering is to focus on love, release, forgiveness, healing and letting go.
- Memorial services that include combinations of the above elements, for the purpose of honoring the departed and the love felt by those left behind.

The approach I have outlined here can be applied to many kinds of losses. These include:

- Death
- Divorce
- Loss of innocence through physical or sexual abuse
- Loss of respect for your body because of abuse
- Loss of love through abandonment or rejection
- Loss of childhood through being required to take on too much responsibility too soon in life

- Loss of health through illness, injury or aging
- Loss of job
- Loss of financial security through investment down-turns and/or changes in the economy
- Loss due to moving away from a home that you loved
- Loss of community because of a geographical move

You may be able to think of other types of losses that you or others have suffered. The important point to keep in mind is that you do not have to suffer from these losses for the rest of your life. You can take charge by moving through your own grief to a point of peace and resolution, becoming wiser and stronger in the process.

GETTING UNSTUCK WITH ANGER

Ray was angry. The only problem was that he was angry with himself. His suicide attempts had been violent and extreme. He once said maybe the reason he had lived through them was that he wasn't ready to put himself out of his misery until he had suffered some more.

Ray was very resistant to doing anger work. My thought was that he secretly knew it would help. His guilt would not allow him to get better. Finally he agreed, only because I gave him permission to direct the anger toward himself in the words he used.

We were in the Grief and Loss group at the hospital, and the other group members were very supportive of Ray releasing his anger. One of the most significant parts of this type of healing is the love and support of fellow patients who have cried, raged, laughed and loved together. I feel this was an important key to the process that got Ray onto the mat that Tuesday morning.

"Come on, Ray, you can do it! Get mad, you'll feel a lot better." This came from a man who had his first rage release experience in the preceding Anger Management group. All the members were leaning forward, cheering him on. Ray sat on his heels with fists clenched, staring at the mat in front of him.

"Hit the mat and say 'It's my fault!'" I coached from the sidelines. I knew he could only express anger toward himself at this point. My strategy was that he would eventually get past this belief and connect with the deeper anger he had toward his father for leaving him at home to care for his mother while he and Ray's brothers went to football games and had fun.

After several sessions of this nature, Ray suddenly screamed in the middle of pounding the mat, "It was *not* my fault! I was too young to be doing that! It was your job, you good-for-nothing son of a bitch!" (Language in anger work often gets quite colorful.)

I knew Ray was going to make it now. He had gone back to the beginning point of his guilt and was shaking its foundation. He still had a lot of work to do, but the self-hatred had ended. His anger had been a tool to break through what was the biggest wall of guilt I had ever witnessed. He was beginning to experience anger on his own behalf for the first time in his life. This was his first movement in the direction of self-love, which was essential for resolving his lifetime of guilt and arrested grief.

EXTREME CASES OF GRIEF

When unique circumstances arise around losses in our individual lives, the grief process can become confusing mentally and overwhelming emotionally. Following are some examples of complications that can arise:

- **Multiple losses.** When we lose several loved ones in a relatively short period of time, or experience death of a loved one in close proximity with divorce, job loss, a move or other major life transitions, our system might just go into overload and shut down. This is a natural reaction to excessive grief. All that is required is knowledge of the grief process, a willingness to work through each of the losses and patience with yourself in the process. Remember, grieving is all about love, and does not have to be considered a bad thing.
- **Loss of a child.** This is known to be one of the most if not the most painful loss a human being can experience. It is highly complex, for many reasons. The pure shock of a child's death is huge, as you never expect those younger than you to go before you do. As parents and older loved ones, you also feel a strong sense of injustice when this occurs. Consciously or unconsciously railing against the injustice can stop the grief process and make it difficult to recover. Anger at God is also quite common in such circumstances. Guilt by parents and caregivers is also unavoidable in the death of a child. A strong spiritual focus, a supportive community and good therapeutic support are often essential to help us through such devastating losses.
- **Death by suicide.** When someone close to you commits suicide, the grief process is highly complex. Guilt and self-doubt are inevitable, and if left unchecked could paralyze the grieving process and leave you stuck in depression for years. One of the baffling aspects of such a loss is that the victim was also the perpetrator. The good friend murdered the good friend, or the family member murdered the family member. The anger and sorrow in such cases can crash into each other, leaving us stymied and unable to move in any direction. Counseling is almost always necessary in such cases.

• **Death due to terrorism or hate crimes.** The mix of grief and anger in such circumstances is tremendous. Both emotions are totally normal and healthy, and yet they can form a kind of deadlock that prevents healing. When unexpressed anger becomes bitterness and a seething rage, the deep experience of sorrow and release is virtually impossible. Resolution depends on the healthy channeling of anger and some degree of forgiveness.

ANGER, GRIEF AND FORGIVENESS

One of the biggest mistakes most of us make in our minds about forgiveness is that it somehow lets the "bad guy" off the hook. It doesn't. Forgiveness is simply the healing of your own mind and heart. Holding anger, resentment and hatred toward another injures your mind and heart; therefore, it follows that releasing those emotions through forgiveness would bring healing. Here are some points to consider about forgiveness:

• Forgiveness is for people, not despicable actions. Some actions are unthinkably horrible and absolutely unforgivable. Human beings can be worthy of forgiveness, even if their actions are not.
• Forgiveness does not absolve the wrongdoer of the wrongdoing. Forgiving someone is merely the decision to release the pain, fear and anger from your own mind and return to love. You can easily see the relationship to grieving here.
• Forgiving someone does not imply approval of their behavior or wrongdoing, nor does it assume that they will not do harm again in the future.

- Forgiveness is best accomplished through recognizing that each of us must "meet our maker" and experience an accounting of our actions on earth. Thus we have the opportunity through forgiveness to give the job of justice over to God.
- Forgiveness is a return to love, just as effective grieving is a return to love.
- Forgiveness will set you free from the illusion that you have to somehow punish the wrongdoer(s) in your mind by staying angry, or even carrying hatred. Hatred hurts the hater. Long-held anger and/or resentment hold no one accountable; they just harm the person holding it.

I want to be very clear here that anger is healthy and absolutely must be felt, experienced and expressed when loss and injustice occur. It is a healthy emotion that you must move through to be a healthy human being. Anger is a good place to visit, but you don't want to live there. Love is a great place to visit, and I highly recommend that you live there. And grief is a necessary part of loving.

There is much more that could be said about grieving and the grief process. The focus here has been on the role of anger in the grief process, and how to bring about resolution in grieving. I encourage you to educate yourself on the grief process and work toward resolution in your own life. The skills described in this chapter can be learned and mastered, so you do not have to live in fear of loving, or of losing those you love.

AFFIRMATIONS

- *To love means to risk the pain of losing.*
- *Grieving is a process that I am willing to learn and experience as a natural part of my life.*
- *The joy and fulfillment of loving and being loved are worth the pain of losing.*
- *Only love lives on as sorrow comes and goes.*
- *Love is the deepest of all emotions.*

10

Female Anger:
The Emergence of the
Powerful Woman

I will address women directly in some parts of this chapter, for the purpose of clear and effective communication. Male readers, please exercise your empathy and take advantage of this opportunity to better understand women's issues and how they may have affected you.

In the U.S. culture as in many others, there seems to be little or no permission for women to be angry. In our stories, movies and mythology, females are usually relegated to submissive roles, or roles that give them power only through their beauty, sexuality and intuitive abilities. This has only begun to change over the past few years.

A large-scale research study entitled the "Women's Anger Study" found that there are three common roots to women's anger: powerlessness, injustice and the irresponsibility of other people (Thomas 1993). Another study found that compared to men women stay angry longer, tend to be more resentful and are less likely to express their anger. It was also discovered in this research that women were more likely to "write off" a higher number of people, planning to never speak to them again (DiGiuseppe and Tofrate 2003). If this applies to you, you will find it helpful to apply some of the skills found in chapters 12 and 13.

VICTIM, PERSECUTOR AND RESCUER

In our families and workplaces, a common drama is one in which we find 1) a persecutor—the proverbial "bad guy," 2) a victim—who is usually portrayed as vulnerable and innocent, and 3) a rescuer—the proverbial "good guy (Steiner, 1990)."

Victims are most often portrayed as female, while persecutors and rescuers are usually portrayed as male. If females are going to show up in another role, it is most likely to be that of rescuer.

So where's the most anger? That emotion is usually ascribed to the perpetrator, although the rescuer quite often is "righteously angry" when coming to the aid of the victim. Here we see that the roles most likely to be played by females are least likely to involve anger. Of course, there are many exceptions to this, particularly in real life as distinguished from our fictional scenarios. The point here is that women seem to have been culturally programmed to believe that they are not supposed to be angry—and worse, that they are bad, wrong or evil if they are angry.

The emotions that are traditionally acceptable in the victim role are fear, pain and sorrow. So indirectly, these emotions have been designated feminine. I have had many female clients tell me over the years that when they get angry they cry. This can be very frustrating, since anger is designed to spur action and protect; yet the emotion being displayed is often seen as a sign of weakness and helplessness. This seems a direct indication that the cultural program has been effective. These women can't claim the power of healthy anger because their bodies know the "rules" ... that women are supposed to be helpless and vulnerable, and if protection is to come it should come from a man with his "righteous anger."

But what happens when the victim has had all she can take? You got it. She gets angry and she doesn't cry. That solves one problem, and takes us head-on into another one.

THE "ITCH" WORDS AND OTHER LABELS

A woman who is angry is often at great risk of being called a "bitch." In stories and even in U.S. history, we also find that powerful women have frequently been labeled "witch," whether they actually practiced any magical arts or not. These words are not always entirely negative in meaning (bitch can refer to canine females and witches can be good), but when they are used as epithets or accusations they are always negative. We also find the word "shrew" sometimes applied to angry women, as in the classic Shakespeare work entitled *The Taming of the Shrew* (1992).

So many women feel they are not supposed to have any anger, and there's something wrong with them if they do. Wrong on both counts. Women, here's your opportunity to set yourself free from some damaging cultural myths.

You have anger as a woman because it is a natural human emotion with tremendous value. When you feel angry, there is a very good reason for it, whether you know what the reason is or not. You need your anger as much as men need their capacity for fear and sorrow.

The division of emotions into masculine and feminine categories has done great damage to our bodies, minds and families. It is time for us to wake up and understand the emotions we all share as human beings, and how we can use them in healthy ways.

MYTHOLOGICAL IMAGES

There is a wonderful fairy tale in which a young prince is sent to seek an answer to the question, "What does a woman want more than anything else?" After his long and arduous journey in which he risks his life many times, runs into dead ends, and faces disappointment and despair, he finally finds someone who can tell him the answer.

The wise old woman says the one word for which the prince has searched most of his life.

"Sovereignty."

The prince goes home and finds that this is indeed the correct answer to the question, "What does a woman want more than anything else?"

Here is a suggestion that what women want, more than to be loved, more than to be protected, more than to be well provided for, is to have sovereignty over their own lives. The dictionary definition of sovereignty that best suits our context here is "complete independence and self-government." Whether you feel this applies to you or not, it certainly suggests that women want to have some degree of control and power over their lives. This is virtually impossible without the power of healthy anger.

Let's look at some images from classical mythology:

- **Athena**—Quiet and calm in peaceful times, fierce and deadly in war. She was known as the goddess of wisdom, handicrafts (especially weaving), war and agriculture. It is said that Athena sprang from her mother's womb in full war armor.
- **Artemis**—Known as the goddess of the hunt and moon, Artemis (also known as Diana) was patroness of unmarried women and youth, childbirth and wild animals.
- **Persephone**—Goddess of the underworld and the bringer of spring. Kidnapped by Hades and taken to the underworld, Persephone spent much of her life as a prisoner. When she emerged once a year, spring would return in celebration.
- **Medusa**—A once beautiful maiden who was turned into a monster. Her gaze could turn a man to stone, as legend has it, and live serpents adorned her head. A victim herself of a cruel spell, Medusa became something feared by many.

These classical figures can be helpful as images of powerful women. We also need some examples that are a little closer to home.

Oprah Winfrey provides an example of a powerful female figure. As an African-American businesswoman, she became one of the wealthiest individuals in the world. With a powerful spiritual focus, she takes positive action to right wrongs and speak out on topics that have great meaning to her. She supports individuals and causes she believes in, and uses her substantial power for the betterment of humankind.

Female political and civil rights leader Aung San Suu Kyi in Burma provides a significant image of peaceful and yet highly effective power in action. Rosa Parks demonstrated the same kind of courage and effectiveness in her simple and forthright refusal to submit to an oppressive system, in the process starting the American civil rights movement. Reformer and activist Erin Brockovich provides a wonderful model for the power of confidently directed energy and action on the behalf of injured and oppressed workers and their families.

In our movie and television "mythology," we find a heroic image of female power in Sigourney Weaver's character as the star of *Aliens*. Here we have leadership, courage and the raw physical energy that comes only from sheer determination. For *Star Trek Voyager* viewers, the half-Klingon B'lana and the former Borg "Seven of Nine" also provide some images of women with power, sovereignty and occasionally a lot of anger. The captain of *Voyager*, Janeway, is also female, and offers some potent role modeling for leadership in many of the episodes.

There are many examples in which we find women coming out of the victim position to finally overcome their perpetrator in a murderous rage. Farrah Fawcett's character in *The Burning Bed* shows how deadly this can be. While it always feels good to see the victim set things straight, what we're looking for here is a way that women can claim their power before they become victims.

You can probably come up with many more examples from your own experience, now that we are slowly waking up to the value and beauty of female power in the U.S. and global culture.

ANGER OF THE STAY-AT-HOME MOM

Most of us know the beauty and value of a warm, safe, nurturing home. We know, if we take the time to think about it, that creating and maintaining a home that is vibrant, welcoming, full and rich is a talent and skill that only some of us have. These abilities require mental, physical, emotional and spiritual qualities that are priceless in their value.

We know how much we love to come home and settle into comfort and peace after an afternoon, day or week in the hustle-and-bustle world. We know that our home needs to be a resting, healing, rejuvenating place, filled with laughter and love.

So why is it that most women who are homemakers dread the question, "So, what do you do?" Why does the answer "I'm a homemaker" seem to carry no worth, dignity or value?

We know the value of our children, and how they will be the creators and shapers of our future. We know that parenting is one of the most challenging and difficult things we can do as adults, and requires tremendous wisdom, flexibility, patience, strength, fortitude, love, forbearance and willingness to learn.

So why do so many women feel embarrassed, ashamed or "less than" when they tell someone that they are a "stay-at-home mom"? Why is the response from the other person so often an awkward "Oh . . ." followed by a change of subject? I'm sure this is why homemakers and stay-at-home moms usually prefer hanging out with each other—they know exactly how hard their job is, and they don't have to be embarrassed or ashamed of saying what they do. This safe atmosphere might just give them the opportunity to express their anger.

"I just don't feel like making love with him anymore," Kani stated emphatically and with more than a little anger. She and her husband Murphy had been married for seven years and had two small children. Kani had come for counseling to deal with her anger and to see if she could retrieve some of the passion she had lost in her marriage.

"I just feel so unimportant. It seems like his work and his life are valuable and a source of pride for him. He's the one with the profession, and he makes all of the money. But I swear I work harder than he does!" Kani was leaning forward now, and her eyes had fire in them.

"He expects me to take care of the children, pay the bills, clean the house, run the errands and do everything else that makes his life so easy. All he does is go to work and come home."

In a quieter tone, Kani continued. "I know he works hard, and sometimes his job is really difficult and I wouldn't trade places with him for anything. And he makes good money, which I really appreciate. But I don't tell him any of that because he doesn't seem to appreciate what I do. I know how important my work is, but no one else seems to, except the other stay-at-home moms. My kids would be lost without me, and there's no way to measure the tremendous value they have. They and my husband enjoy the benefits of all I do to keep our house working and comfortable. And they never say anything. Occasionally I get a 'Thanks, Mom' from one of the kids as they run out the door, but it just doesn't seem like enough. Sometimes I just want to run away. Then they'd know just how much I do!

"And my passion for making love with Murphy is just gone. I'm too tired, and I'm too angry. I know it's not all his fault, but I can't help but blame him. The longer we go without being intimate, the more distant we become." Kani seemed to be winding down a little, as she sighed and sat back in her chair.

Over the next few weeks, Kani told of her history of watching her mother struggle with the same feelings she was experiencing. "She never did anything about it. I knew she was angry, but she never said or did anything about it. She died a very unhappy woman, and I'm afraid I'm headed in the same direction."

Through the telling of her story and releasing the grief and anger she was carrying for her mother's plight, Kani's mood and attitude began to shift. I could see more energy in her face, and I began to hear optimism in her words. She had started telling her husband what she wanted, and to her surprise he was actually listening.

"I'm doing what my mother never did," Kani stated with a look of pride and determination. "I love my life and wouldn't change anything about it—I just want to be appreciated for what I do. It's funny, but as soon as Murphy started telling me how much he loves me for all I do for him and the children, it became easier for me to tell him how much I appreciate his hard work and the financial security he provides. We actually made love last night!"

The story doesn't always end as happily as this, as many of you well know. The purpose of providing resolution and positive outcomes in this book is to let you know that it can happen, and it does happen every day. The good news doesn't always reach our ears. But right now, all over the world, there are good people treating each other with kindness, respect and appreciation. It can happen for you too.

Here's another story that may be familiar to some of you.

TAKING CARE OF KING BABY

Betty had always been a pleaser. Her parents, her three sisters and her brother were all pleasers. It was very pleasing to be around her and her family, because it was their pleasure to make sure that everyone was pleased. This may sound a little ridiculous, but it really happens. And it happened in Betty's family.

They were nice people. They didn't dominate or try to control each other. They didn't vent anger or blame each other when things went wrong. They checked with each other before making decisions and tried to include everyone in plans that affected the family. This all worked fine for Betty, until she became an adult and moved out into the world that was not quite like the home she grew up in.

And then Betty met Ralph.

Ralph was different from Betty's family. Quiet, brooding and sometimes withdrawn socially, Ralph presented a challenge to Betty that she somehow embraced fully and mistook for love. She knew the kind of love she felt for her family, and something in her sought the new and different feelings that she felt with Ralph.

Ralph had no trouble making decisions. He was an engineer and owned his own highly successful construction company. He liked Betty's passivity because it left him plenty of room to dominate the relationship, their lives and ultimately Betty's every move.

Betty liked Ralph's decisiveness and authoritative approach to his work and his life in general. He knew what he wanted and had a clearly defined plan for reaching all of his goals. This was refreshingly different to Betty from what she had grown up with, and it allowed her to stay with her comfortably familiar pattern of cooperating, pleasing and going along with Ralph's plans.

Betty spent a lot of time doing Ralph's laundry. He liked his socks folded just so, and arranged in his drawer according to color and thickness. His underwear too had to be folded perfectly and placed in the "correct" pattern in his dresser. He demanded that his shirts be ironed by hand, arranged perfectly in the closet with exactly two inches of space between each one. And it went on from there.

Eventually, especially after their daughter and son were grown and off to college, Betty grew tired of pleasing Ralph all of the time. As a matter of fact, she wasn't very pleased at all. There was little pleasure in her life, as she had spent the last twenty-two years deriving pleasure from her children, and now they were gone.

Ralph did absolutely nothing inside the house, other than eat, sleep and watch television. He expected to be treated like a king, and Betty complied, to keep the peace. When the king

didn't get his way, he became "king baby" and threw a temper tantrum. In a calm and controlled manner, he would reit-
erate again and again what his expectations of Betty were. If
she argued, he got louder. If she continued to argue, he would
go away and pout. Sometimes he would not talk to Betty for
a week at a time. This bothered Betty so much she almost
wished he would scream at her instead.

Once, and only once, he did scream. And worse. In the heat
of their worst argument ever, Ralph backhanded Betty across
the mouth, knocking her down to the floor. On her way
down, she hit a side table and cut her head. When Ralph saw
what he had done, he went to his office and closed the door,
retreating further than ever into his shell of withdrawal and
pouting. Betty had to get the medical treatment she needed
on her own.

They never talked about what had happened. It horrified
them both so much that they found it easier to pretend it had
not happened and go on. But it made Betty want to get out of
the house more than ever.

Betty became very active as a volunteer at the local animal
shelter. She was so devoted to the animals and the staff that
she became almost indispensable to them in running their
operation. She loved her work. She was receiving praise and
recognition for the first time in her life. She started feeling
confident and strong within herself. You probably know what
came next.

Ralph didn't really like Betty being gone from the house so
much. Things were not getting done, and sometimes she
didn't have dinner on the table like he wanted when he came
home. When that happened, Ralph would just sit at the table
and stare at his empty plate until Betty put his meal on it.
Betty read about the "king baby" syndrome that men sometimes fall into, and realized that the label fit her husband "to
a tee."

Tension continued to mount in Betty and Ralph's home. It was no longer a warm, nurturing place to come home to, for either of them.

"Why don't you get your own dinner when I'm late?" Betty was crossing a line she had never crossed before. "I'm gone all day to the shelter, and then I get home and I see you staring at your empty plate like I'm some kind of servant who hasn't done her job! I can't take this anymore." Betty waited after her outburst, watching Ralph to see what he would do next. Her heart was pounding and her throat was dry. She remembered that day he had hit her, and she could almost picture him doing it again. She just didn't seem to be able to control the anger that was boiling up to the surface.

"I want you home" was all that Ralph said before going into his office and closing the door. The pouting and silent treatment had begun again.

Now Betty was furious. Thirty years of rage bubbled up from within her, and she had no idea what to do with it. This time, she did what she had always done. She made every effort to please her husband, burying her anger deep inside. She even quit her volunteer work, which made her feel like her heart was breaking.

Then Betty got sick. Her anger became toxic to her system, and she developed early symptoms of chronic fatigue syndrome. While lying in bed one afternoon reading about emotions and their impact on health, she realized that her anger was making her sick. She had not expressed it by continuing her work and doing what she knew was right for herself, so it turned into an illness, which got her out of the old pleasing pattern in another way.

Betty learned what all of us will learn eventually. At its best, anger is part of love and wisdom and is designed to further our health and happiness. Yet, when it is not honored and expressed in healthy ways, anger becomes unhealthy and dangerous.

Fortunately, Betty and Ralph finally sought counseling, and with significant effort on both their parts, they greatly improved their situation. After the initial period of venting and voicing anger, they began to talk through their issues in a safe and respectful manner. As they got it all out on the table, they gradually came up with a plan that would work well for both of them. Betty was finally able to voice all of her grievances and get her feelings out in a healthy way.

Almost immediately, Betty started to recover from her illnesses. She went back to work at the animal shelter, this time as a paid employee. Over time, she advanced in the organization and eventually started a related business of her own, through which she experienced tremendous success and fulfillment.

Ralph began to realize that he loved Betty more than he loved his habits and compulsive patterns. Though it was like pulling teeth for him at times, he began to take care of himself around the house. He learned to talk about his feelings when he got upset, and he stopped the pouting routines. King baby grew up and got his feet on the ground and became a responsible adult man who respected his wife as a person.

In Betty and Ralph's story we see an example of what happens when individuals overdevelop one aspect of themselves at the expense of another. Ralph was excessively masculine and greatly handicapped because he had not developed his feminine qualities. The "king" was the overdeveloped masculine, and the "baby" was the underdeveloped feminine.

Betty was the opposite, always receptive, supportive and nurturing and never direct in taking charge in her marriage. Their relationship was a great example of the old saying, "opposites attract." A positive way to look at this is that both saw their undeveloped self in the other and married it, hoping to learn how to develop their unrealized aspects.

In the outcome to their story, we can see how both Betty

and Ralph became more balanced, taking responsibility for their undeveloped selves. This was to their benefit individually and as a couple.

LET ME SHOW YOU THE DOOR

Sometimes anger shows up simply as powerful, effective action taken in a dangerous situation. This is a true story told to me by a very dear friend.

Leigh was in her pajamas, reading in her college dormitory bed. It was 11:30 P.M., and her roommate had gone home for the weekend. She had the feeling someone was watching her. Out of the corner of her eye she saw a pair of legs about three feet from her bed. A young, tough-looking man in his early twenties stood there holding a crumpled paper bag. He was mumbling something to the effect of "Wanna buy somethin'?"

Without thinking about what she was doing, Leigh, a small woman of slight build, stood up and took the much larger man by the arm. With a calm and dogged determination, she led him out of the room and down two flights of stairs, asking only, "How did you get in here?" Foul profanity spewed from the man's mouth all of the way down, which Leigh ignored, set on her mission to remove him. When they reached the front door, she opened it and he was gone.

When she got back to her room, one of the three girls from the room next door said, "He came to our room, and we told him we didn't want anything. We watched him go into your room and were waiting for you to scream."

All three girls were there, giggling and looking a little embarrassed. These were childhood friends from Leigh's hometown, and they had done nothing to warn her or intervene in any way. Leigh just looked at them for a few seconds, went in her room and closed the door.

She was not afraid at all during the entire episode. She did feel angry, however. A righteous anger that she described to me as a kind of "How dare you!" was directed toward the intruder. She was even angrier toward her so-called friends next door. They knew she was alone in her room and a strange man was entering, and they did nothing.

Leigh never raised her voice. She made no threats or took any violent action. She simply took effective action and got the job done.

This is the power of healthy anger in action. One of the greatest fears that many women have is of being victimized by a male intruder or assailant. Leigh was not a victim; she didn't become a perpetrator, and she didn't need a rescuer. When healthy anger is channeled into effective action, the victim-perpetrator-rescuer triangle is broken.

This is an account of someone's experience and is not to be mistaken for a recommendation of action. Every situation and every individual are unique and require unique courses of action.

PHYSICAL POWER AND THE POWER OF PRESENCE

In explaining their fear of men, many women will refer to men's superior physical strength as a basis for their fear. Yet in our example above, Leigh did not use physical strength to remove the intruder from her dormitory. It was the power of her presence that dominated the foul-mouthed man so that he apparently felt he had no choice but to comply with her will.

Anyone who has studied martial arts knows that it is not physical strength that determines the victor in a combat situation. It is clarity of purpose, skill and the ability to focus on the desired outcome that determines dominance and superior performance. While mastery of skills can be very helpful, without confidence and clarity of focus, knowledge and ability are sometimes useless. A good martial arts or self-defense instructor will tell you that your ability to be calm and confident is at least as important as your level of skill.

Author Carlos Castaneda's character Don Juan describes human will as fibers of light that emanate from the body just below the navel. He suggests that this largely unused human capacity can actually extend for great distances out from the body and effect physical changes in people and objects (Castaneda 1974). A woman who had absolute confidence in her physical and metaphysical power told me once that she had pushed a dangerous-looking man away from a distance of thirty feet.

These are possibilities to consider. If you have no experience to validate these ideas about the power of will and presence, don't allow your skepticism to close the door to your mind just yet. All that is being asked of you here is that you consider that you may have more power than you ever dreamed, and that you can use that power to enhance your protection and effectiveness in your world.

The power of presence and the strength of will are aspects of human capacity so vast that they may never be completely understood or fully tapped. When we open our hearts and minds to these magnificent realms, we are inviting not only the best of who we are as human beings, we are inviting our very Creator to participate as well.

LOSS OF POWER THROUGH PROJECTION

All of us were victims as children. The very fact of our size and limited mental ability made this so. We were victims of the circumstances around us, victims of what others did and did not do. All of this was outside our control.

Many female children experienced a particular type of victimization. In U.S. culture and even more so in some other cultures, some families favor and even revere male children over female children. Whether direct or indirect, spoken or unspoken, this inequity does great damage to children.

As a little girl, you may have felt that you would have more value if you were male. You saw privileges, opportunities and freedoms granted to males that were not available to you. This has an inevitable impact on self-image and identity when it occurs. In these cases, the beauty and power of femininity are ignored and denied.

One of the results of this all-too-prevalent dynamic is the projection of superior value and worth onto males. This is reflected in many ways, only a few of which include preferential treatment in business leadership opportunities and political office. On an everyday scale, many women are often subject to gender discrimination in retail sales and sometimes in conversation with friends and family.

As a woman, you need to be aware of the messages coming to you from the external world. You need to be aware of the internal beliefs that provide fertile ground in which these suggestions can take root.

Here are some suggestions for working with and reworking these messages and beliefs:

- Complete the unfinished sentence "Men are . . ." as many ways as you possibly can. Write from your old beliefs, and be sure to include all of the negative as well as positive references.
- Complete the unfinished sentence "Women are . . ." as many ways as you can. Write from your old beliefs, and

be sure to include all of the negative as well as positive references.

- Think of the spoken and unspoken messages from your parents, and what you learned about women and men from that powerful and primary source. Write these messages down as well.

- Look at the words and phrases you have used for women and men and see where the power, strength, potency, worth and value are—in both the positive and the negative references. Examine the judgments you are making, and look for the fear and anger references.

- Using your notes from the above exercises, write a list of what you consider to be your old beliefs about women and men, in full sentences.

- Try turning each of these statements around so that the meaning is opposite, and notice any feelings that come up. For example, change the belief "Men are angry" to "Women are angry," or "Women are weak" to "Women are strong." Journal about any feelings that arise.

- Continue with this exercise until you arrive at the new beliefs you want. Work to anchor your new beliefs in what you know to be true, making them balanced and realistic for you.

- Read and reread your new beliefs until they become a natural part of your subconscious belief system about yourself and others.

When you as a woman project anger, strength or power onto males and do not claim these assets as your own, you are giving away power that is rightfully yours. This is the nature of projection. If these qualities were not in you, you could not project them onto another. As an exercise, think of all of the people, women and men, whom you perceive as powerful in any way. Imagine that the very best part of this power is yours. How would you be different in the world if this were so? See yourself moving through your world as if all of that power you see in others were in you, and soon it will be so.

Claim the strength of your will and the power of your presence. They are your natural birthright, and you were meant to have them.

THE POWER OF THE FEMININE

One of the biggest challenges both women and men will face in reading this section is to remember that when I use the term "feminine" I'm not referring to women exclusively, and when I use the term "masculine" I'm not referring exclusively to men. Femininity and masculinity are mental, emotional and spiritual qualities we contain within ourselves, while our physical gender is a biological and physical aspect of our humanness.

Each of us, women and men, has both masculine and feminine power and energy. Masculine power can best be characterized as penetrating, direct, focused and initiating. Feminine power can best be characterized as receptive, open, nurturing and responsive. Most men tend to lead with their masculinity, and most women tend to lead with their femininity.

Anyone, female or male, who has not actualized her/his feminine power does not listen well, is not open to others' ideas, does not know how to nurture and has to be right all of the time. Anyone, male or female, who has not actualized his/her masculine power has trouble making decisions or forming an opinion, does not take initiative, is unclear in communication, and is easily dominated and controlled by others. We are seriously handicapped as human beings in either case.

I am addressing the power of the feminine here because I believe it has been undervalued in U.S. culture and in many other cultures throughout the world. Masculine power has been overvalued and overused, to the great detriment of us all. This has affected women very directly and personally, and has greatly contributed to women's anger.

Feminine power can be seen as the ability to wait, to watch, to listen and to learn. The feminine gathers information and is open to a variety of input from many different sources. The powerful feminine can hold and nurture children, adults, information and emotions. One way to understand this power is in the metaphor of the womb, which holds and nurtures life itself.

We have plenty of good talkers in the world and not enough good listeners. We have plenty of opinions expressed and decisions being made, and not enough information-gathering, contemplation and assimilation.

Here are some images and ideas for you to use in developing a vision for the woman you want to be. Use these ideas as goals, and outline steps you can take to reach them. Many of the exercises in this book, including the ten-step plan, will help you get to where you want to be.

THE HEALTHY ADULT WOMAN

She knows where she stands in the world. She has a clear sense of her physical body, and she is comfortable with it as it is. She takes care of her body, mind and spirit because she knows that's her job, and if she doesn't do it no one else will.

She loves her role as caregiver to her friends and family, yet she rarely if ever fulfills this role at her own expense. She is wise enough to know that when she cares for herself she is caring for the wife, mother, friend and businessperson that relates to others.

She is comfortable with her femininity. She knows how to grieve and hold loved ones in their grief. She enjoys relationships, and enjoys a variety of intimate connections with friends and family. She cultivates the depth and richness of her own soul through the care she gives to her body, clothing, home, plants and animals.

She laughs freely, openly and easily. She seeks pleasure for its own sake, and makes time in her schedule for play, rest and relaxation.

She reads, journals and meditates on a regular basis, as a way of continuing on the endless journey of self-discovery. She embraces her own wisdom, and she knows that she has much to learn. She is always growing.

She is comfortable with her own masculine spirit. She makes decisions when she needs to, and can be decisive, clear and direct in communication. She can take charge of situations, and does so on a regular basis as needed. She knows how to penetrate a complex problem and get to the bottom of an issue.

She values her relationships with women and men alike.

With women, she explores and celebrates the joy of sisterhood, and plumbs the depths of the sacred feminine in friendship, growth and knowledge.

With men, she dances with the tension and the passion of the male-female combination, celebrating the creativity and joy of complementary relationship. She loves openly and honestly, and does not give herself away.

She is deeply aware of her sexuality, and embraces it totally and without shame. She preserves her most precious gifts for the partner who approaches her with the utmost gentleness, respect and power of presence. She preserves sexual contact for the safe container of a loving, committed relationship or marriage.

With children, she is light and playful, steady and wise. Children are drawn to her naturally, because they know they will be accepted and loved exactly as they are. They also know she will keep them safe and let them know where they stand. She sets the necessary limits with children and allows them the freedom they need to grow and learn. And she knows how to enter their world and let them guide her in their magical world of play.

She has a sense of her purpose and mission in life. It does not have to be big, but it may well be. She is as comfortable and fulfilled in her garden or reading her favorite novel as she is in important meetings and conversations about future plans and large sums of money.

She does not let the biases, fears or expectations of others determine who she is or what she does. She is governed, guided and directed from within.

Her spiritual focus is a central and essential part of her life. She has a spiritual practice that she maintains through regular prayer, reading and meditation. She is connected with a spiritual community, either through her friends and associates or through the religious organization of her choosing. She knows that she is a child of God and that this is the original, final and pervasive reality in which she lives, thinks, breathes and moves.

AFFIRMATIONS

- *I am glad that I was born female.*
- *My female gender is a beautiful and precious aspect of my identity and my existence.*
- *As a woman, I am powerful and at peace with myself.*
- *I am constantly learning, growing and becoming who I was born to be.*
- *I accept the healthy roles that I choose to play, and I am not defined or confined by them.*
- *I am aware of others' expectations of me, and I am not governed by them.*
- *I take charge and make things happen.*
- *I know how to surrender, let go and allow life processes to unfold.*
- *I am guided and directed by my Creator from deep within my being.*
- *I am at peace with myself.*

11

Male Anger:
The Awesome Power
of the Gentle Man

I will be talking directly to male readers for much of this chapter. Female readers, please use this opportunity to better understand some of the issues that men face, and what impact these dynamics may have had on you.

The goal of this chapter is to help you better understand yourself as a man, and how to deal with your male anger. We will look at the dark and the light side of what it means to be male, and discuss what it means to be healthy and whole.

When we think of anger, the face of a furious, raging man often comes to mind. The thought of an angry man is not a pleasant one. Throughout history, we have been taught to fear, avoid and even hate this image of male anger. This is for good reason. Wars have been caused by such men, corrupted by power and controlled by their emotions—acting out their rage on millions of human beings they never met. This same image is associated with abuse of women, children and others. How can we as men ever feel good about our anger in the face of this image of a violent, raging maniac who has done so much harm? How can we face our own suppressed emotions when we fear that such a violent rage exists deep within us? We need new images of maleness.

Thanks to education, healing and media access, we have become painfully aware of how many men abuse and molest their children and wives. There seems to be a collective reluctance among men to face this dark inner realm that is at fault for so much suffering. The shame and fear a man feels at the mere prospect of facing and embracing his anger and potential for violence is tremendous and seemingly insurmountable. So the suppression continues.

Suppression, of course, leads to a couple of different alarming consequences. One is the inevitable explosion and loss of control that comes when the rage reaches a boiling point. In such cases, suppression leads to more abuse and violence. The other result of stuffing anger is illness and eventually premature death (Webb and Beckstead 2003; Stoney 2000). It is my opinion that the reason men die younger than women is related to our tendency to suppress our emotions and—even worse—hate ourselves for having them. To get a feel for this, go visit a rest home sometime. You will find that the majority of the residents are female and widows.

So here we are, on the horns of a dilemma. To live longer, to claim our emotions, we must face our fear and shame associated with male anger.

THE DESTRUCTIVE
POWER OF HELPLESSNESS

One of the most striking realizations I have come to in my thirty-plus years of work as a psychotherapist is that rage and violence often come straight out of a sense of helplessness and powerlessness. The violent man often feels like a helpless victim inside, and that feeling is totally unacceptable to him. He then resorts to the primitive action of violence, determined to change his circumstances and put a stop to the cause of his distress.

Perhaps a more familiar version of this is total frustration. You've tried everything you know to solve the problem, and nothing seems to be working. That's when some of us as men find ourselves turning to anger as a last resort when all else has failed (as in the following example).

Jim had worked all of his life to provide well for his family, and succeeded. They never wanted for anything materially. "I just don't understand why they're not happy. I give them everything they want, and it's just not enough. My wife's depressed, and all my kids want is more money and freedom to be away from home. Sometimes it gets to be too much for me, and that's when I lose it."

He came to see me because his anger outbursts were getting all too frequent. Madge, Jim's wife, never complained. She just got more depressed. And ate more. And slept more. Jim was getting close to retirement, yet was dreading the thought of spending more time at home.

"She never cleans the house unless her family is coming to visit. We live in this huge expensive house, and it's filthy most of the time. I'm not comfortable in my own home. I try to be patient. As a matter of fact, I didn't say anything about it for years. I tried asking nicely if she would pick up a little more between the cleaning lady's visits, and that didn't seem to help either. Lately I've just been getting mad and screaming at her." Jim looked at the floor as he spoke.

"What do you say when you're screaming at her?" I asked.

"I don't know," Jim replied. "I just ask her why she doesn't do more for the kids and why she sleeps all of the time. I get so mad I can hardly remember what I said after I calm down. It's like I blank out or something."

This was a familiar story to me. I have often found that men who go into extreme anger episodes are often not fully conscious of what they're saying or doing. This is why it is so dangerous. This is how we can forget that the person we're angry at is also the person we love more than anyone else in the world.

In a joint session with his wife, Jim suddenly blurted out to her, "You're killing me! Can you see this, doc? Can you see how she's killing me?" Jim's wife and I were silent for a moment. His words seemed to echo in the room.

"How is she killing you, Jim?" I asked.

"She just gets more and more depressed, and the doctors can't seem to do anything about it. I can't stand the way we're living. It gets me so mad that I can't sleep at night and have a hard time concentrating at work." Jim was leaning forward, holding his head in his hands at this point.

"So for you, getting Madge to change is a matter of life and death." Jim was silent in response to my words. He knew there was something wrong with that line of thinking. And yet that's exactly how he thought.

A few weeks later, in an individual session, Jim asked, "What does it mean when a picture keeps popping up in your head and you can't make it go away?"

"Well, let's consider that it is your mind trying to tell you something that might be helpful in your healing process. What is the picture?" I responded.

"I must be crazy. It just doesn't make any sense. I keep see-ing my mother's face in front of mine, and she looks horrible. She has so much hatred in her eyes, and it feels like she's got her hands around my throat. See what I mean? It makes no sense!" Jim was trying to laugh at this point, hoping I would agree that the vision he was having made no sense and should be disregarded.

"Let's just go with it for a minute. Tell me as much about the picture as possible. Also tell me everything you can remember about any circumstances, feelings or memories that seem to go along with it." I waited quietly after speaking, knowing this was not going to be easy for him.

Over the next few weeks of individual sessions, Jim revealed that his mother had gotten pregnant with him before she and his father were married. They felt they had to marry because of the pregnancy, and did so even though nei-ther really wanted to. Subsequently, Jim's parents had fought almost constantly. Jim slowly put together the possibility that his mother had blamed him for having to marry his father, and for all of the misery she had felt in the marriage.

During this time in Jim's therapy, a memory began to re-surface. Though he had not thought about it in a long time, he recalled a scene in which his mother threatened him. Over a few weeks' time, he put this memory together with the "pic-ture" that had been coming to his mind.

"I thought she was going to kill me," he stated quietly after putting the memory together with the image for the first time.

"I even have a hard time breathing sometimes lately, like there's something tight around my throat. Could this all be real, doc? I feel like I'm crazy thinking about this stuff!" He seemed to be pleading for reassurance, and yet not really wanting his experiences authenticated as a valid memory.

"I want you to trust your own mind and heart on this, Jim. I know you don't want to believe it. And yet another part of you wants an explanation. The truth will come to you over time. Meanwhile, you and I need to keep an open mind and explore the possibilities." He seemed somewhat content with my statement.

During this time, Jim spontaneously stopped thinking or saying that his wife was "killing" him. His anger toward her began to subside. Without the oppressive anger from her husband, she began to make progress in dealing with her depression, which was helpful to both of them.

In therapy, Jim and I worked with the vision of his mother choking him as if it was a real memory, and he got some emotional release and relief from this process. He never decided whether this event actually occurred, but he knew he needed to deal with the feelings he had about it.

As Jim's anger toward his wife subsided, he began to work on his skills of showing love and support to her for every effort she made. I encouraged him to talk about why he loved her, and what he appreciated about her. Through this process, aided by her recovery in her own therapy, Jim began to feel and show respect for the woman he loved. The chest pains he had been having when he first started therapy were starting to subside.

"It's funny, but I feel more powerful and more like a man when I'm kind and caring toward my wife. Inside, I felt like a little boy when I used to rage at her. I always thought it was tough and manly to be angry, and kind of wimpy to be loving. Now I'm realizing it's just the opposite." Jim was relaxed as he said this, and had a slight smile on his face.

"Madge treats me with a lot more respect these days. I am starting to look forward to going home. The kids are going to be heading off to college in the next couple of years, and I think it's going to be great. Our sex life is even starting to rekindle." Jim spoke quietly. "I know I have to keep at this, but I think we may be out of the woods on the worst of it, doc."

I had watched this man move from an angry, blaming abuser to a powerful, gentle man. He was devoted to mastering the art of being a loving husband, and a strong provider and protector. Most importantly, he had learned to protect his wife from his own anger. He was demonstrating the essence of what it means to be an emotionally healthy man.

NO GURLS ALOWD

Remember those books when we were kids about the boys building secret clubhouses where the girls couldn't come? There was a period of our late childhood and early adolescence when (God forbid!) girls were actually bigger than us. Word had it that they got smarter earlier than we did, too. No wonder we had to develop some camaraderie among ourselves just to maintain a little dignity as guys! Cub and Boy Scouts provided some of these opportunities, but many of us just worked it out in the neighborhood. We weren't ready or able to date yet, and forming same-sex social groups was natural and easy.

There is a popular theory of developmental psychology, presented by H. S. Sullivan (1953) in *The Interpersonal Theory of Psychiatry*, which says that boys and girls both go through a stage during preadolescence when they prefer the company of the same sex. Some kissing and sexual play often occurs during this phase of development as a natural and even healthy way of safely experimenting in the mysterious world of physical intimacy. If you remember such experiences, you may have some fear and guilt associated with them. It is very common for men in particular to have strong fears of being homosexual because of childhood experimentation. If you have such fears, take this opportunity to relieve your anxiety. It is okay. It was just a stage that many of us go through as a part of growing up.

DEVELOPMENT OF THE AMERICAN MALE

If our fathers were absent, drunk or otherwise emotionally unavailable, we had little support in working through this somewhat confusing aspect of development. It was Dad's job to provide a role model for us, showing what it means to be a man, to be masculine. Of course, he most likely did not receive this from his own father, which is why he wasn't there for us.

In the absence of Dad's guidance, we had to wing it, which means we got it from TV, movies, video games and comic books. We learned about being men from stereotypical images from John Wayne to Steven Seagal. Even if we did have a father figure around, he most likely had role models with the same kind of limitations.

So, coming out of this developmental stage, we had to get tough (like our heroes) and we had to show this to each other and to the girls. Thus came the birth of macho in the American male. Remember how cruel some of us were to each other as adolescents (and this applies to both male and female), particularly in junior high school? This is one of the ways we worked our way out of the awkward stage of development when we didn't like the opposite sex. What a price we paid! Some of my worst memories are from those years when social acceptance seemed a matter of life and death.

Behind the false front of the macho man is a scared, confused little boy who was never supported and guided through his own emotional, sexual and social adjustment. You are probably aware that the macho male social scene includes jokes and slurs about women and homosexuals. This seems to follow naturally from the unresolved sexual development of early adolescence and the absence of appropriate male role models.

Afraid of our own tenderness and sensitivity and determined to convince ourselves and the world that we aren't "momma's boys," we surge hard into the tough, aggressive image of a man. We leave so much behind when we do this. It's too great a sacrifice. In many ways this process prevents us from growing up. There are a lot of little boys in grown-up bodies running around, running our companies and our countries.

The situation becomes pretty serious when you consider the consequences of immature men playing with billions of dollars, world politics and nuclear weapons. It is also sobering to look at the kinds of fathers and husbands so many of us turned out to be. Being stuck with a seriously lacking macho male image to fulfill, we find ourselves severely handicapped when it comes to expressing the true, intimate feelings necessary for healthy relationships.

THE PROTECTOR/PROVIDER ROLE

One of the primary driving forces in men is the role of protector/provider. Our natural and genetic predisposition is to focus outside the home in this mode, protecting our families from external intruders and going out into the wilderness of the business world to bring home the proverbial bacon.

One of the greatest and most common causes of male anger occurs when this role is somehow threatened, doubted or questioned. An all-too-common response to a wife's unhappiness, regardless of the real reason, is, "What's the matter? Don't you like the house? Don't we have enough money? I put food on the table and clothes on your back. What more do you want?" This is a result of very narrow thinking. The role of protector/provider is much broader and deeper than just providing financial comforts and warding off would-be intruders.

We have to bring our role as protectors and providers into the home, and into the relationships we have with our families. The role of protector includes protecting your family from your anger, sarcasm, criticism, judgment, irritability, blame, projection, constant doubting, questioning and second-guessing. The role of provider includes providing love, support, romance to your spouse, humor, fun, creativity, empathy, patience, nurturing, caregiving, forgiveness, emotional safety, financial health and spiritual leadership. That may sound like a lot, but that's what it takes to have a happy, loving, healthy family with vibrant, growing spouses and children.

The main point for our context here is to provide your family with emotional safety and protect them from your anger. Without these basic elements of the protector/provider role, the provider becomes the intruder, and far too many men have been taken out of their own homes in handcuffs already. It's time we do some serious growing up as men, and a major part of that is becoming mentally, emotionally and spiritually healthy.

THE ONLY TWO EMOTIONS ALLOWED

As males, many of us got the message that it is okay to be angry. We may have also learned that it is not okay to show fear or pain or sorrow. We were shown plenty of male anger on TV and in the movies. It was almost always violent and aggressive—even deadly. As a matter of fact, male anger was often what saved the day for the good guys. The only time we saw fear or pain was in the faces and voices of the bad guys, just as the hero was about to "get" them. The implication is, of course, that if we show or even feel fear or pain, we are weak and will be destroyed.

Most of us rarely, if ever, saw our fathers cry. If we did, it was by accident, and he was most likely ashamed of himself for "losing control" or "breaking down." The powerful suggestion of this role modeling is that we are never to be vulnerable or acknowledge our deeper, more private feelings. This means basically that we can't be emotionally close to another person, male or female.

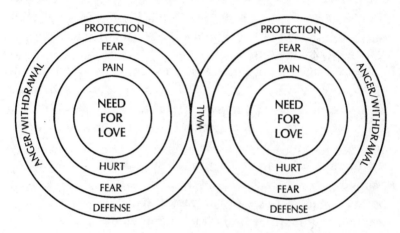

Figure 11.1 The Wall of Defensiveness

If you look at Figure 11.1, you will get a picture of what happens when intimacy stops at the level of defense and protection. Sure, we get to hide (and deny) our fear and pain, but look at what is in the center. In hiding our fear and pain, we severely limit our ability to love. Another way of saying this is that if we can't face our own fear, we are not strong enough to risk the vulnerability of opening our hearts in true intimate love.

Many of us as males were also only allowed a limited kind of love. It had to be love for a female, and it had to be sexual. With only anger and sexually oriented love as acceptable

emotions, we have been at risk of becoming emotional crip-
ples as men, with a tremendous amount of unmet needs.
Getting aggressive or having sex were our only two options
for emotional release and relief of tension. When we combine
these two emotions, sexual love and anger, we have major
problems.

I believe this explains much of the physical and sexual
abuse perpetrated by men on women and children. It cannot
be overemphasized how important it is that we deal with this
as men. It is something we have to work out together—we
can't get it from women.

Just as many of our fathers were absent, most of our mothers were very present, and we were dependent on them to
meet our needs. They had to try (and, of necessity, fail) to
meet the needs that our fathers were neglecting by their
absence. I think this made us angry with our mothers and
therefore at women, even though it wasn't their fault. We
blamed Mom for Dad's absence, in many cases, simply
because she was there and an easy scapegoat. Dad may have
been out saving the world and bringing home the bacon, but
he was nonetheless equally responsible for what was going
on in our home.

Now the picture is complete. We have groups of immature
men playing with expensive toys and making derogatory
jokes about women and sex. Consequences range from world
war and wife-beating to boring social lives and lousy marriages. Consequences also include depression, anxiety and
early death due to stress-related illnesses. It is time we did
something about this, men. If we don't, no one will.

Fortunately, we are starting to break free from the stifling,
ugly, limiting and even deadly image of the American male.

AWAKENING THE WILD MAN

As an author, poet and facilitator of men's work throughout the United States, Robert Bly has contributed greatly to the development of a healthy image of maleness. Along with author and master storyteller Michael Meade, psychologist James Hillman and others, Bly has truly broken new ground in this area. With the help of a growing number of associates, they are paving the way for the creation of a completely new set of ideas about what it means to be male.

The work of these pioneers is now being carried forward most effectively by a group called *The ManKind Project*. Devoted to healing the dysfunctional or nonexistent images of maleness that many of us grew up with, this not-for-profit organization also provides an initiation experience entitled *The New Warrior Training Adventure*. For more information, visit *www.mkp.org*.

One of the stories Bly tells is the myth of Iron John, which is also the title of one of his books (1990). The message is that within the male psyche is an ancient, deep and powerful masculinity. Contacting the wildness of our nature is risky and scary.

As the story goes, Iron John is under the water of man's soul, and no one has visited there for a long time. Our experiences with anger and violence cause us to fear that the Wild Man will be violent and aggressive. But he is neither.

As symbolized in the image of the Wild Man, the healthy male is forceful and acts with resolve. He is not cruel, nor opposed to others. He is also not controlled by others and their expectations. The healthy male is at times unpredictable, not necessarily set in his ways. He is guided by an inner spirit that is uniquely his own, as manifested in his thoughts, words and actions. The dark watery moistness of the Wild Man's home at the bottom of a pool in a forest represents the sensitive, receptive aspects of the male, so long rejected by most cultures as not being masculine.

Becoming a healthy man means facing all of the emotions surrounding love—including love of life, music, poetry, art and nature. The word "wild" in the context we are using it here implies untamed, uncontained and uncontrolled by external forces. In his book *The Middle Passage*, James Hollis (1993) refers to a "second adulthood," in which we become more directed by our own values and sense of integrity than by what others think, feel and want of us.

Each one of us as men can awaken the spontaneous, creative spirit within, whatever our background may have been. To make the mysterious journey within to accomplish this awakening, we must be willing to face and deal with all of our emotions, including our anger.

It seems we are caught between fear of being the embarrassingly adolescent macho male and the seemingly worse alternative, the dreaded "wimp." The fear associated with both of those images—macho and wimp—comes from our concern about what other people will think of us.

The real question is, what do you think of yourself? How do you see your own strengths and weaknesses? Do you live according to your own values, or are you driven to perform according to someone else's or society's standards?

Fortunately, we don't have to choose between macho and wimp. We saw Jim choosing another alternative at the beginning of this chapter. Slowly, the image of a new healthy man is beginning to emerge. You will find that image deep within your own soul. Here are some ideas to consider about what it means to be a healthy man.

A HEALTHY ADULT MAN

He laughs easily. His smile is relaxed, as if it belongs there on his face. He is at home in his body. He may not be in perfect shape, but he is not extremely out of shape either. When alone or lost in his own thoughts, he looks interested and thoughtful, not worried or afraid. He takes care of himself.

He works hard when he works, but he knows how to stop. He is successful at what he does, and he enjoys doing it. He wouldn't do it if he didn't enjoy it.

He is motivated by a sense of purpose, by his own values and ideals. He is not governed by the demands and expectations of society or even those close to him. He is sensitive to what is required to be a part of a functioning society, and he does not break the law. He is also sensitive to the emotional needs of loved ones and responds skillfully and effectively.

He is devoted to becoming a master of expressing love and appreciation, for his own health and for the health of his relationships. He does what he feels is right for himself and others concerned, based on the situation at hand.

He is capable of feeling desire and following this feeling. He trusts his own intuition and judgment, and also takes full responsibility for his mistakes. He is guided by a profound sense of spiritual purpose that emanates from deep within his being. He knows where he is going, and he is constantly reworking and expanding his plan.

His friends and associates consider him reliable. They know he would not agree to something if he did not intend to follow through. He knows how to say no. He is consistent and flexible at the same time.

Some aspects of his life are structured and disciplined, while there are times when he seems to be a totally new and different person. He is capable of surprising even those who know him best. He is always growing and changing. He is not afraid of change and the challenges brought about in transition.

He can lead and he can follow. He does not seem to care which he does, but he does want to move. If the available leadership is ineffective, he will not follow. If no one follows his own leadership, he will reevaluate his direction and focus. If he finds that he is still committed, he will continue alone.

He is fully and completely an adult man. He is learning from his childhood and past experiences and uses them as a resource for self-knowledge and understanding. He knows how to meet his own emotional needs, yet is able to receive emotionally from others. He feels no guilt or shame. He can talk openly, when appropriate, about his own pain, fear and need for love. He expresses his love openly for those who are important to him. He also expresses his anger.

When angry, he becomes clear and precise in his communication. He may raise his voice, but only slightly, so the listener will get the message. He always combines his expressions of anger with a positive emotion. He can be smart and angry at the same time. He can be angry and respectful at the same time. He can even combine his anger with humor in a way that serves his purpose but harms no one. The person on the receiving end of his anger always knows that he means what he says.

If his anger builds and he feels tense and irritable, he withdraws to a safe place and works out the physical tension and mental turmoil in a way that suits him. Then, when he is calm and clear on what he wants to say, he goes back and expresses his feelings verbally to the appropriate people. He does not blame others for his feelings or his problems. He takes full responsibility for himself as a person and for his needs and feelings. He is fully aware of both his personal freedom and his responsibility. He has very high integrity.

He is creative. Being creative is a spiritual process for him.

He believes creativity is something that flows through him, using the resources he has available for expression. His creativity comes out in his conversation, his clothing and routes he takes to get from one place to another. He enjoys many forms of creative expression through music, art and verbal expression. He is creative because he loves the energy of new life and meaning, and is only moderately concerned about others' opinions of his outcomes.

He is spiritually focused, though he does not talk very often in spiritual terms. He may be a part of an organized religion, though if he is, he does not restrict his beliefs to the confines of the organization and its doctrine. His spiritual faith is a private matter to him, although he does share his views with a select group of people. He has nothing to prove, and he has no need to convince anyone of anything. He respects the right of everyone to believe as they choose and expects the same respect from others. His spiritual life is the center of his existence. His deity is loving, all-knowing and all-powerful. He is aware of eternity.

He knows how to play and be childlike when the time or mood is right. A sense of joy periodically and regularly rises from within him. He is comfortable with children and with animals, and they enjoy him as well. He can feel at home in the penthouse of a New York skyscraper or alone on top of a mountain. The world is his home, and he is comfortable in his own skin. He is glad to be alive.

AFFIRMATIONS

- *As a man, I am a vast mystery.*
- *I love and embrace my natural sense of adventure.*
- *I am in the process of discovering what it means to be a joyous, healthy man.*
- *I accept all of my emotions, my pain, fear and anger.*
- *By claiming my pain, fear and anger, I am taking charge of them.*
- *When I am in charge of my feelings, I am in charge of my life.*
- *I fully claim my power as a healthy man.*
- *As a man, it is important that I be open and receptive.*
- *I am sensitive and responsive in relationships with women and men.*
- *I know the power of being a gentle man.*
- *I am in charge of my life.*
- *I am open to the deep and magical aspects of who I am.*
- *I am at peace and at home in the world.*

12

Releasing Anger
in Healthy Ways

The two ways in which we express emotion are through release and communication. This chapter is devoted to teaching you methods for healthy and safe release of anger and the related emotions.

ANGER LIVES IN YOUR BODY

We have all heard the phrase "talk it out" as a recommended way of resolving anger and other difficulties in relationships. This does work, but only if the physical and emotional components of the anger are in a state of balance and there is an internal sense of equilibrium. When you get angry, your body gets hot, your muscles are tense, your heart pounds and your thoughts race out of control. This is not a time for trying to verbally communicate your feelings.

In his groundbreaking book *Emotional Intelligence,* Daniel Goleman explains how extreme emotion can actually shut down the higher functions of the brain, making rational thought virtually impossible (1997). Most of you have learned that it is best not to make any important decisions while extremely angry or afraid.

During experiences of extreme anger, it is time to attend to your own internal physical and emotional needs until you can relax enough to think clearly. Only when you have relaxed and regained full access to your brain's capacity can you begin to communicate effectively with another person about what is going on. Your emotions live in your body, and your mind is merely an interpreter or messenger describing the feelings that are pulsing within you from your head to your toes.

ANGER RELEASE
METHODS AND TECHNIQUES

There are some simple exercises you can use to release the physical tension associated with your anger. By doing this, you will become more relaxed and better able to think and communicate verbally. The buildup of physical and emotional tension actually blocks your mind from clear thinking and prevents effective communication. Therefore, the first thing you must do when you are extremely angry is to release the physical energy or "blow off some steam." This is done primarily through the use of the two types of approaches I will describe below.

Please be aware that any exercises that you try from this book are undertaken at your own risk. If you have any doubt whatsoever as to your emotional readiness or mental stability, please consult a qualified professional before actually attempting the exercises.

Nonaggressive, Socially Friendly Methods of Anger Release

Often we feel anger at times when we have to or choose to deal with it internally—for example, in traffic, a public place or in the presence of someone who would be hurt by our anger if we were to release it. Following are some methods for managing, processing and/or releasing anger when some kind of physical expression is inappropriate or undesirable. Please understand that these methods will not work for everyone. It is extremely important that you understand that it is not being suggested here that you simply suppress your anger and be done with it.

1. **Breathe into it and let the emotion expand outward into your body.** Do this by imagining that the energy of your anger is getting bigger and bigger. Create an image of your anger as a cloud, a fire, a fist or whatever fits best for you. Breathe deeply into your stomach and exhale slowly as you feel and imagine this image of your anger getting bigger and bigger until it expands outside your body. Keep going with your image until it gets so big that it disappears. This is very effective, and yet may be only a temporary release for some people.

2. **Create an exaggerated image in your mind of someone or something giving full and complete expression to your anger.** It is essential that this image not include violence. The use of imagery is a form of rehearsal, and can in some cases perpetuate behavior similar to what is being imagined (Samuels and Samuels 1975). Here are some examples of images that have worked for others:

- A tornado ripping across an open field. Let the power of this force give expression to your emotion.
- A gigantic being thrashing about, grabbing thunderbolts from the sky and tossing them into huge black thunderheads.
- A martial arts master taking charge of a situation without harming anyone.
- A magnificent dancer swirling, sweeping, swooping and flying about, twirling and spinning with tremendous energy and power.

3. **Send love and justice to the person or situation toward which you feel anger.** Imagine that the power, clarity and justice of divine perfect love is shining like the brightest of all lights directly on and into the person(s), requiring that they face the truth and reality of their actions. Watch sobriety and realization dawn across their face as the light of justice prevails. Examples include:

- See the driver who is endangering his own and others' lives being pulled over and getting a huge ticket, or having his license revoked. Watch his face as he realizes the insanity of his actions.
- Imagine deep truth and clarity dawning across the mind of the tyrants and abusers who have wrought terror and suffering on your and others' lives. Watch what happens in their eyes as perfect love is revealed and ultimate justice is done.

4. **The first chance you have after your anger has come up, write or journal about your feelings.** The main point to emphasize about this technique is to let the angry part of your mind have full and pure expression on the paper, holding nothing back. Do not censor or edit in this process, or you will not get full release. Do not be reasonable or civilized. This allows full purging of the anger and

gives you a chance to see the depths of your emotion clearly. It also gives you a place to put your anger, out on the page where you can look at it consciously and examine it with your logical and reasonable mind.

Physical and Vocal Anger Release Methods

The space, equipment and supplies needed for these methods are usually available in most homes. These exercises need to be done in private, unless you are with a trained professional or in a therapy group with a professional present. Your family and friends usually won't understand, and you don't need to be questioned about what you are doing. As much as possible you need to feel safe. I usually advise clients who choose to do this at home to do so when they are alone in their house—unless their spouse or roommate understands and supports the anger work.

Here are some considerations:

1. A mattress or large overstuffed pillow is usually helpful. If you're using an exercise mat, you definitely need a pillow, as most mats are just not soft enough. It is very important that precautions be taken to avoid injury. After all, the point is to provide an experience of expressing anger in a way that doesn't hurt anyone, including the person doing the anger work.

2. Some people do anger work alone in their car. Although this is better than taking it out on another person, it can be dangerous and I don't advise it. If you feel you are going to explode, however, it may be healthier to scream alone in your car than to suppress your anger and hurt yourself—or stuff it until you explode at someone you love. I strongly recommend that if you do this, you at least stop your car first.

3. Another piece of equipment sometimes useful in anger release work is a bataca or "encounter bat." These are foam-padded bats that can be ordered through special supply houses that handle therapeutic equipment. The bat is sometimes helpful to people with back problems that might have a problem hitting a mat or pillow with their fists or arms. It also allows an opportunity for the person to feel more powerful and in control. Tennis rackets also work well for this exercise. When using any of these items it is wise to wear gloves to avoid causing blisters.

4. If a "body bag" or sand-filled canvas punching bag is used, it is important to use some type of gloves to avoid scraping the skin off your knuckles. Using gloves may also be necessary if hitting a vinyl mat with your clenched fists. The upright bag, either suspended from the ceiling or leaned into a corner, is sometimes helpful for those who would rather stand than kneel in the anger release process. If the bag is suspended from the ceiling, it needs to be somehow anchored to the floor. This is to prevent the delay in your release work as you wait for the bag to swing back in your direction. To achieve a complete release, you need to be able to have a full-blown explosion, and this can't be accomplished if you have to wait and plan your blows to a swinging punching bag.

POSTURING AND POSITIONS FOR PHYSICAL RELEASE OF AGGRESSIVE ENERGY

The Upright Position

In the early stages of anger work, many people are stuck in blaming someone else for their anger. This is natural, of course, particularly when we have been hurt or abused by someone else's behavior. When this is the case, people usually want to do their anger work standing up and want to picture the face of the person they are blaming on the mat or bag. I do not encourage this, but it is better to allow a person to try this method of release than to cause them to continue suppressing their anger.

The following example is extreme, and it may not relate to you directly. We are all affected by the increasing incidents of violence in our society, however, and it is good to know that there are ways of possibly preventing it. This is a true account of using anger work to prevent workplace violence, with details altered for protection of privacy.

Matt checked into the hospital to keep from killing his boss. He was certain that if he had stayed out and continued to go to work, he would have committed murder. When he came to my Anger Management group, he insisted that his anger existed only because of what his boss had done. He refused to claim responsibility for his emotions and refused to try any of the anger-release methods I recommended. As his discharge date approached, I gave in to his request for a private session in which he planned to hit a mat up against the wall while picturing his boss's face and body on the mat. He did this with lots of profanity and seething hatred. He did not experience any type of emotional release, and he told me the next day that he didn't feel any better. As a matter of fact, he said he hated his boss more than ever.

This is an example of the results of blaming. When we blame others for our anger, fear and pain, we are giving them all of our power. This is a difficult lesson. It seems we each need to learn it over and over throughout our lives. Matt was beginning to learn this lesson for the first time.

He was so afraid of leaving the hospital with his feelings of rage and hatred unresolved that he finally agreed to try some anger-release work in the ways I recommended. In the seclusion room the last day before his discharge, I got him to talk about his feelings toward his father as he was growing up. Immediately the same feelings of rage and hatred began to surface. This time, however, I got him to acknowledge that the feelings were his responsibility alone, that they had been with him all of his life.

Before I conclude Matt's story, I want to make a few more comments about the upright methods of anger release. I still recommend this position for those with back problems or for those to whom the other positions are too threatening at first. My primary concern about this position is that it requires people to use their fists. This does not allow the powerful release that is accomplished in the two methods I will describe below. There is also serious risk of injury to the wrists, knuckles and fingers with a straight-on punching technique. If this position is used, cautious advice should be given and the person should be encouraged to move to one of the safer positions as soon as possible.

The Power Position

I refer to this technique as the "power position" only because I have seen so many people claim their power over their lives and emotions while using this method. It seems to be the position that most people are the least uncomfortable with when first trying anger-release work.

The power position first involves kneeling on the end of a bed, mattress or soft mat. The person's knees should be on the mat, not on the floor. Many people are not accustomed to resting their weight on the knees, and a cushion helps to relieve some of the pressure on the joints. The ideal arrangement is to have a large, well-stuffed pillow directly in front of the knees. This position is difficult or impossible for those with back trouble, and it is necessary to be aware of these types of problems before trying this technique.

After the person is kneeling on the mat, I usually tell them to raise their arms directly over their head, make fists with both hands and come down on the pillow or mat as hard as they can. I recommend that the actual blow be struck with the entire lower arm, from the elbow to the fist. This allows for a more powerful energy release than using fists.

The power position can also involve standing over a bed or other soft structure about waist high. Usually a tennis racket, bataca bat or other similar item is needed for this technique, so that the person doesn't have to lean over as far. In some cases, however, this position can safely include the use of fists or open hands.

I only have an opportunity to give this coaching, by the way, in a few cases. Most of the time, once a person has hit a few times, the anger and rage surfaces and they are not hearing or seeing anything. If a person is using their fists, I don't stop them to correct the procedure. I try to exert as little control in their process as possible. The point is to offer support and safety for them while they "lose control" for the first time without hurting themselves or someone else. If there is a pause while they are catching their breath, I will advise them to try using their entire lower arm if they have been using their fists. Again, hitting with fists presents the risk of injury to knuckles and wrists.

Occasionally I have found some individuals more comfortable sitting on the mat with their legs extended in front of them. In this position there is less stress on the knees, but for some it may create more back strain. The hitting in this position is actually done on the mat between the extended legs. I have also known some people to use open hands in this position, which is an option to using closed fists. I usually recommend using closed fists, because it is a more powerful hand position and because hitting with open hands is sometimes painful, particularly on a vinyl mat.

I have had a couple of experiences with facilitating anger work for individuals with severe back, hip and leg problems. For these individuals, sitting in their chair or wheelchair while hitting another chair with an encounter bat seems to work fairly well. I have also found that some people are more physically comfortable holding a pillow in their own lap and hitting it with both fists or open hands.

Matt finally agreed to use the power position. Kneeling on the mat, he began breathing heavily. It was as if his body knew it was about to explode and release a lifetime of rage. He exploded all right. By the time he was through, he was sweating and breathing so heavily it took him half an hour to recover enough to stand up and walk out of the room. But now he was smiling. He didn't explain his smile, and I'm not sure he could have if he had tried. The smile wasn't coming from his brain; it was coming from his body. His heart was relieved of more than forty years of pressure, tension and pain. The next day he gave me an update.

"Well, I'm still angry at those guys, but I don't want to kill anybody. I know what I'm going to do about the situation at work, and I'm doing it for me and my family, not for revenge on my boss. I feel more in touch with myself than I have since I hit my first home run at fourteen." Matt shook my hand and thanked me, but he did not give anyone but himself credit for what he had accomplished—and rightfully so. He did his part, so he was able to reach his goal.

The Temper Tantrum Technique

This posture for anger release allows a full body rage release that seems to go deeper into the body and thus deeper into the subconscious mind. When a person is having difficulty with the power position or if they have used the power position several times and still have not reached the "bottom" of their rage, I strongly recommend this technique. It is based on the position and method many of us have seen demonstrated by very young children. Some of us may even remember doing it ourselves.

This method of rage and anger release involves lying on one's back on a mattress or mat that is wide enough to allow at least eight to twelve inches clearance on both sides of the body. This is to provide space for pounding with both hands without going off the mat. While releasing anger in this way, the person's body will sometimes drift off to one side or the other or up or down on the mat. If the mat does not allow enough room for this, the person will go off the edge or ends of the mat, which will interrupt the flow of their emotional release.

The procedure begins with the person closing their eyes. I then instruct them to raise their feet up on the mat so their legs are bent and their feet are flat on the surface of the mat. The next step is to begin pounding alternately with both hands and kicking alternately with both feet. For most people this involves hitting with the right fist while kicking with the right foot, then hitting with the left fist while kicking with the left foot. For a full release, the person must do this as rapidly as possible until their body takes over and they don't have to think about what they are doing at all. Usually not much instruction is needed, since the subconscious mind remembers everything, including how to throw a good temper tantrum.

Vocal and Verbal Components of Anger Work

Nonverbal vocal components: Voice tone and volume, as well as words and phrases spoken, are extremely important components of anger-release work. Regarding volume, the rule is the louder the better. The reason for this is that greater volume tends to open up the entire vocal capacity, allowing the voice to come from the diaphragm and chest region rather than from the throat. There is also less likelihood of damaging the throat or vocal cords when the throat muscles are relaxed and the voice is being projected from deep within the midsection. The deep vocal release is best accomplished with a process beginning with a growling exercise that helps to relax the throat muscles. The desired roaring effect that provides the greatest emotional release and experience of power is then achieved by simply forcing greater volume of sound into the growl until it becomes a roar. Many people are inhibited about doing this where others can hear it, and have an easier time letting go when roaring into a pillow. This can be a highly effective form of emotional release in many cases.

Your voice has always been a primary means of expressing your emotions and your self. It is the suppression of emotion and the suppression of self that leads to the need for anger-release work. Many of us were told to "shut up" or "be quiet" as children, and we need to overcome this message to our subconscious mind. As our anger and other emotions are suppressed, there is an inevitable suppression of our sense of self-worth. Thus in doing anger work we are not only beginning to reclaim our emotions, we are beginning to reclaim ourselves.

Verbal components: There are infinite variations in the appropriate words and phrases to use with different individuals, and the decision-making process I go through to choose the best words for effective release is based on my entire career of practicing psychotherapy. For this reason, I am not going to try to give you a list of the best verbalizations to use in your own or your clients' anger work. It is simply too complex to go into in this introductory volume. I emphasize this point so readers will not believe that after learning about these techniques, they will be prepared to provide intensive anger- and rage-release interventions.

If you want to try these techniques on yourself, you can obviously accept full responsibility for the results. Experimenting with these powerful techniques on another person's emotions is another matter altogether, and I definitely do not recommend it. Trust your intuition and try only those methods that feel right for you. You may also want to consult with a counselor or therapist who is familiar with this type of work before attempting the techniques.

Verbalizations

Appropriate verbalizations during anger work fall into three general categories. They are as follows:

1. Simple anger-release phrases for the purpose of claiming the emotion, such as, "I'm angry!" (It is very common at this point to move into hatred toward the abusers or the people who abandoned or neglected them. If the person insists on saying, "I hate you," I will allow this. I move them on to more empowering statements as quickly as possible, however, because hatred is an insidious form of anger that is more harmful to the person feeling it than to the person being hated.)
2. Statements of fact that the person needs to acknowledge, as in the case of an incest or physical abuse victim saying, "It was wrong!" or "It wasn't my fault!"
3. In the case of a person who is having recurrent memories or flashbacks of an incident of abuse, it is sometimes helpful to have them visualize the incident while hitting the mat and say, "Stop it!" "Get away!" or "No more!" while picturing the abuser ceasing the abusive behavior. This is a powerful technique, as it couples the physical and emotional power of the victim's anger with an assertion against the acts of the abuser. This is often a

corrective process, which eliminates flashbacks and recurrent nightmares. By claiming strength in this way, the person is for the first time moving out of the victim position in relation to the abuser.

4. If there is fear, shame, self-blame or another type of interference to the effective release of anger, a statement of the fear or mental block can sometimes help to remove it. Examples of such block-removal statements would be, "I'm afraid!" "I can't feel!" or "It's my fault!" To go even deeper into the shame and to release it, the statements, "I'm bad!" "I'm worthless!" or "I'm a mistake!" can be used. After these statements are repeated over and over, the block is usually removed, the truth begins to emerge and the fear or self-blame dissipates. The negative or block-removal statements are replaced with the appropriate alternative, such as, "I'm strong!" "I can feel!" or "It wasn't my fault!" The simple and powerful words, "No!" and "Yes!" can also be very effective.

5. Other statements that are messages to caregivers in cases of neglect and abandonment are, "Where were you?" "I needed you!" or "Please love me!" These statements are particularly helpful in getting individuals in touch with their pain in order to facilitate the healing process that must always follow effective anger work.

6. The final category of statements to use in anger work that is specifically for the purpose of empowerment falls under the general heading of affirmations. In such cases it has been determined therapeutically that the person is ready to claim power and affirm it emotionally and physically. Statements would be made such as, "It's my life!" "I deserve to be angry!" "I deserve to be loved!" "I am lovable!" "I'm a good person!" "I was a good child!" "I am innocent!" or "My body is good!"

If the person is not ready to fully accept the truth of these affirmations, they will not fully exert all of their physical and emotional energy while making the statements and hitting the mat. At that point they may be aware of a new block or interfering thought, which needs to be stated forcefully and worked through. Whenever the opportunity presents itself, anger work ideally ends with loud, forceful statements of self-affirmation, in order that the body and mind are directing their energy in a positive direction. This may be done at the end of a session with someone who has made a major break-through, or at the end of a long period of treatment with someone who has been working through long-term healing in the process of dealing with major childhood trauma.

When using any of these verbalizations in anger work, one statement should be chosen at a time. This statement is repeated with each blow to the mat, with primary emphasis being placed on key words such as "my" and "good" and "deserve" in the examples above. This seems to work best when the emphasized word is spoken forcefully at the instant the mat is hit. I usually have the individual repeat this process with as much power and momentum as possible, over and over until they are physically exhausted and need to rest.

The verbal statements described above are ordinarily used while the person is in the power position, and not in the more primal temper-tantrum posture. In the latter position, I usu-ally encourage individuals to open their mouths as wide as possible and roar as loudly as they can. As mentioned above, the instruction is to roar for the purpose of a more complete and primal release, as well as to avoid injury to the throat or vocal cords.

When someone is on their back, hitting the mat with both hands and kicking with both feet while roaring from deep within their chest, most of the time an effective release is occurring. People often report a lifelong tension or pain in their stomach or chest is gone or reduced after this exercise. Better than any other method I know, this one seems to effectively get to the "bottom" of suppressed anger and rage.

EMOTIONAL REACTIONS
TO EXPECT AND BE READY FOR

The reason I recommend caution in using these techniques is that I have seen almost every possible reaction occur according to individual physical, mental and emotional differences. Here are some considerations and possible outcomes in cases of less extreme trauma:

1. **Emotional breakthrough.** This, fortunately, is one of the most common responses to anger-release work. People feel the power of their own emotional and physical strength, and they break through the fear. The pain is contacted, but as is shown in the concentric circle diagram in Figure 6.1, pain is directly connected to the need to give and receive love. The experience of feeling the pain is therefore experienced in conjunction with compassion for the inner child. As the person recognizes the injustice of what happened to them and the depth of the pain it caused, open crying or sobbing may (and often needs to) occur.

2. **Holding anger.** Some people stop in the pain and hold on to the anger, with new awareness of how they were abused, neglected or abandoned. This is encouraged as long as it is needed for empowerment. The anger ultimately needs to be released, however, in order for the person to be free from the victim position on an emotional and psychological level. Some individuals move more easily into a self-nurturing posture, which will be described in further detail below.

3. **Release, relief and return to joy.** Occasionally, though not often, an individual will break all the way through to the emotional center and contact joy, at the heart of their need to love and be loved. This is accompanied by experiences of empowerment, feelings of elation and a general sense of well-being. This rarely happens in the first anger-release exercise, but if someone is consistent in his or her therapeutic work, it usually occurs at some point in the healing process. This is the goal of emotional release and regressive work.

   A risk worth noting, however, is the tendency for therapist and patient alike to assume that this means therapy is over or that little remains to be done. Although this is indeed sometimes the case, it is far more common that contact with well-being and joy is simply a breakthrough from one stage to another, and there is still more work to be done.

   As a matter of fact, these periods of well-being are sometimes followed by depression when the person is not cognitively ready to maintain an ongoing state of happiness. Guilt and shame sometimes flood in like a tidal wave if the person never had permission to feel these feelings of joy and self-love or if the family script was never to do better than the other family members. Once a person has had a taste of this, however, they know it is possible, and it provides motivation for further investment in growth and recovery.

In cases of extreme trauma or more complex and disturbed anger and rage issues, you might experience one or more of the following:

1. **Paralysis in fear.** Some people can only go into their emotions as far as the fear and cannot penetrate far enough to

reach their pain. Once again referring to the concentric circles of emotion in Figure 6.1, you can see that the empowerment of the anger only took the person as far as their wall of fear where they became paralyzed. When this occurs, it is essential that the individual be encouraged to do more anger work to empower themselves past the fear. This may happen in minutes, days or weeks after the first fear reaction, but it is the therapist's responsibility to see that the person does not stay stuck in fear. With persistence on the part of the therapist and encouragement to the patient, anger work for empowerment can always break through the fear, contact the pain and connect with the loving and lovable core of the individual.

2. **Dissociation from current reality and possibly from current identity.** In most cases this can be effectively managed with sophisticated therapeutic techniques. However, in the case of individuals with dissociative or identity disorders, the dissociation may need to continue temporarily until reintegration is possible and appropriate in terms of the patient's needs. Extreme caution and qualified supervision should always be employed when working with individuals with dissociative and identity disorders.

3. **Self-destructive thought and behavior.** Often victims of extreme physical or sexual abuse will become suicidal during or following rage work. The guilt they feel after becoming so enraged at their caregiver (even though that person was an abuser) throws them into shame, guilt and even self-hatred. John Bradshaw, in *Healing the Shame That Binds You*, makes the point that the abuse victim often will identify with the abuser to avoid the unmanageable conflict of hating a caregiver (Bradshaw 1988). Such people may sometimes try to injure themselves physically, thereby taking on the actual role of the abuser. It is the

therapist's responsibility to ensure the person's safety from self-harm. When this type of response occurs, I immediately stop the rage and anger work and move into inner-child healing work or other therapeutic interventions to provide reorientation and nurturing to the client.

4. **Nausea and possibly vomiting after deep rage release.** This reaction is the body's way of symbolically representing the process of purging and release that is occurring on an emotional level.

VERBAL AND VISUAL MEMORIES AND HEALING WORK

While doing emotional release work, it is very common that a person will have sudden memories of events and conversations that were connected with the intense emotions being experienced. This is very helpful to the therapist as it provides material for healing and emotional reconstruction.

The most accurate term to describe the methods I use after intense anger work is inner-child healing work. I do not have to induce any type of regression or trance state as the person is already in an altered state of consciousness due to the emotional release. I usually move directly into a visualization process in which the person pictures a traumatic childhood memory. This memory sometimes occurs spontaneously as mentioned above.

Sometimes I facilitate the process by saying, "Can you see yourself as a child at a time when you were hurt or afraid and needed love?" When the patient has indicated that the memory is there, I have them fill in details until the picture is complete. Then I have them enter the situation as a powerful, loving adult. The task then is to move the abuser completely out of the picture in a firm and yet nonaggressive way. I encourage patients to do this by simply placing a hand near the chest of their abusers and pushing them out of the picture until they are completely gone or out of view.

Next I ask patients to carry their newfound love and strength to the frightened, wounded inner child. I encourage them to pick up the child and offer nurturance, love and protection. The statements often used for the nurturing adult to offer to the wounded child are, "You're okay now. I've got you. I won't let them hurt you anymore. I love you. You are my precious child, and I'm here for you. You can count on me." These self-nurturing statements are usually well received, and an effective integration with the inner child can be facilitated.

Sometimes, however, the patient will go back into fear, or will flash to another abusive memory. This is simply an indication that there is more work to be done. It does not detract from the significance of the healing that has occurred up to that point.

AN EXPERIENCE OF
BEING WHOLE AND COMPLETE

The goal of healing and therapeutic work is to become whole. This is accomplished emotionally through the integration of the current adult with the wounded child of the past. The current adult, in the form of a nurturing, strong parent, goes to the wounded child in times of need as presented by the subconscious mind in the form of visual and verbal memory. New awareness of the child's basic innocence and need for love is the motivation for the nurturing parent. Strength is derived from the experience of healthy, appropriate anger directed at the injustice of what happened to the child.

As the adult becomes stronger in the role of the nurturing parent, that adult goes to each painful memory with strength, love and healing for the wounded child. Before this, the wounded child had been emotionally frozen at the points of trauma. Through the healing process, the child is set free from these trauma points to allow full and complete emotional energy to move into present adult experiences. This allows for the development of emotional maturity. This is a primary foundation for personal spiritual wholeness.

AFFIRMATIONS

- *I have all that I need to be whole and complete.*
- *My anger is my ally in my journey past fear and pain.*
- *My feelings live in my body, and I am open to all that I feel.*
- *All of my memories are here for my healing and growth.*
- *My subconscious mind provides me with all the information I need in order to become whole and complete.*

13

Managing and Expressing Anger in Adult Relationships

HOW ABOUT A NICE KISS?

NICE KISS! is a mnemonic device I use to teach and remember a simple process for identifying and expressing feelings. This chapter is for those who have made significant progress in their own growth and healing and are ready to begin communicating their feelings in adult relationships. It will also be useful for those who have few unresolved issues and simply need skills for better managing and expressing emotions.

Here's how the NICE KISS! works:

Notice the feeling
I dentify the feeling
Claim the feeling
Express the feeling
Keep
I t
Simple,
Sweetheart!

Now I will elaborate on the intimate details of this NICE KISS!:

Notice the feeling. Ask your stomach, your heart, your chest, your neck, your shoulders, your back and even your head (if you have headaches) what you are feeling. Don't expect the answer to be in your brain. Your brain will give you silly answers like, "I don't feel anything," or "I think I feel..." or "I feel confused." (Confusion is in our thinking. It's not a feeling.) Right now, ask the part of your body where you carry your stress to tell you how you are feeling. Before putting the answer into words though, wait until you finish your NICE KISS!

Identify the feeling. To do this, you want to start applying your KISS! (Keep It Simple, Sweetheart!). One of the ways we get out and stay out of touch with our feelings is by being too "headsy" and abstract in the words we use to describe them. By using simple, clear words, we express more feeling in the process of speaking the word.

Try choosing from the feeling words used in the concentric circle diagram. That gives you anger, fear, pain, hurt, love and need for love as options for feeling words. If none of these fit, but you know the feeling is not a positive one, see if the word you would use to describe your feeling might be a part of anger, fear, pain or a need for love. Lonely, for example, is definitely a need for love. Anxious, tense and stressed out are all abstractions of anger, fear and pain. If you are having a positive feeling, let's assume it fits in the center with the need to love and be loved.

I suggest you expand your repertoire for positive feeling words as much as you can, while limiting your repertoire of negative feeling words. Some examples of positive feeling words are: happy, glad, peaceful, joyful, exuberant, ecstatic, excited, enthusiastic, thrilled, pumped, pleased, grateful, blessed and honored.

Claim the feeling. This is instead of blaming the feeling on someone else. One of the best ways I know to do this is to imagine your inner child having the feeling. That is, picture your inner child hurting, afraid, joyful, lovable or in need of love. If anger is the feeling you identify, try to find the fear or pain that is beneath it. Claim the anger as a protective feeling, felt by the nurturing parent for your hurt or frightened inner child. Next, pick up and embrace your inner child, feeling the deeper, more vulnerable feelings within yourself. Allow the child to move into your heart, which is its home. The feeling is yours; you have claimed it. You're in charge.

Express the feeling. Everything up to this point has been an internal, private process. Now it's time to talk about your feelings to someone else.

There are two basic reasons to talk about your feelings. One reason is because it is healthy for you. Suppressing feelings is unhealthy; expressing them is healthy. You are expressing your feelings for yourself, not for an expected result. You have no idea what the result will be, and there are no guarantees that it will be received in the way you want it to be.

To suppress your feelings is to deny your worth and value as a person. You are past that now. Part of your commitment to yourself is to express your feelings in a healthy manner, in an environment that is as appropriate and safe as possible. Another reason is for the purpose of making a connection with another person. Intimacy is established through honest, open communication of feelings. Again you are not looking for results; you are just doing your part of allowing for intimacy by expressing your feelings.

"I" statements are the key here. Use statements that begin with "I feel" and insert feeling words. Avoid "I feel that you . . ." or "I feel like they . . ." Since the purpose is to express your feelings, then do that and express your thoughts about others later. You will find an expanded version of this process complete with problem solving in Appendixes II and III.

This is where it becomes particularly important to:

Keep
I t
Simple
Sweetheart!

You want the person listening to hear you, and possibly reflect back what you have said. If you ramble from one thought to another until you have expressed several paragraphs without stopping, your partner in communication may well have stopped listening.

IT ALL BOILS DOWN TO LOVE

We are most likely to have intense feelings, including anger, in our more intimate relationships where there is more need to give and receive love. The more we love someone, the more vulnerable to being hurt we are and the deeper the pain when we are hurt. This is not bad or a problem to be solved—it's just the way it is. Because the pain is greater (at least potentially), the fear is usually greater also. Thus it follows that the anger in intimate close relationships is more intense than in casual relationships in which there is less love, pain and fear. As we have already mentioned, there is more violence in the home than in any other sector.

There is, fortunately, a level of emotional maturity we can reach where our intimate relationships do not contain much pain, fear or anger. Most of us are still working toward that goal. So the more love there is, the more potential we have for pain, fear and anger. It is also true that the more love there is, the more potential we have for resolution of pain, fear and anger.

SELF-MONITORING ON THE 0–10 ANGER SCALE

Many of my clients have benefited from developing an awareness of their anger level in order to make choices before it escalates out of control. The following scale may be helpful to you in becoming more aware of and managing your anger effectively. Most people find that they can still make good decisions up to level 2 or 3, and after that the emotions start taking over and interfering with clear thinking. Here's how the scale might look:

Anger Scale

0	You are feeling totally calm and relaxed. You may feel happy and excited about something or not. You have no anger or irritation at any level.
1	You feel a very slight anxiety or irritability, but it's not affecting your behavior. You can barely notice it when you try. Your mind is open, and you're very aware of the "big picture" perspective.

Anger Scale (cont'd)

2	The irritation/anxiety is a little higher, but still not enough to bother you or affect your behavior. You can still see the big picture.
3	You are starting to notice negative responses to people, places and things around you. You are still keeping it all inside, but you're just not settled. Your focus is starting to narrow slightly, but you can still think clearly and make good decisions.
4	Now you are starting to think about yelling at that other driver, or calling that talk-show host and giving him or her a piece of your mind. But you don't act on the feelings. Your tone with others might be just a little short, or you might try to cover your feelings by being extra nice. Tunnel vision is starting to set in.
5	Now you are definitely not having fun. You are mad at yourself, others or the world in general. You're still in control of your behavior, but others can tell you're not feeling that great. You are moving into a single-minded focus and your decision-making process is impaired.
6	You start thinking about getting away from the situation. You might fantasize about escaping somehow. You might also tell someone off at this point, but you make an effort to be controlled and even somewhat considerate. Your mental clarity has become erratic. You have lost sight of the big picture.
7	You are starting to say things to yourself like, *This is driving me crazy. I can't stand this anymore. That person is driving me up the wall. How can they be so* (fill in the blank)? *If I could, I'd like to really let them have it!* Your thoughts are racing, and your muscle tension is becoming noticeable. Your vision is narrowing further.

Anger Scale (cont'd)

8	At this level, a plan of action starts to form. Now your anger is so high that you are ready to do something about it. You are so upset that you really have no choice. Your thinking is not clear, and your plan of action might include revenge and retaliation, or just a desire to hurt someone you perceive as a threat or problem to you or someone you love. You have become almost completely irrational.
9	Now you're acting on your anger. You are telling someone off, and possibly trying to hurt them or "put them in their place" with your words. You also might be planning how to abandon, neglect or reject them. Your thoughts are obsessed and totally focused on your pain, fear and anger whether you know it or not. You are ruled by your emotions and starting to lose control.
10	At this level you are dangerous to yourself and/or others. You are in the depths of fight-or-flight, and your primitive survival-based brain has taken over. You have tunnel vision and single-minded thought. All you can think about is how to make the pain and/or stress stop. You are desperate, and you are willing to take desperate action. Your fear and anger are doing your thinking for you.

If you have major anger issues, you may escalate straight from 0 to 10 without any awareness or self-control. If you have successfully suppressed your anger, you may live constantly at a level 3, 4 or 5, never taking action or feeling any better. Many people are mildly irritated much of the time.

Being emotionally healthy means living around a level 0–2 most of the time. In extreme circumstances a healthy person may escalate to a 3 or even a 4, but will take positive, effective action to resolve the problem and return to a sense of well-being.

EXPRESS YOUR FEELINGS
FOR YOU, NOT FOR RESULTS

The point has been well made that suppressing feelings is hazardous to your health. It is also clear that expressing them in appropriate ways is healthy. For this reason it doesn't make sense to only express your feelings if you think the listener wants to hear them. Many times the listener will not want to hear your feelings. They may be too full of their own emotions to be able to clearly receive what you are offering. So you have to do it for you! Timing for this type of communication is important, however, and I will elaborate on that at a later point in this chapter.

If you are looking for certain results when you decide to express your feelings, you will usually be disappointed. It takes a really healthy person to be truly open to hearing about your pain, fear and anger. You may find it just as rare for someone to be open to hearing about your joy and excitement.

One of the most common statements I hear in my practice when I encourage people to express their feelings to their loved ones is, "I tried that and it didn't work . . . ," or "I did that and he just blew up . . . ," or "I tried that and she didn't change. . . ." In other words, we try this business of being open with our feelings and telling our loved ones what's really going on, and they just don't act right. So we give up and go back to suppressing our feelings and being depressed, constantly angry, passive-aggressive or periodically explosive. The material in chapter 5 dealing with creating healthy boundaries and commitment priorities may be helpful here.

I often tell my clients to preface expression of their feelings with any combination of the following statements:

• I don't want you to fix me or give me any advice.
• I'm not trying to change or fix you.

- I just want you to listen to me and be here.
- You don't even have to say anything if you don't want to.
- I am telling you about my feelings because they are an important part of who I am, and it's good for me to express them.

This doesn't guarantee any results, but if the other person is paying attention and is fairly clear with their own issues, it could help to create a productive interaction. If the other person responds well and the relationship benefits, great. If the relationship can't ultimately handle your being open with your feelings, it is not a healthy relationship for you. Remember, you are doing this for you.

Your feelings are who you are inside. To deny them is to deny yourself. To express them is to accept and love yourself and to claim responsibility for who you are. When there is no more shame, there is no more reason to hide your feelings. As you claim your feelings and learn to express them, it gets easier to claim ownership over your own time and energy.

SORRY, I'M NOT AVAILABLE AT THIS TIME

Part of self-love and self-preservation is knowing how and when to say "No." This skill is a part of being healthy emotionally and having access to the useful energy of anger. Without it, you are subject to—or even victim to—whoever wants a piece of your time, energy or money. Let's use telemarketers as an example.

Seth's time and energy are very important to him. He doesn't buy products or services he doesn't need, but he is basically a victim to anybody who calls him on the phone or shows up in his workplace with a sales pitch. He spends far too much time listening to salespeople telling him about

products he does not want. He is afraid of hurting others' feelings, and this has been his cross to bear throughout his life.
He is angry much of the time, but does his best to keep this
from others.

The phone rings, and Seth answers. He always answers,
afraid of what will happen if he doesn't—that it might be an
emergency, or someone might be mad at him. "Hello, Mr.
Thompson [Seth's last name is Thomas, but he says nothing].
I would like to tell you about a new opportunity we are offering especially to you. This is your chance of a lifetime to . . ."
Caught once again like a fish on a hook, Seth listens for an
opportunity to speak. He waits, and waits. When he finally
gets a chance, he says his "No, thank you." Of course, this
doesn't stop the salesperson, who has been well trained to
overcome objections. So he listens and waits some more. His
time and energy are being stolen, and he feels helpless to do
anything about it. Sometimes he even buys products he
doesn't want, just to end the conversation. A couple of times
in the past he just hung up the phone, but the guilt bothered
him too much to keep doing that. These kinds of things happen to Seth ten to fifteen times a week.

If you have a problem like Seth's, you might want to take a
course on assertiveness. In such classes, you will learn to
express yourself clearly, freely and even respectfully without
being overly concerned about the other person's feelings.
Learning to communicate honest feelings *with* respect will
provide the freedom you need to claim authority and control
over your life. You will need to develop a repertoire of skills to
deal with the various situations in which someone wants a
piece of your time. Here are some examples of ways you can
learn to protect your precious time and energy:

• Let the answering machine, voice mail or caller ID be your
  screening device. You do not belong to your telephone; it
  belongs to you.

- Learn to powerfully, confidently and assertively say "No" with a smile on your face.
- Learn and practice statements such as the following on the telephone:
  - "No, thank you, I'm not interested." You can interrupt the sales pitch as soon as you have realized that's what it is—after all, they interrupted you, didn't they? Immediately hang up the phone after your statement, or you will most certainly be giving away some more of your precious time and energy.
  - "I'm not interested. Have a great day!" Then hang up.
  - "No, thanks. Good-bye." And hang up.
- When it's a live salesperson at your door or in your office, it gets a little tougher, especially for those of us who are caretakers of others' feelings. That's why the smile is so important. You can look this person right in the eye, smile and say, "I'm not interested. You have a great day! Good-bye." And close the door gently but firmly, or show them to the door if they've entered your place of business.
- Get a friend to role-play some of this with you, and be sure to play both roles. Practice the assertive skills for ending the conversation, and play the role of the salesperson on the receiving end. This will show you how it feels to be on the giving and receiving end of respectful and assertive expression. You need to know that the salesperson will live, and that you are not doing them any harm by being assertive and healthy.

Is this anger? You bet! It is healthy anger channeled into effective communication. It feels great to have ownership over your own time and energy, and it feels awful to feel like your time and energy belong to anyone who shows up in your life or on your telephone line.

When you learn and apply these skills, you will feel more like your life belongs to you. You may still worry at times about other people's feelings, but you won't let this stop you from taking care of yourself. You will find that the more you claim your time and energy as your own, the more content you will be. The more content you are, the more others will be attracted to you. By taking care of yourself and respecting others to care for themselves, you are doing yourself and everyone else a great service.

MAKING THE CONNECTION

Since our basic emotional need is to love and be loved, it follows that we need to make connections with those who are important to us. Expressing feelings is essential to this process. Most of us have believed that if we can only please the other person, they will love us, everything will be fine and all these feelings will just go away. With these expectations, we have probably had several failed relationships. Perhaps we learned about codependency and decided we didn't want to live like that anymore. Now it is time to get down to the business of learning to build and maintain healthy adult relationships based on openness, honesty and mutual respect. With these ingredients, and some love and basic skills thrown in, all we need is persistence.

It is important to point out the difference between trying to connect with the other person and going for results. This is a very subtle distinction. If there were not some desire to connect, we could express our feelings to a cup of coffee. Here's the difference between trying to connect and going for results.

When going for results, we are trying to get the other person to do something or to respond in some particular way. This can only lead to disappointment and misery. When connection is the goal, we are simply offering our expression to the other person in the way we feel they will be most likely to receive it. That's all we do. We are offering ourselves. What the other person does is his or her own business. When this offering is made with no expectations or demands, the other person is free to respond in the way that is best for them in that moment. If we truly love and respect them, that is what we want.

Here is a poem I wrote about the journey to connection:

The Journey from Me to You

My words stumble and stagger
From garble
To meaning
On their way from in here
To you
Out there, listening.

Why is it so far
From my feelings
Through my thoughts
To your mind?

Why do I try so hard
To reach you
Who seem so far away?

Aahh, yes
The connection . . .

Your eyes are sparkling
Our souls have touched.

It was well worth the journey.

It is a difficult journey at times, but the rewards of true connection are great, and they cause us to embark again
and again.

Let's consider some guidelines that seem to work for making the journey as smooth and effective as possible.

Be current. This only means expressing those feelings
while they are fresh. Being current with your feelings is as
much for your own sake as for the other person. Suppressed
feelings hurt the suppressor. Old, suppressed feelings are no
fun to hear about when they do come out. Support groups or
therapy may be the best place to let out the suppressed feelings so you can be current and fresh with the people you care
about the most.

Be clear. This goes back to the NICE KISS! Use words that
are easily understood by the listener. Get clear within yourself before trying to connect emotionally with another person.
Look at the concentric circles of emotion in Figure 6.1, and
move from the outer circles into the center. In other words:

1. **Use your skill, strength and knowledge to take down the
   defenses by talking about them.** "I'm very angry right
   now, and I feel like leaving" (anger and withdrawal). "But
   instead of doing that, I'm going to tell you how I feel."
   You may want to use the prefacing statements described
   earlier in the "Express Your Feelings for You, Not for
   Results" section.

2. **Talk about the fear you are feeling.** "When this happens,
   I tell myself that things will never change and it will be
   like this forever. I'm afraid that everything will just get
   worse, and you will leave or I will leave or we will stay
   together and be miserable. In the past I have always tried
   to fix or change you at this point, but now I am just
   telling you how I feel." You've taken down the defenses
   and now you are being vulnerable, which is a sign of

strength and maturity. You might also talk about the other kind of fear, the one we call shame. "I'm also afraid that it's all my fault and I'm screwing this up just like I have everything else. I feel like I am bad, and that's why the bad things keep happening. I know in my head it's not true, but that's what I feel." Shame lives in the shadows. Bring it out into the light of day, and it is not so powerful as it once seemed to be. It might just go away.

3. **Talk about your pain.** Now you are really showing a commitment to the journey. You are getting closer to the heart of the matter, the center of the circle. "I'm really hurting right now. This feels just like those times in my childhood when I was hurt or rejected. I can handle my pain, but I want you to know what's going on with me." (This is always a good time to reassure the other person that you don't need them to fix you.) "I don't want you to do anything, just hear me." You are now showing trust—of yourself primarily. This is an important point. Ultimately, as we learn to trust ourselves, we are better able to trust that we will be safe with others. This sharing of pain and hurt should only be done when you feel confident that you can take care of yourself, no matter how the other person responds. They may simply not be able to support you. They may even attack you out of their own fear. They may be hurting so much themselves that they can't talk. That's why you have to do it for yourself, just in case the other person has nothing to offer you in that moment.

4. **Talk about the love.** If you don't feel like using the word "love" in such a moment when you are feeling angry, hurt and afraid, tell the other person you are doing all this because they are important to you. If they were not important to you, you would not be having all these feelings. "I'm telling you all of this instead of leaving or trying

to drive you away because you and this relationship are important to me. I care about you and I want this relationship to last. I don't want to hurt you. I do want you to understand me because that helps me to relax and be myself in your presence." Or if it fits, you may be more intimate with a statement like "I love you. I want you to love me. This is the most important relationship in my life. I want you to know how I feel inside because I want to be close to you to feel connected."

Be sensitive. This is a matter of paying attention to timing. Being sensitive in this context also involves being aware and using your intelligence. Expressing your feelings effectively does not mean letting your feelings be in charge. Our thoughts need to be in charge so we can make decisions and act on them. This is also essential if we are to be sensitive to the important element of timing in communication. If you have been at home all day or evening building up a plan for telling your spouse how you feel, it may not be wise to lay it all on them when they walk in the door. To ignore the importance of timing is to set yourself up for failure and to sabotage your own success in communication. We also have to be careful about the other extreme. I have often heard the statement "There just never seemed to be a good time to discuss these things." That can be a defense against the fear of risking in open communication. Somewhere in the middle of these two extremes is a time that may not be perfect but is the best we have to choose from for now. Here are some points to consider in timing when you express your feelings:

• Late at night is usually not the best time. It may be your only time, however, and talking about your feelings then is better than not talking about them at all.
• Family members of drug addicts and alcoholics usually

know it is useless to talk to the addicted person during a using binge or while their system is highly toxic. If there are no periods of relative sobriety, it may be time for an intervention, which can include many of the expressions of feelings outlined above.

• When the other person is hungry, angry, tired or generally stressed out, you are not likely to be received. You may want to schedule a time to be with your significant other when you know they are most likely to be open and receptive.

• When the feelings between you are fairly pleasant and relaxed, it may be a good time to share your emotions in an intimate way. A risk here is that you may think, "This feels good. I don't want to spoil it by talking about all those yucky feelings. I'll wait until later." The problem is that later will not be good either, for the reasons we have discussed. This is one of the ways we keep ourselves stuck and never express our feelings until something makes us explode.

• Sometimes we just have to pick a time and go for it. If you can't find what appears to be a good time, do it anyway.

BE RESPONSIBLE FOR YOURSELF

Remember, you are not doing this to change the other person. You are expressing your feelings because it is healthy for you to do so. You are in the process of learning to love yourself, and doing what is healthy is a big part of loving yourself.

This means that if the other person doesn't respond the way you want them to, you still know what to do. This is when your skills for self-nurturing need to kick in. You didn't get the support you needed, so you give some support to yourself. Your words to your inner child may be something like, "I love you, no matter what they say or do. I think you are wonderful, and you are the best part of me. You are my precious child, and it's okay for you to feel anything you want. I love you right now, while you are hurting and scared. I'm angry because you have been hurt, but I won't let my anger make things worse. My anger is for your protection, and that's how I am using it. I'll keep you safe, and we won't try talking to them again until you feel secure. You are my top priority, and you can count on me."

Taking responsibility in this way prevents blaming or attacking the other for their insensitivity. Blame and attack puts you in the victim role and only adds to your pain and fear. If you find you are filled with anger or even rage, you may be comfortable using some of the anger-release methods described earlier. If you are not or this doesn't seem to work for you, you may want to find a therapist who does this type of work and schedule a session. The point is to notice, identify, claim and express (NICE KISS!) your feelings without blaming or attacking anyone and without hurting yourself.

You deserve support and love; if you don't get it from the other person, give it to yourself. This is also a good time for returning to a spiritual focus, which is a source of support and love that is unconditional and unlimited. Sometimes loving yourself in the form of nurturing your inner child opens the door to your heart and allows spiritual love to enter, however you may define this for yourself.

KNOW WHEN TO WALK AWAY

Part of being responsible includes being sensitive to our own needs and feelings. We need to know when our emotions are just too intense for us to try to communicate. We need to know when to withdraw in a healthy way. This does not mean emotional withdrawal, where we shut down and try to act as if everything is okay when it's not. What we're talking about here is physical withdrawal to another part of the house, outdoors to take a walk, or even taking a break for a few days or weeks to become emotionally and intellectually integrated enough to communicate effectively.

Here are some examples of situations that might require a period of healthy withdrawal:

1. You can't think straight. No matter what you try, you are just not getting your point across.
2. You are so emotional you feel you are going to explode or you can't stop yelling or crying. You're stuck in a pattern of arguing or blaming. It's time to nurture and care for yourself. Staying with the other person is not going to help unless they just happen to be very healthy, balanced and skilled in helping you through such intense emotions.
3. Physical, sexual or emotional abuse is occurring. Leave the situation immediately. You know that it is only going to get worse before it gets better. By withdrawing in a healthy way, you are saying, "I deserve better treatment than this, and I will not stay in a situation where I am being abused." If you are the one who is doing the abusing, it is essential that you stop the abuse and withdraw yourself in a healthy way. Perpetrators of abuse are hurting themselves as well as their victims.
4. During periods of illness, withdrawal from interaction with others is sometimes helpful so we can listen to what our bodies are telling us. Illness and pain can be great teachers if we allow them to be. Our bodies have great wisdom that comes only in silent, still moments without distraction.
5. Sometimes withdrawal is important even if there are no major problems. Healthy intimate relationships involve

a movement like breathing, which allows an open, expansive period in which the connection is the top priority, followed by a more closed, distant period when one or both people are more focused within. Withdrawal from intimate communication is essential to allow for centering and self-nurturing. Another way of saying this is that in order to maintain our friendship with ourselves, we must spend some time alone. When we are alone, we get in touch with feelings that are otherwise not as noticeable because of the distractions provided by the other people present.

Here are some statements we might make in withdrawing from communication with another person:

- "I'm not happy with the way I am communicating with you right now. I need some time to figure out what I am feeling and what I need to do about those feelings. I will talk with you some more about it this afternoon." (Or tomorrow, next week or when you're ready—whatever is appropriate to the circumstances. It is important that you get back with the person so your withdrawal doesn't just seem like some form of punishment.)
- "I deserve to be treated with respect and so do you. Neither of us is doing that right now. I am taking a break to figure out my feelings and my needs. I will talk to you when I figure out what I want to communicate to you."
- "I haven't been feeling well lately. I don't think it is just a simple illness, and I don't think I am a victim of some outside force. I need to find out what my responsibility is for what's going on in my life, and I need some time alone to do that."
- "It's not about you. I'm just feeling a lot of emotion right now, and I need to be thinking more clearly before we talk."

Sometimes you just have to leave. You may be in such a state that you can't think of anything to say that you have not already said, and it is time for action. This may be the healthiest option in some situations.

The other person will often feel rejected, hurt or angry when you do this or when you make any of the above statements. Respect them enough to let them have their own pain, fear and anger. You simply can't fix them or how they are feeling. They may try to stop you or make you feel guilty out of their own fear of abandonment. You may or may not want to reassure them that it is not their fault, depending on the health of the relationship. If you let them convince you not to take care of yourself in this way, you are simply contributing to your problems and to the problems of the relationship.

When you practice healthy withdrawal, you are sending a very clear and positive message to yourself. The message is, *I deserve my own attention. It is time for me to give some quiet, focused attention to my own feelings and needs. I have nothing to fear within myself. I am a friend to myself, and I am now choosing to spend some time with my friend.*

THE REWARD OF CLOSENESS

Close, warm, intimate relationships are fantastic. The feeling of true connection with another person is well worth the journey. It seems to me that developing close, intimate relationships is one of the most challenging and rewarding frontiers of personal growth. It also seems that truly healthy, loving relationships may be one of the highest forms of human experience. The love that can grow in a deep commitment between two healthy individuals is a fulfilling, uplifting and healing experience.

According to Dr. Dean Ornish, in his book entitled *Love and Intimacy*, healthy intimacy is good for and even essential to our overall physical health. His research further shows that isolation can greatly impair health functioning, reinforcing many of the assertions about the need for love and connection in this book (Ornish 1999).

An essential ingredient in a healthy relationship is a positive spiritual belief system of some kind. Each of us needs a focus for our expectations and projections of perfection so that we don't ask too much of each other. This prevents us from making a god or goddess out of our loved ones, attaching great expectations to their behavior and their ability to make our life wonderful. You can make your own life wonderful through a commitment to a healthy body, mind and spirit. Then when you come together with someone who is doing the same thing, the results are tremendously uplifting and fulfilling.

AFFIRMATIONS

- *I am responsible for my feelings in each of my relationships.*
- *My first commitment is to myself, then to my role in the relationship and finally to the relationship itself.*
- *The only connection for which I have full responsibility is my emotional and spiritual connection with myself.*

14

Healthy Anger and Your Health

FROM THE WARRIOR SPIRIT
TO THE SPIRITUAL WARRIOR

Each of us developed a warrior spirit soon after our
birth. Your first anger development occurred after
the first few months of your life, coming to a head
around the age of two, which is how the idea of the "terrible
two's" developed.

In this chapter, we will look at the process that took you
from your birth as an innocent child to the development of
the warrior spirit as protector of the child. We will then
explore the development of the warrior's "sword" and
"shield" and discuss how they show up in your body and in

223

your actions. This will lead to an understanding of how illness, aggression and violence relate to the sword and shield,
and how the warrior spirit disconnected from love and intelligence becomes a "destructive protector." Finally, we will
explore how this destructive part of your personality can be
transformed into a "loving protector" and ultimately into a
spiritual warrior.

This will provide you with a road map for following and
understanding the process we will explore together.

THE CHILD IS OLDER
THAN THE WARRIOR SPIRIT

The child and the warrior both represent examples of
Jungian archetypes, which are well illuminated in the work of
Carol S. Pearson's *Awakening the Heroes Within* (Pearson 1991).
The picture that comes to mind when you think of a warrior
is no doubt an adult image—powerful and focused. Yet the
warrior spirit was born later to protect the inner child.

The idea of the child as wise elder is reflected in the familiar aphorism, "Out of the mouth of babes," which brings to
mind a story from my own experience.

Several years ago my family and I rented two houseboats
for a thirteen-day family vacation on an Arkansas lake. Two of
my brothers, my five-year-old niece and I were up late, and
everyone else in our fifteen-member group was asleep. My
brothers and I were playing guitar, mandolin and harmonica
and singing some of our old favorite songs. It was a sweet
time, and the music flowed well.

On a break between songs, my older brother John shared a
thought. "At times like this I think about the four of us (one of
my brothers was asleep) renting an old bus and traveling
around the country, just playing music and having fun." We

joined in with more ideas about how we could quit our jobs, cash in our life savings and take off. My niece Becki was silent, lying on her back in the middle of our group of three and listening. We enjoyed our fantasy for a while, and then when it was winding down, Becki sat straight up and said, "Why don't you just do it! Right now!"

All three of us had the same reaction. We were struck silent. Something about her timing and her tone caught us completely off guard, and the truth of her words went deep. It was beyond the idea of living out the fantasy of touring the country on an old bus; it was about taking action. Her wise little warrior spirit spoke a truth that soared past our playful reverie and found a home in our hearts.

We were so moved by the experience that we wrote a song about it, which we still sing today.

THE BIRTH OF THE SWORD AND SHIELD

The warrior spirit in general develops because the child needs protection. The child is innocent, open and vulnerable and needs the protective energy of the warrior for its safety in the world.

A useful way of understanding the development of your warrior spirit is by working with the imagery and energy of the sword and shield. The sword projects, penetrates, pierces and protects against anything that threatens or opposes you. The shield deflects, conceals, separates and distances you from the perceived threat or opposition. Both are natural and highly useful.

You can see that the sword and shield are metaphors for the defense mechanisms of anger and withdrawal, which we have thoroughly explored in this book. The metaphor and mythology of the warrior's sword and shield will ground your understanding and take you further into the healthy power of these natural processes.

This world does not respond well to the warrior's sword. The piercing, penetrating energy of your anger was most likely punished, overpowered or ignored, causing you to withhold your sword and put it somewhere that it could not be seen or heard. Or you may have been raised in a family where there were "sword fights" going on all of the time, and you had no choice but to join in the fray as best you could. So you either became withdrawn and quiet, never showing anger, or you became aggressive and outspoken for your own survival. Your sword is either hidden inside you, or it's out for the world to see, hear and feel. No matter what, it didn't go away completely.

- **The sword in action.** If you use the sword of your anger openly and have not learned to temper its steel and carefully direct its focus, it has both protected you and caused you and others harm. Since your parents most likely did not know how to honor and develop your warrior spirit, you really had no choice in this matter.
- **The sword in the body.** If the sword of your anger was punished, overpowered or ignored, you had to put it away. There was nowhere to put it but in your body. Unlike the sword swallower in the carnival who has developed adaptive mechanisms, most of us don't digest our swords well at all.

We have no choice but to develop our warrior's shield, whether we learned to fight with our swords or keep them concealed. There have always been and will always be other warriors with their swords out, and we would literally die without our shielding.

• **The shield in action.** Hiding, pretending, closing off and numbing out are all aspects of the shield in action. When you learned to be "seen and not heard," to form a frozen face mask that conceals your emotion and vulnerability, to grit your teeth and tense your muscles to keep from crying, you were putting your shield into action.

• **The shield in the body.** The shield shows up in our bodies in many different forms. Muscular tension and occasional spasms, restricted breathing, digestive problems, circulation and/or heart problems, slumped shoulders and excessive weight can all be seen as manifestations of the warrior's shield showing up in the physical body.

THE DISCONNECTED WARRIOR SPIRIT

The original purpose of the warrior spirit, its very *raison d'etre* is to protect the child. As life and relationships become complicated and the sword and shield are not honored or cultivated, the warrior spirit becomes distracted and desperate, choosing destructive forms of protection that actually do more harm than good.

If your warrior is disconnected, you may find the following to be true for you. The fiery temper that you originally developed to give you some power and control in the world becomes a weapon that harms you and the ones you love the most. The aggression and forcefulness that you developed in order to make a place for yourself in an unsafe world becomes a handicap that causes others to fear and avoid you. The fierce determination to protect yourself by "winning no matter what" becomes your nemesis as you abandon your integrity in order to "come out on top." The sword that once worked so well for you now seems to have a mind of its own, and you can't seem to stop its self-destructive course.

The skill of being invisible that once made you safe from negative attention is now a curse that keeps you from being seen and heard by those whose attention you want. The wall of stoic silence that you developed to survive in a home where vulnerability was punished now becomes a prison from which you cannot escape. The protective barriers of numbness, detachment and dissociation that allowed you to survive abuse are now an impenetrable fortress that prevents you from knowing yourself and letting others know you. The shield that once served only to protect now threatens your connections with yourself and your loved ones, and even threatens your life itself.

Clearly, the sword and shield of the warrior spirit are necessary and important. Yet when your world failed to educate you on their use and function, you were on your own to figure out how to use them. The development of your sword and shield was therefore unconscious, without the guidance of wisdom and experience.

The warrior spirit in most of us can thus be seen as lost, primitive, wild, unfocused and beastlike. Beastlike because it had to retreat into our bodies without the education of our minds, and our animal nature is alive and well in our physical bodies.

Your warrior spirit can only develop into the noble and powerful spiritual warrior with the help and participation of your brilliant mind and your open heart. Most of us have not had the opportunity for that development, but it lies before you right now. You can retrieve your sword and shield from the shadows of your being and bring them into the conscious light of day. Then, combining them with your love and wisdom, you can shine them until they reflect the pure light of health and beauty, for the fulfillment of your true spiritual purpose.

First, let's assess the damage they've done while operating in the unconscious shadows of the soul and society.

ILLNESS, VIOLENCE AND
THE WARRIOR GONE AWRY

Author and anthropologist Carlos Castaneda, who has written much about the warrior spirit in the context of particular Native American traditions, said, "There's a primary knowledge that we all carry, directly connected with the two-million-year-old person at the root of our brain. And we do our best to suppress it, which makes us obese, cardiac, cancer prone" (Castaneda 1994). He is suggesting here what has now become established knowledge based on scientific research regarding the relationship between our minds, our emotions and our health (Sarno 1999).

- **The sword in our bodies.** The American Heart Association has sponsored research that indicates, "People who are highly anger-prone are nearly three times more likely to have heart attacks than those who aren't" (Goodman 2000). Metaphorically, we might conclude that when your sword is out of control, it might just pierce your own heart. Other ways that the misguided sword can injure us are reflected in this quote from a health-care professional with the Vanderbilt Health and Wellness Program. "Anger impacts us physiologically, making itself known to us through muscle tension, headaches, rapid breathing, increased heart rate, stomach distress, elevated blood pressure and even flushing of the skin."
- **The shield in our bodies.** The effects of shielding, or complex unconscious psychophysiological defense mechanisms, are diffuse and multifaceted. It is clear that chronic tension in large and small muscle groups throughout the body can lead to a variety of acute and long-term physical ailments. Gastrointestinal disorders, upper respiratory

illness, and cardiovascular problems are all related to and effected by hypertension (Kasparov et al. 2001). We are looking at interactions between emotional and physical processes here, not implying specific cause-and-effect relationships.

When we look at the problems in the world, the warrior's sword and shield are not hard to find.

- **The sword in the world.** The piercing, penetrating energies of angry words, sarcastic cuts, racial slurs, bullets, missiles and bombs are all too prevalent in today's twenty-first-century world. With war, terrorism, hate crimes, workplace violence, school shootings, domestic disputes, rape and child abuse occurring on an ongoing basis in various locales across the planet, we don't have to wonder about the seriousness of this problem. The unconscious, unclaimed warrior of the human soul is on the loose in our world, at times intimidating and at times claiming our minds, hearts and homes.
- **The shield in the world.** Stoic faces, no eye contact, awkward silences, cold and flat voices, uncaring responses, and miles of distance between people who are physically inches from each other are but a few of the manifestations of the warrior's shield in the world. Children with thoughts of violence and suicide who are not speaking to their parents, parents who don't know how to talk to their children, husbands and wives who don't communicate, the woman afraid to set foot outside her front door, and people everywhere with unexpressed love in their hearts show us examples of the walls that painfully separate us from each other.

THE DESTRUCTIVE PROTECTOR

The warrior spirit who is disconnected from love and wisdom becomes the destructive protector. Still making a misguided effort to protect her inner child from pain and suffering, the woman continues to drink too much, harming herself and her family in the process. Driven by his will to win approval through being successful and making lots of money, the man continues to work sixty hours a week against his doctor's recommendations and at the expense of intimacy in his marriage.

All of the compulsive-addictive disorders can be seen as the destructive protector at work. These behavior patterns create a "high" or "rush" or reward that gives temporary relief (protection) from pain, and yet creates far more pain than they ever relieve. In the effort to protect, they become destructive.

Other forms the destructive protector may take include:

- **The inner critic.** That voice in your head telling you what is wrong with you, reminding you of your limitations and flaws, is actually trying to protect you from harm. Therapeutic dialogues with inner critics consistently reveal that their original purpose was to prevent pain, suffering and loss. The more frustrated their efforts became, the louder and more desperate they became, until they were far more destructive than protective.
- **The inner tyrant.** Also known as the taskmaster, this aspect of the destructive protector will never let up on you until all of the work is done. And the work is never done. Many successful, competent and intelligent people are ruled by an inner tyrant. It gets great results in the outer world, yet wreaks havoc on the inner world.
- **The cynic.** That voice in your head that tells you what is wrong with the world and everyone in it was originally

developed in an effort to keep you safe. Yet if allowed to run its course and have its way, it will cause you to become isolated, withdrawn and nonfunctioning. The cynic will seduce you with the idea that the world is not good enough for you, and make you a prisoner behind your own walls of bitterness and distrust if you let it.

• **The fear mind.** This aspect of the destructive protector will convince you that it is just not safe out there. It's not safe to take that risk. It's not safe to get close to that person, to make that investment, to start that business or to take that vacation. In a misguided effort to protect, the fear mind can create absolute paralysis.

• **The angry victim.** Constantly convincing you that your problems are those other people's fault, the destructive protector in this form can actually lead you into abusive and violent behavior. The protective part is pointing out the things others are doing to hurt you, and the destructive part is telling you that you need to hurt them first. I'm sure it's clear how dangerous this can be, possibly leading to paranoia and even homicidal behavior.

We can see the sword and shield of the disconnected warrior in each of the above examples of the destructive protector. All of these can exist in one person, feeding off each other's fear and anger until catastrophe strikes. The destructive protector's ace in the hole is death. Homicide and suicide are the last-ditch efforts of a misguided, disconnected destructive protector warrior spirit. Our job here is to prevent any of us from ever going near such tragic outcomes, by reconnecting the warrior spirit with its original purpose of loving protection.

RECONNECTING THE WARRIOR WITH LOVE AND WISDOM

The healing of the warrior spirit requires a return to the pure innocent child whose protection was its original purpose. As this happens in the therapeutic process through imagery, journaling, voice dialogue and experiential release work, the destructive protector shifts her focus from destruction to protection. As the connection with the child grows through continued processes such as those described in this book, the protector becomes a loving protector. This is the beginning of the birth of the spiritual warrior, and gives us a metaphorical context for exploring healthy anger.

The story of Lora in chapter 7 gives a picture of this reconnection process. At first when she saw the little girl inside, she didn't like her. This was the destructive protector repeating the parents' pattern in an effort to connect with their love and avoid the pain of losing it by being emotional like a normal healthy child. When Lora started contacting her anger, and took the laser "vitamin pill," she immediately had a dream in which she was connected with the child. The healing of her anger (warrior spirit) created an automatic and spontaneous connection with her inner child.

THE LOVING PROTECTOR

When your anger becomes healthy, your warrior spirit is intimately connected with the power of love. The protection of your precious inner child is therefore always a matter of love more than fear-based anger. With the spiritual power of love as an ally and empowering force, your warrior is now far more capable of providing effective protection for your child self without sacrifice or loss.

The development of your sense of faith and optimism is a natural and essential part of this process. A belief in positive outcomes and an overall attitude that "Things are going to be okay" will bring stress relief and comfort to your inner child. In extensive research conducted over many years, Herbert Benson, M.D., found that individuals with a strong sense of faith and optimism recovered more quickly when they became ill, and were less likely to get sick in the first place (Benson 1997).

During a speech in Dallas in 1998, author Thomas Moore said, "The only real change occurs in the imagination." Right now, imagine a positive outcome in some situation that concerns you. Believe it. Feel it. You may notice your body relaxing a little. You might even experience a sigh of relief. If this happened for you, you just got healthier and improved the functioning of your immune system. Your loving protector wants you to have faith and hope, because of the wonderful benefits it brings to your body, mind and soul.

Here are some ideas to consider about your loving protector:

- The loving protector focuses inward, while the spiritual warrior's focus is external.
- The loving protector is completely devoted to caring for the inner child and all of the inner aspects of your being.
- The loving protector accesses and utilizes more brain capacity than the destructive protector.
- The loving protector sees all that you are and embraces you in your totality.
- The loving protector is like a guardian angel in your own mind, heart and body.
- The loving protector is equipped with a magnificent sword and shield that shine with a spiritual light that radiates from within you.
- The loving protector rarely if ever needs anger or aggression to protect you.

- The loving protector accesses your brilliance and wisdom, the depths of your love and the power of your spirit.
- The loving protector is your spiritual warrior focused internally on you.

In my book *Anger Among Angels*, you will find an entire chapter devoted to the loving protector, providing example dialogues in a journaling process (DeFoore 2000). To strengthen your loving protector consciousness and your connection with it, try this journaling process. To shift from the destructive protector to the loving protector as your predominant internal mode, follow this process on a daily basis.

1. First write from the destructive protector to purge the negative consciousness and allow a clearing for the expression of love. This can be seen as "draining the swamp" so you can get rid of the "alligators." Let your anger, fear, resentment or whatever negative thoughts and emotions you have flow out onto the page, uncensored. Don't hold back. Make sure you are only writing from the negative emotions without editing the content. Remember, this is for your (and possibly your counselor's) eyes only. Keep writing until you can't think of anything else to say or until you feel an internal shift or release.

2. In response to the destructive protector's purging, write, "Thank you for telling me how you feel. I appreciate the effort you are making to protect me. You have a place here inside me. You are not in charge, I am. I am going to give you some help now from another kind of protector" or something to that effect.

3. Now try to imagine that you are someone who loves you unconditionally. Perhaps a grandparent, parent, aunt, uncle, spouse or friend who sees your flaws and loves you anyway. If you prefer, create an imaginary image in your mind of the "perfect" loving elder who has known you all

of your life and sees the beauty, worth and value in you.
4. Write to yourself from this place. Your writing will perhaps go something like this:

"I know who you are inside. I have always been here, watching and listening. I know your heart, and it is a good heart. You have always tried so hard. You mean well, and you care deeply. You have accomplished many things in your life and overcome some tremendous obstacles. You have done some things you didn't think you could do. I know about your suffering and your pain. I have always been here. I know how afraid you are sometimes, and how angry you can be. I love you exactly as you are. My love for you is unconditional and freely flowing.

"My message to you now is to keep doing what you're doing. You are on the right track. Keep learning, growing and expanding your mind. I have faith in you. I know that when you learn of a new and better route to take to the fulfillment of your purpose, you will take it. I will always be here, believing in you, supporting you, encouraging you. Thank you for listening to me. The more you listen to me, the more clearly I will speak to you. I am a part of you that is merely waiting to be developed. I am your best friend, and you get to take me with you everywhere you go."

This journaling process, in conjunction with other healing and therapeutic processes, will eventually help you to become your own best friend instead of your own worst enemy. When you are having a hard time, you will reassure and comfort yourself, making it easier for you to get through to the other side. When you do something that causes you or someone else pain, you will take responsibility, acting reasonably and appropriately to correct the situation without blame, shame or guilt. You will be comfortable in your own skin, and more at home in the world.

THE SPIRITUAL WARRIOR

So how does this look to the world outside us? As the loving protector develops within, the spiritual warrior begins to develop in our relationship with the outer world. To get a sense of what a spiritual warrior is, think of the people you admire the most. You can use historical figures, celebrities, fictional characters or someone from your own life experience. What do these people have in common, and what sets them apart from others? Here are some of the qualities that come to mind:

- They know who they are and where they stand.
- They are comfortable with who they are and where they stand.
- They are humble souls, always learning and growing.
- They go their own way, led by an inner knowing of their purpose and mission.
- They enjoy life and all of its little daily pleasures.
- They are at home in nature, and have an abiding love of animals and the outdoors.
- Music, art and poetry are important to them.
- They are creative, in their own unique way.
- Children are naturally drawn to them.
- They love and honor the elders on the planet.
- They laugh heartily, often.
- They weep openly and without shame when sorrow strikes.
- They have a vision of their own place in life and the unfolding of their future.

- They manage their finances well and successfully.
- They are aware of the beauty in other human beings, and treat each one with respect.
- They automatically engender respect from others wherever they go.
- Their very presence creates good behavior from most of the people they are around.
- They are above no one, and no one is above them.
- When they are upset, they take action.
- Their physical health is robust.
- They take good care of their bodies by staying active and eating well.
- They are aging beautifully and gracefully.
- Their touch is healing.
- They have a strong relationship with the God of their choosing, and impose their views on no one.
- There is a deep peace in their eyes.
- They realize their own greatness and insignificance.
- They have an optimistic view of human existence on planet Earth.

The spiritual warrior has the courage to be creative and to express abundant positive emotion. This is not easy by any means. It is much easier to "stick with what you know" and adopt the "safer" negative attitude of "expect the worst and you'll never be disappointed." The problem is that approach may literally make you sick. A research project that has come to be known as the Nun Study suggests that individuals who are the most creative in their thought processes and who express the most positive emotion are the least likely to develop Alzheimer's disease (Lemonick and Mankato 2001). It has also been found that expressing love and appreciation helps the human heart to function better (McCraty and Childre 2003). Clearly it is possible that the effort you make to develop the spiritual warrior within you will greatly benefit your physical, mental and emotional health and well-being.

Set your vision of the spiritual warrior you choose to become. See yourself already there, as you go about your daily activities. Feel it happening. Know that it is so, and act accordingly.

HEALTHY ANGER

So what does anger look like when it's healthy? Effective action. Healthy anger may not look, sound or feel like anger as we have come to know it. It is purely and simply the raw energy of emotion channeled into action to accomplish the desired outcome. It shows up as determination, enthusiasm, clarity, focus, energy, drive, consistency, fortitude, guts, courage, commitment, persistence and resilience. Healthy anger necessarily works in conjunction with humor and love, wisdom and intelligence.

Healthy anger grabs the store clerk's attention so that you get better service. All it takes is an enthusiastic, "Excuse me, could I get some help here?" with a smile, a clear voice tone and a lot of good energy. Healthy anger incorporates a tremendous set of skills, which you will find described throughout this book. Seth's assertive behavior described in chapter 13 is a good example of healthy anger. Also, the discussion of mature, adult anger in chapter 7 gives further detail on healthy anger.

Use your healthy anger to say "No!" to the messages you have received about aging. See yourself right now aging like you would like to. See yourself strong, fit, vibrant and well ten, twenty, thirty or more years into your future. Make up your mind you're going to fulfill that vision. Write out a plan to make it happen. Use the healthy power of your anger to stick to your program, and don't let anything stand in your way.

Embrace the aspects of the spiritual warrior, the healthy man or the healthy woman that work best for you, and make it happen. Read Henriette Anne Klauser's book *Write It Down Make It Happen,* and do what the title suggests (Klauser 2001). This is your life, and no one can or will live it for you. No one is going to come and make everything okay for you. But you can. And there are many people willing and able to support you when you do.

You can live the life you have always dreamed of, and the pure, powerful energy of your healthy anger can help you get there.

AFFIRMATIONS

- *My healthy anger is one of my greatest assets.*
- *When my anger is healthy, it helps me to do what needs to be done.*
- *I can access and utilize the powerful energy of my anger to reach my goals and follow through on my commitments.*
- *My healthy anger is good for my health.*
- *Healing my anger is one of the best things I can do for my body and my mind.*
- *The healthier my anger is, the more freedom I have to express my love and tenderness.*

15

Overcoming
Workplace Violence

Eruptions of deadly violence in places of business in the United States seem to be at an all-time high at this book's release. This is a distant concern for some of you, and yet others reading this book may be currently employers or employed in companies where this has occurred or could occur. You may have an angry, abusive boss or coworker. Or you may be currently looking for a job and wondering if this company where you are applying might be the next site of a violent incident. Whatever your situation may be, there are things that each of us can do to address this alarming problem, and the need is great.

What is the message that these workers are sending? It

seems fairly simple, clear and direct. They are angry, they feel they have been victimized and unjustly treated, and they're not getting what they want. This is not complicated or new. What is new is the frequency of multiple murders and in some cases suicides in these first few years of the twenty-first century. What is complicated is how to address and resolve this problem on a large scale.

In this chapter, we will look at 1) the psychology of the violent person, 2) perceptions that others have of the violent person, and 3) the responsibility and ability to respond that coworkers, business leaders and the rest of us have.

THE PSYCHOLOGY OF THE VIOLENT PERSON

The perspectives offered in this section are based on my personal and professional observations over the past thirty-one years and research in the area (Toch and Karon 1992; Langone 1984). You will find other information on violence and the psychology of violence at *www.questia.com*, the world's largest online library.

I will use the masculine gender in referring to the violent person because that reflects most of my experience and because males have committed the most violence throughout history (Toch and Karon 1992).

Violence comes from a place of psychological chaos, confusion and a deep sense of powerlessness. However calm and assured such a person may appear at times, he is carrying a profound sense of psychological disturbance at some level, or he would never be prone to violence. Violence simply cannot arise from a place of peace and harmony.

The violent person is or feels that he is excluded. He may be extremely isolated. He feels misunderstood and mistreated, and often is. Whether he knows it or not, he sees himself as a victim of other people, systems and circumstances that are out of his control—thus the sense of powerlessness and helplessness.

He is deranged. He thinks that somehow he must penetrate the impenetrable, break through the walls that have shut him out, get the attention of those who won't listen to him and punish the guilty for their wrongdoing. He is delusional and at times borders on grandiosity, thinking he has the duty to bring justice to an unjust world. He doesn't trust anyone else, and certainly not the system, to administer justice for him.

Yes, all of this is true. And yet he is human. He is a child of God. And he responds to love, care and attention because he needs that as much as we all do.

He makes it hard for you to love him, or even spend time in his presence. He lives out his self-fulfilling prophecy that no one likes him and might even relish the idea of your being afraid of him. He is at times unpleasant, rude, abusive, unsociable or just socially awkward, saying the wrong thing at the wrong time. He will most likely offend you and embarrass you. He may deliberately try to hurt you. Why would you want to have anything to do with him?

You don't. I don't. Nobody does. So he is isolated and alone, cooking up his ideas of violence. This is the problem. The violent people are the outcasts and misfits of the world. They don't fit, they're no fun, and they hurt, offend and bother us, so we cast them out. The thing is, that approach is not working. They are breaking into our inner circles with bullets. They are entering our hearts and minds with violent explosions of unthinkable cruelty, ripping innocent people's lives away as an expression of their helpless rage.

And he does not like himself. That's why he often kills himself after he has killed his victims.

MISGUIDED PERCEPTIONS
OF THE PROBLEM AND SOLUTION

A common or familiar perception might be something like this:

"Let's face it. These people are weird, crazy; they ought to be locked up and punished. If we just keep killing (executing) those who don't kill themselves, maybe we will finally be rid of them. Meanwhile, when you see one of these dangerous folks, stay away from them.

"We don't want to include them in our circles, conversations and socializing, because that would reward their bad behavior. Ignore them and maybe they will go away."

We might also hear reasoning like:

"The problem is the guns. If they just didn't have those guns, none of this would be happening. We need to legislate to get rid of the guns."

If this approach worked, we would have solved the problem a long time ago. The "reject and punish" approach actually feeds the problem, like fighting fire with fire. It could be that the problem of workplace violence is going to continue and maybe even get worse until we move to a deeper and more lasting resolution. Let's take a look at some different perspectives and examine a few approaches to resolution.

COWORKERS' RESPONSIBILITY
AND OPTIONS FOR HELPING

From my experience in studying business processes and doing corporate training over the past fifteen years, it has become clear to me that business systems are the true culprit when it comes to workplace violence. Systems that oppress, ignore, exploit and abuse workers, and/or focus only on the bottom line and pleasing shareholders create hostile work environments that breed anger and violence.

Everyone working in such systems is affected. No individual is to blame, and yet "management" and "owners" are the usual scapegoats, and in some cases rightfully so. In an oppressive and abusive system blind to workers' needs and concerns, every worker will feel and live with the effects. Shadows of discontent loom large in such organizations, and tend to concentrate and come to focus in the employees with the most tendencies toward confusion, delusion and violence.

Relatively sane employees with loving families and decent lives can survive in such work environments, because they can retreat to the counterbalancing domain of their more loving and healthy nonwork world. Such people can "let things slide," or "let things roll off their back" and "not take things so personally." Yet where do those things slide and roll off to?

I think there's a very good possibility that the disturbed, isolated workers prone to violence pick up on the anger and discontent all around them, and make the fatal mistake of thinking that murder is some kind of answer. Just as in families where one child is the scapegoat or identified patient and carries other family members' unclaimed anger, fear and pain, I am suggesting that violent workers are the "shadow bearers" of a disgruntled workplace family. This is no one's fault, yet it is every worker's responsibility. Here are some things you can do in your workplace:

• Look around among your coworkers and ask yourself the question, "If anyone in this group were most likely to become violent, who would that be?" Most of the time you will know immediately. If not, ask some of your friends what they think.

- Spend one-on-one time with the most unhappy and isolated of your coworkers.
- Ask them what they are thinking and feeling.
- Reflect what you have heard them say. You don't have to agree, disagree or solve their problem. Just hear them and tell them what you have heard them say.
- Then say something like, "I hear you." "I see where you're coming from" or "Thanks for telling me what's going on." Many angry, upset people want and need to be heard more than anything else.
- If you can empathize and offer understanding, by all means do so, with comments such as, "When I put myself in your shoes, I can see why you would feel that way" or "That makes sense to me." Only say this if you sincerely mean it. Patronizing can do more harm than good.
- As a general rule, do not offer solutions or even different perspectives. If and only if you feel a rapport with the person, or if you sense that they might be open to your viewpoint, then provide information, perspective and/or resources that you think might be helpful. *Do not try to change a person's mind*—that will only feed the hostility.
- If you have a group that is healthy enough to embrace this person, invite him to join you for lunch, at a party or a ball game. The idea is to include him to counter his feelings of exclusion and isolation that contribute to his tendencies toward violence.
- Be playful and humorous with those who are having a rough time. This requires that you have some degree of rapport, or else the effort could backfire and add to the hostility. If you think there's a chance it could bring a smile,
  - Tell a harmless joke.
  - Put a flower on his desk or in his workstation.
  - Rearrange something at his workstation in a humorous way.

- ▪ Put a toy or smiling face somewhere that will surprise him and maybe bring a laugh.
- If you have the opportunity or authority to do so, put this person on a committee or offer him a position of leadership on some task.
- Do this consistently, with anyone who seems angry, extremely cynical, withdrawn, isolated, outcast, quiet, off to himself, depressed, or openly violent and aggressive. You may be saving lives, perhaps even your own.
- If you do not feel that you can do any of these things for whatever reason, then just wish the best for this person in your mind. Every time you think of them or see them, send them love and give them your silent blessing. If you pray, then pray for them. This can be as effective as overt action, and in some cases more so.
- Unless you believe it would do more harm than good, alert management to your concerns.

BUSINESS LEADERS' RESPONSIBILITY

In the late '90s I did a significant amount of work in corporate communications training and development. During that time I learned a lot about the value and importance of a kind of communication that is not ordinarily considered appropriate in a business environment: talking about feelings.

Through a simple process of expressing and reflecting the basic negative emotions of fear, sorrow and anger and the positive emotions of love, appreciation and happiness, great healing occurred and important business information was revealed. Though we have no way of knowing for sure, we may have prevented violence from occurring.

It was the business leaders who made this training program happen, and it was only in their power to do so. Many employees simply do not have the authority or funding to provide education or communications training programs in their workplace.

It is the responsibility of business owners and managers to either 1) implement open communication systems within their organizations, or 2) bring in outside consultants and trainers to facilitate the development of these systems. An excellent source for emotional intelligence in leadership processes is the book entitled *Primal Leadership: Realizing the Power of Emotional Intelligence* (Goleman et al. 2002).

FIFTEEN YEARS OF HEALING IN TWO HOURS

As the in-house expert on our consulting team for dealing with anger-related problems, I was sent to this particular location because of their long-standing union-management disputes. When I arrived at the initial briefing, I was informed that union workers were currently working without a signed contract. After seven months of negotiations, company managers and union leaders had failed in their attempts to come to agreement on salary, benefits and termination packages.

I also learned that the plant manager had received death threats directed at him and his family during the past year. He sat in on the training most of the two days, even though he had already been through the program at corporate headquarters. I knew this was not required of him, and I was impressed with his leadership and courage. His presence surprised several of the workers present. The tension in the hotel meeting room where we met was heavy and thick.

Over lunch on our first day, one of the managers told me that this particular plant had been known for disputes, conflict, strikes and a few riots dating back over twenty years. He implied that they did not really expect much good to come from the training.

My associate and I spent two days initially teaching and facilitating learning processes around communication and the development of communication tools. We also focused on interdepartmental dynamics and business processes, all to lay the groundwork for actual communications training.

Here's the setup and process for part of the communications training between management and nonmanagement workers:

- Ten empty chairs were placed in the middle of a large room in two rows of five. Each chair was facing another directly across from it.
- Five designated managers were asked to sit in five of the chairs, each facing an empty chair across from her/him.
- The remaining group of fifty-plus employees in the room was invited to come and occupy any of the five empty chairs and express their feelings on anything at all to any or all of the managers. The instructions were as follows:
  - The worker sits across from the manager and says, "I feel (mad, sad or scared) because . . . [then complete the sentence however they choose]."
  - The manager then says, "I hear you saying that you feel (mad, sad or scared) because . . . [repeating exactly what the worker said]."
  - Then the manager asks, "Is that correct?"
  - If the worker is satisfied with the manager's reflection of what she said, she responds, "Yes" and takes her seat. If not, she repeats her original statement and they try again until the worker feels heard. Then she takes her seat.
- This process was repeated as long as there were any workers with something to say. On this particular day we went for two and a half hours before stopping.

One of the most poignant moments in that afternoon was when a union steward who had been particularly hostile and outspoken came and sat in front of the plant manager. The room was very quiet and still. It seemed the union worker was having a hard time thinking of the right words to say.

"Mr. McAfee, I feel real sad because of what happened to you and your family over this past year." I heard a few sniffs around the room as we waited for the manager's response.

"Henry, I hear you saying that you feel real sad because of what happened to me and my family over the past year. Is that correct?" Mr. McAfee's eyes were moist, and he spoke with a slight catch in his throat.

"Yes sir, that is correct," responded the union leader, after which they shook hands and he returned to his seat in the circle with the rest of the workers.

Several other powerful moments like that one occurred, intermixed with humor and some very serious business-related information. One exchange comes to mind that had significant potency and implications.

"Mr. Johnson, I feel pretty scared when I have to go and fix a problem with the breaker box while standing in about four inches of water." The man speaking was an electrician in his middle forties, and he looked very serious as he spoke. The manager across from him was in total shock.

"Matt, I hear you saying that you feel pretty scared when you have to go and fix a problem with the breaker box while standing in about four inches of water. Is that correct?" Johnson looked like he couldn't believe that it actually was correct.

"Yes, Mr. Johnson, that is correct." Matt went back to his chair. No questions were asked, no solutions or explanations given.

Next to speak was Sara, a woman in her thirties with a ball cap worn backwards on her head. She sat down in front of her supervisor, Joe, and said, "Joe, I feel mad when I see the men in this plant being promoted twice as fast as the women." She was smiling as she spoke, but everyone could tell she meant exactly what she was saying.

"Sara, I hear you saying that you feel mad when you see the men in this plant being promoted twice as fast as the women. Is that correct?" Joe looked a little embarrassed, as if he knew that her complaint was legitimate.

"Yes, Joe, that is exactly correct." Sara stood and walked proudly back to her seat, while a few of her coworkers applauded.

Following this exercise, we asked for comments and questions from the group about the process we had just completed.

A woman in her mid-fifties, after blowing her nose, said, "I feel like I've just witnessed fifteen years of healing in the last two hours."

Mr. Johnson said, "I'm determined to communicate better with all of you. I feel responsible for the fact that we had to have this off-site workshop for me to learn about a life-threatening situation in the plant."

Mr. McAfee, the plant manager said, "I want to thank those of you who expressed your personal concern for me and my family. It means a lot to me."

Another manager, Mrs. Bronson, said, "I have just received more important information about the running of our plant in the last two hours than I have in the last two months." Several of the other managers nodded in agreement, and Mrs. Bronson added, "I have also made some notes, and plan to begin making some changes tomorrow to correct some of the problems you have pointed out today. Thank you."

When violence is prevented, nothing happens. You won't be reading news headlines that say, "Violence prevented for fourth straight week in Detroit." We therefore have to make our efforts at prevention on faith.

As a result of the work the participants did that day, you could see and feel the tension melt from the faces and bodies of the people in that room. Lives may have been saved by what happened. The important business information hidden behind feelings of sorrow, fear and anger may have improved overall leadership and communication when shared openly. After this kind of process, friendships begin, and respect and trust levels grow, contributing to the overall level of openness, optimism and humor in the workplace. Productivity levels and teamwork can greatly increase as a result of eased tension and increased camaraderie.

If all organizations implemented this simple exercise on a consistent basis, with appropriate communications training and education from time to time, violence in the workplace might be greatly reduced. This training process and communication exercise is inclusive without being intrusive. It is simple and yet allows groups and individuals to address complex issues.

Why does it work? Because great tension and hostility is resolved when the person who feels offended or oppressed is allowed to speak and be heard. Also, and very importantly, the structure of the exercise provides safety for the navigation of "troubled waters" involving sorrow, fear and anger. Ordinarily, conversations around these emotions would lead to arguments, or would not occur at all.

In Appendix III, you will find a set of guidelines for "Respectful Conflict Resolution for Workplace Problem-Solving," which is designed specifically to help individuals successfully navigate emotionally charged territory.

If you look at the information shared in this chapter and in this book, you will see that there is something you can do to help prevent workplace violence and/or violence everywhere. The choice is yours.

AFFIRMATIONS

- *My work is an expression of my spiritual purpose in life.*
- *My work is an act of love and service.*
- *My work is my vocation, my calling to serve the higher good for humanity.*
- *My workplace is an important aspect of my life, and I choose to care for it with love, understanding and compassion.*

16

A Picture of
Emotional Wellness

Looking back over the various diagrams presented
in earlier chapters, you will find that the innermost circles of the concentric circle diagrams
contain the need to love and be loved, and a commitment to
self, the inner child and a spiritual focus point. Ultimately,
healing involves an expansion of these inner dimensions so
that our most innocent and loving self becomes the predominant aspect of who we are. Everything presented in
this book has been leading toward an expansion of love and
healing from within. This is the function of expressing emotions in healthy ways.

THE INNER JOURNEY OF HEALING

We might see Figure 16.1 as representing a road map for the journey within. As you begin taking quiet time each day to develop an inner focus, you will be better able to listen to your body and take responsibility for your own health and happiness. As you venture into your inner world, you will encounter your own walls, defenses and anger. By using the processes outlined in this book to make an ally of your warrior spirit and develop the spiritual warrior, you will have the power to move beyond these barriers and face the powerful inner realms of your soul.

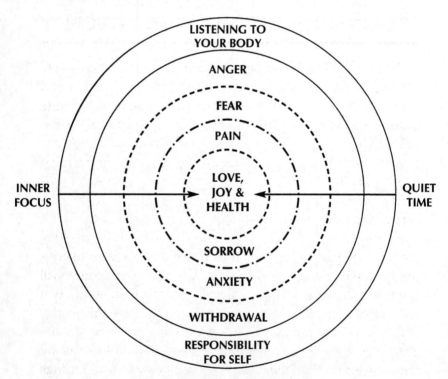

Figure 16.1. The Inner Journey

Empowered by anger at the injustice of our childhood injuries, we break through the wall of fear and encounter the inner realms of hurt, sorrow and pain. The healthy anger we have gained as an ally is based on compassion for the wounded child. When we contact the pain of the child, we automatically feel love for this innocent being who has been abused, neglected or abandoned by adult caregivers. This is where the journey always leads. The more we make this journey, the more healing occurs and the more the wall of fear and the realm of pain diminish. Each time we contact the inner circle of love for the inner child, it expands, dissolving the pain and fear. Eventually the inner world begins to transform entirely.

PERSONAL INTEGRATION AND INTEGRITY

One way of looking at who you are as a human being is to see yourself as an integrated system of thought, action and feeling. In the diagram in Figure 16.2 you will see that thought, action and feeling are analogous to the parent, adult and child relationships as described by author Thomas Harris (1976).

As the nurturing parent provides protection, support and love for the inner child, the inner child begins to trust the nurturing parent. This was illustrated in chapter 8 in the dialogues with the inner child. This of course makes the adult more effective with all of the internal resources working together. As your thoughts about yourself become more positive, you will begin to feel more secure and your actions will become more powerful and focused. If you look at the two sets of three circles in Figure 16.2, you can see how this works.

It follows that nurturing your inner child is a way of more effectively integrating your thoughts, actions and feelings. By the same token, thinking positive thoughts about your feelings is a way of nurturing your inner child. The more internally

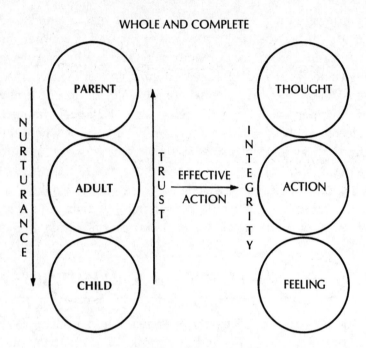

Figure 16.2. The Goal of Healing

integrated you are in your thoughts, actions and feelings, the more integrity you will demonstrate in your relationships with others. It follows that your relationships with others are ultimately a reflection of your relationship with yourself.

To effectively take charge of your thoughts, actions and feelings, you must examine what patterns and habits already exist. One of the best ways to do this is to take a look at your family of origin and examine the messages you received there. Figure 16.3 shows a way of identifying some of those messages and how they affected you. As you can see in the diagram, the spoken words you heard as children affect your thoughts of today. The behavior you observed in your parents to a large extent determines your actions today. The

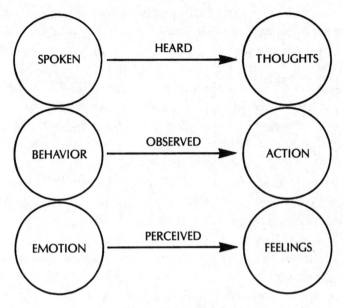

Figure 16.3. Origins

subtlest influence your parents had on you was emotional.
You were picking up on feelings even before you came out of
your mother's womb. The emotions you perceived from your
parents had a profound subconscious effect on how you feel
about your world and yourself today.

UNLOADING FAMILY BAGGAGE

From the points made throughout this book and from your
own life experience, you probably know the value of resolving issues relating to your family of origin. We must each
examine the thoughts, actions and feelings we subconsciously soaked up during our formative years at home.

Much of what you learned was useful or you would not

have the intelligence and skill to read this book. It is just as important to recognize what you received that was valuable as it is to unload what you don't need anymore. If you don't acknowledge the gifts, you may feel guilty in the process of identifying the baggage you want to unload. Take an inventory of what you picked up. Separate out what you want to keep and what you want to give back. Be grateful for what you got that is useful. Return to your parents/caregivers what you received that is getting in the way of your being the person you want to be. They never meant to pass on their hangups to you anyway. Taking them back is no hardship on them, because they never really gave them up in the first place.

(By the way, I am not implying that this be done in person, face to face with your parents/caregivers. They neither need to be physically present nor even living for you to resolve these issues for yourself. It may be helpful to involve them in your healing process if they are healthy and ready to participate. Otherwise, you may be adding to existing problems instead of unloading baggage.)

This business of giving back unwanted baggage to your parents may sound strange to you, but it really is possible. It usually is done in a therapeutic context in which Gestalt techniques are employed to create a valid emotional release from abusive and shaming childhood experiences. There are also workbooks available such as Dr. Charles Whitfield's *A Gift to Myself*, which is designed to help with the process of healing the inner child (Whitfield 1989). John Bradshaw's *Homecoming* is also designed for this purpose (Bradshaw 1990). These workbooks often include exercises for resolving family-of-origin issues, along with the other healing and affirmation methods.

As a result of this inner healing work, walls begin to disappear, and we become more clear and open to ourselves and to the world around us.

A DYNAMIC BREATHING SYSTEM

In comparing the diagrams in Figure 16.4 with those in Figure 16.1, you can see that the inner and outer circles have expanded until they connect, removing the walls of fear and pain. You will also notice that the system is an open one, indicated by the broken lines in the top diagram. This allows more expression of love and joy in relationship to the world. It also allows for more receptivity to input from others. This is a flexible, breathing system of healthy boundaries.

In the diagram on the bottom of Figure 16.4, there is more protection and more privacy from the world. We each need this for self-nurturing, rest and spiritual focusing. When we are rejuvenated and ready, we open to the world again, expressing and receiving openly as in the top diagram. This is my idea of how we maintain our health and happiness in a demanding and changing world. We have times when we are open and expansive and times when we are quiet and private, more focused within. This is as natural as breathing in and breathing out.

As discussed in the preceding chapter, we each need the opportunity to be close and intimate with others, while maintaining responsibility for our own needs and feelings. With the flexibility indicated in the opening and closing pattern of Figure 16.4, we can give and receive nurturing in a close relationship without being dependent on the other. We can also withdraw and have time to ourselves as needed without being isolated. While in the open mode, we may express our anger, fear and pain (yes, it is still there, but it is not like it used to be) without losing touch with love and compassion. The backlog of pain, fear and anger from the past has been healed so the current emotions are manageable and can be easily communicated. From a clear, healthy place,

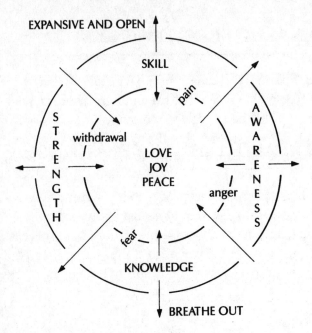

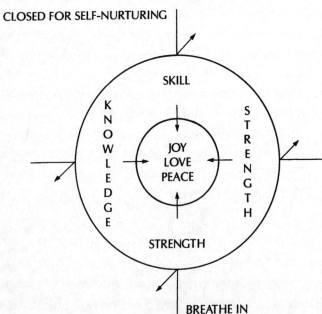

Figure 16.4. Open and Private Circles

the simple expression of feelings clears the emotions. Connections are easily made, and they are not threatening. This is the rest of the establishment and maintenance of healthy, flexible boundaries.

THE HEALTHY ADULT RELATIONSHIP

For more perspective on how this dynamic system might work in a healthy adult relationship, take a look at the diagram in Figure 16.5. Both individuals represented have a nurturing, trusting relationship with themselves. Therefore, there is internal stability and balance within both people, allowing for free expression of intimacy at all levels. As indicated by the arrow connecting the two sides at the adult level, the primary connection is adult to adult.

The two are, however, able to communicate at the level of authority and responsibility, which is needed for raising children or taking charge of any demanding situation, such as paying bills or solving problems. Because of their personal freedom and flexibility, however, they can also connect emotionally at the child level. This is essential if there is going to be fun, spontaneity or lovemaking in the relationship.

Both individuals must be healthy in order to freely allow the true intimacy and healthy withdrawal necessary for a healthy adult relationship. This dynamic breathing system gives those involved an opportunity to grow and develop as they are compelled to from within. This type of relationship is an enhancement to the lives of everyone involved. It is my belief that this is the type of relationship that each of us truly desires.

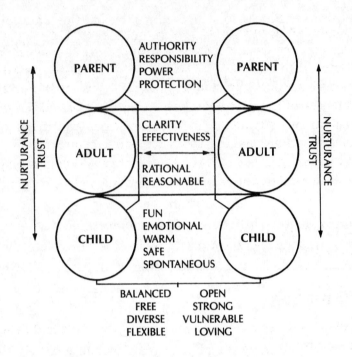

Figure 16.5. Healthy Adult Relationship

SKILLS FOR BEING FULLY PRESENT

To the extent that we are being subconsciously influenced by our past, we are not fully present in any relationship. To the extent that we have resolved past issues, we are capable of thinking, acting and feeling completely within the present moment. This is when we are most effective and most likely to act in ways consistent with our thoughts and feelings. This results in personal integrity, as we discussed earlier in this chapter.

Most of the time we are thinking about one thing, doing something else and completely unaware of our feelings. This disjointed or disintegrated way of being leads to tension and stress because we are actually in conflict with ourselves. We are more likely to have accidents or make costly mistakes when we are out of sync in this way. It follows that once the influences of the past have been released, it would be very much to our advantage to take conscious control of our thoughts, actions and feelings in a positive manner.

In Figure 16.6, you will see three different skill groupings, one each for thoughts, actions and feelings.

AFFIRMATION, VISUALIZATION AND IMAGINATION

Affirmation

All of our lives we have had different thoughts and beliefs affirmed by those around us. Our first thoughts were greatly influenced by our parents. As we moved out into the world, the influences were our peers, teachers and the media. This set of skills is simply designed to help you be an influence on your own thoughts, rather than accepting uncritically the constant influence of the world around you. We are always affirming something in our minds as a natural function of our thinking process. You may have heard the aphorism, "You are today what your thoughts were yesterday. You will be tomorrow what your thoughts are today."

As you can see in Figure 16.6 there are three levels of affirmation. The first deals with the past, the second with the present and the third affirms the new action or experience in the future. I will use one example throughout the skills exercise to provide continuity and to demonstrate how each of these skills can be applied in conjunction to one specific problem or change area.

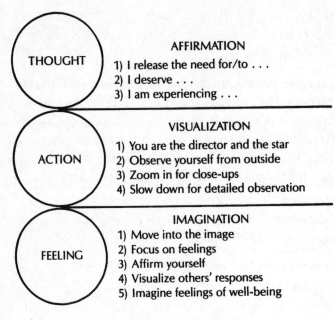

Figure 16.6. Skills

1. I release the need for/to . . . (feel like a victim in my relationships).
2. I deserve . . . (to feel empowered and comfortable with myself in all of my relationships).
3. I am experiencing . . . (more of a sense of comfort and empowerment within myself as each new day unfolds).

Affirmations often stir up major objections from our conscious and subconscious mind in the form of negative and fearful thoughts. These self-defeating thoughts are coming from a frightened part of us. They are not bad or something to be resisted. When this occurs, simply embrace your inner child and say, "It's okay to feel afraid. I've got you and I will take care of you through all of these new changes." Then go back to the thoughts. You don't want to let the fearful mind get the last word. Here are fourth and fifth levels of the affirmation exercise that are helpful for responding to self-defeating thoughts.

4. Negative or contradictory thoughts which arose are . . . *(Every time I try to stand up for myself I get hurt or something bad happens. Besides, I'm afraid of changing. I've always been like this.)*
5. Thoughts in response to the negative or contradictory thoughts are . . . *(It's okay to be afraid. I'm also angry about the way my life is going, and I am determined to use my anger to empower me to make positive changes. I am experiencing a sense of empowerment within myself right now as I think of my healthy anger and how it can help me move out of the victim position.)*

This same exercise can be used to address a wide variety of areas in your life. You will find a copy of the Affirmations Exercise in Appendix I in the back of this book, which you are free to copy and use for your own growth and development. You will find "target areas" listed in this exercise, which are merely suggestions as to how you might focus your affirmations work.

Louise Hay's book, *You Can Heal Your Life,* and Ruth Fishel's *The Journey Within: A Spiritual Path to Recovery* are excellent resources for affirmation work (Hay 1987; Fishel 1987).

As a final note in this section, I would like to say that as human beings we can do anything we set our minds to. Decide what you want and go for it.

Visualization

Have you ever heard anyone say, "I just can't picture myself doing that"? When we hear statements like that, we know for sure the person is not going to do what they can't picture themselves doing. It also follows that if we can picture ourselves doing something, we are much more likely to do it.

This exercise is just that simple. If you want to do something, picture yourself doing it.

1. You are the director and the star. This means you are picturing yourself out there in front of you, engaging in your new behavior. It's as if you were both the director and the star on a movie set.
2. Observe yourself from the outside, from the director's position. You are concerned with how you, the actor, are presenting yourself. To continue with our example from the affirmation section, picture yourself in a situation where you have historically felt uncomfortable and anxious, like a victim of your circumstances. This time, however, you are seeing yourself as you would like to be, calm and confident. Notice how you look from across the room. Look for indicators that you are completely at ease.
3. Now move in more closely and notice how deep and even your breathing is. Your skin shows a glow that indicates good circulation and relaxed muscles. There's a sparkle in your eyes, and you look as if you are right where you are supposed to be. To help with this image, you may want to picture yourself in a situation where it is easy for you to feel relaxed, and then move that image into the challenging situation.
4. Slow the action for a moment and watch yourself as you move about, interacting with others. Notice how you present yourself pleasantly and with confidence. Your head is up and you are looking directly into the eyes of the other person. You are showing a sincere interest in them while remaining centered and focused within yourself.

Remember to stay on the outside throughout the visualization exercise, so your focus is on your behavior. When you have successfully accomplished your goal of seeing yourself as you would like to be, it's time to bring the image in, and to

imag(e) in(e) having the feelings you have been picturing yourself having.

Imagination

This is where you begin to come closer to actually having
the experience. You rise from the director's chair and walk
across the room.

1. Move into the image of the star (bring the image in). The
   director and the star are now one, and you are in the
   situation. You are now seeing what the star was seeing
   during your visualization exercise.
2. Focus on the feelings. Don't allow yourself to be distracted by what you are seeing in the room around you.
   Be aware of what is present while maintaining focus on
   your own bodily sensations of warmth, relaxation and
   comfort. Notice your breathing. You are breathing from
   your stomach in long, deep inhalations and exhalations.
   This is happening naturally with no effort on your part.
   Notice the relaxed, energetic feelings in your body. You
   can feel the pleasant sensations in your body moving up
   into your face, creating a pleasant, calm expression.
3. Affirm yourself. Use some of the affirmations from the exercise above, or create new ones to repeat to yourself as you
   imagine yourself calm and at ease. Tell yourself exactly what
   you would like to hear. Give yourself the support you have
   always wanted. Be your own best friend and supporter.
4. Visualize others' responses. Picture the other person in
   front of you. They may be uncomfortable with your new
   sense of confidence and ease. They also may be very positive in their response. Imagine yourself being completely
   okay with their response, whatever it may be. They may
   try to pull you back into old patterns so they can be more

comfortable since that is what they are used to. Still, you stay relaxed while focusing on the pleasant, soothing feelings of calm moving throughout your body and face. If they persist with attempts to pull you off center, simply imagine yourself calmly announcing that you have other things to do and you will reconnect with them at another time. You may want to go back to the visualization exercise to begin this process of leaving the situation with comfort and ease. You may also want to imagine yourself expressing your feelings in a new way.

5. Imagine feelings of well-being. Notice a feeling of stillness deep within your being. There is a silence in the center of your mind, which seems to arise from this stillness. In that silence, you find that the words you need to say are spontaneously emerging. From the stillness, you find that the feelings you want have spontaneously arisen. Words that seem to go with these feelings of well-being are comfortable, easy, relaxed, confident, calm, empowered, energetic, peaceful, focused, centered and still. Use these words to create new affirmations for yourself to apply to your life in general as well as specific situations in which you would like to improve yourself.

By taking charge of your own thoughts, actions and feelings, you are directing a tremendous amount of energy into the core of your being. This will bring an inevitable expansion of your sense of self-worth and value. You will no longer feel fragmented and incomplete. Maybe this is what is meant by "getting it together."

EXPERIENCE BEING WHOLE AND COMPLETE

While reading through the above exercises, whether you actually applied the exercises to a situation from your life or not, you probably felt some of the feelings being described. The mere process of thinking of the words "comfort" and "ease" requires our mind to recall their meaning. As we recall the meaning of these words, our subconscious mind is busy providing examples from our past when we in fact knew the meaning of comfort and ease. As this process unfolds, sometimes in a split second, some degree of comfort and ease actually begins to occur within our bodies.

Body, mind and emotion are not separate, but intricately interwoven in ways we have only begun to understand. As we make affirming statements to ourselves and think of soothing, empowering words, our emotional body is responding, whether we know it consciously or not. When we picture ourselves in our mind's eye as successful and confident, behaving in ways we are completely comfortable with, our body responds with the appropriate feelings. When we imagine ourselves as actually having the experience we want to have, we are actually having the experience we want to have.

Regardless of what happens in your daily life, practicing these exercises will increase your feelings of well-being and ease. They are designed to give you power and control within yourself, which you are actually exercising by affirming, visualizing and imagining.

When your thoughts, actions and feelings are working together in ways you have chosen for your health and well-being, you are acting in an integrated manner. You are fully present, and your whole being is completely involved in each element of each experience in each moment. This is what we are here for. This is how we maximize our individual expression of this miraculous gift of life that we are.

AFFIRMATIONS

- *I can do anything I set my mind to.*
- *I have a brilliant mind.*
- *I release the need to limit my mind in any way.*
- *I deserve to be the best me I can possibly be.*
- *I am experiencing more of my true, essential self with each new day.*
- *I am becoming familiar with a place of stillness and peace within my being.*
- *When I relax and focus on the silence within my mind, answers to questions and solutions to problems spontaneously arise.*
- *My natural state of being is one of comfort and ease.*
- *I have everything I need to be whole and complete.*

17

Conclusions and Brainstorms

THE END OF THE VICTIM ROLE

I magine with me for a moment what the world would be like if no one ever felt like a victim. This would be a world in which people took responsibility for their feelings and for the situations they found themselves in. Without the victim position, there would be no "bad guy" out there to blame for our circumstances. In this world we would feel empowered from within. When something didn't go our way, we would work through the emotional reactions and then get busy doing what we could to make the situation better. It would not be a perfect world, but it would have much more positive action and much less complaining and self-pity. There would be fewer addictive disorders, since many of these arise from a feeling of helplessness and despair. Helplessness and despair arise from feeling like a victim.

This is why I believe this matter of claiming our power through claiming our anger as a healthy emotion is so important. Experiencing and expressing anger in healthy ways is a first step toward moving out of the victim position. We cannot feel angry—with the full physical components of heat, adrenaline and energy—and feel like a victim at the same time.

Granted, feeling like a victim often gives rise to anger. The problem is that anger coming from a victim position usually goes into blaming, attacking or even hating the persecutor. As I have discussed in previous chapters, this is a phase of healing for those who were indeed victimized in the past. It is not a goal, however. Anger for empowerment comes from a sense of what is right and just, and is used only to heal and to creatively express.

A world in which no one felt like a victim would be a world of empowerment, freedom and responsibility. This world would have more joy and fulfillment, simply because more people would reach their goals and live their dreams. This world would have more love and less fear, since removing victim feelings would also remove a tremendous amount of fear. Fear and love are incompatible. An absence of fear would automatically give rise to more love.

SOCIOLOGICAL AND PLANETARY PERSPECTIVE

The patterns of oppression, suppression and rage are clear and prevalent in our society and throughout the world. Slavery is one of the greatest oppressions known to humankind. Slaves had to suppress their emotions to prevent their oppression from getting worse. Expressing their emotions may even have meant being tortured and killed.

Rage is one of the maladies that always results from oppression and suppression. It makes sense that slavery brought out rage within the people who were oppressed. This is a natural human response to such treatment.

The Civil War in the United States is an example of a nation raging against itself. The civil rights movement involved some rage but also the use of healthy anger. Oppression and abuse of African Americans today have brought further emotional suppression and more rage. This has continued long after the slaves were "freed." As a society, we are still in the healing process from this oppression and its results.

Cultural and social rage is an explosive release from the depths of suppressed emotion. This is just like the rage we have explored in this book, resulting from childhood abuse and abandonment. It is empowered by the years of pain, fear and anger resulting from oppression. It brings about destruction and bloodshed, but it also brings necessary change. We have seen this not only in the rage against racism, but also in the responses of early feminists in their rage against sex discrimination. Adolescence can be viewed as a (sometimes violent) process of breaking free from the "oppression" of childhood. As long as there is oppression, there will be suppression and explosions of rage. It is inevitable. Solving the problems leading to oppression is what empowering a large part of the world's population is about. What we are about in this book is giving rise to healthy empowerment within individuals to minimize suppression and oppression as much as possible.

Long-term constructive change, both personal and societal, comes from the healthy use of anger for effective transformation of oppressive systems. Many individuals who use appropriate and yet powerful means to bring about fair and equitable treatment of all people are now accomplishing this. To me, this is healthy expression of anger.

Many of us are angry at the abuse of this planet, our home. The best way to channel this emotional energy is to put it into hard work for creating a healthy, safe planet. To attack violently those we feel have abused our environment simply causes new problems which distract us from the task at hand. I am not against political and social activism. As a matter of fact I actively support some environmental protection and conservation groups. I am only aware that we all cannot and do not need to become political and social activists to help with the restoring of our planet to good health. Recycling, for example, gives each of us an opportunity to take individual responsibility and put our emotional energy into immediate constructive action.

There are always constructive means for positive action. If you are in a situation in which you feel victimized and powerless, find that blank spot in your mind where the solution to your problem is supposed to be and isn't. Now just be still with that silence and emptiness, in the absence of your answer. Learn to be comfortable not knowing, and you will know all you need to know when you need to know it. The answer will gradually appear in the blank space, or the problem will work itself out. Many times our problems are primarily a result of our emotional reactions to situations. When we become still and silent, we often find the problem vanishes like a cloud on a windy day.

A SPECIES IN RECOVERY

One way of looking at the human situation is to see us as a species in recovery. We are recovering from a wide variety of small-minded, shortsighted, naive views of the world and our place within it. Following are some of those mistakes in thinking from which it is my belief we are in recovery:

- We thought we were better and more important than nonhuman life forms. We saw ourselves as superior and therefore devalued and abused the plant and animal kingdoms. We are indeed glorious beings. Our greatest sin is self-negation and failure to use the magnificent gifts we were given. When we begin to see ourselves as better than other life forms, however, we lose sight of reality. We are totally dependent on this planet and all of its life forms for our physical existence. All of the life forms on this planet are mysterious and wonderful, and they deserve respect, whatever our relationship to them may be.

- As a result of the belief that we are better than other life forms, we have struggled to develop power over them. This has led to great destruction and grief. We are like an ignorant, untamed being who is given a beautiful home filled with magnificent possessions. In this analogy, the untamed being systematically destroys all of his possessions. Through our own ignorance, we destroy and neglect our gifts until they are worthless. We are in recovery from just that same type of ignorance, in terms of how we have treated the earth and its life forms.

- We thought that some human beings were better than others. We have neglected, abused, robbed and killed our fellow human beings. We have unleashed blind, ignorant rage among ourselves and suffered greatly for it. Our wars have been helpless reactions to fear and oppression.

- We have divided up our planet into sections and attacked each other across the lines. This is just one small planet. We are all sticking off the sides of it, held into the center by a force we call gravity. We are each equally powerful and equally insignificant. Our existence is the result of a fragile, delicate balance, the likes of which we have not found anywhere else in the universe. We have to learn to live together, now. It is time. We are all the same in the ways that really matter, and each of us deserves to live as much as the other.

• We thought our sexuality was bad, and as a result both genders have rejected the other in a subconscious attempt to avoid being led astray. We have managed to get ourselves totally confused where gender and sexual relations are concerned. Sexual abuse, sex addiction, sexism and the dissolution of the family are some of the devastating results of this confusion. Our sexuality is as natural and beautiful as the flowers and the sunshine. The differences between the genders add to the mystery and the wonder of life and relationship. The act of making love is a sacred communion between two people, which is ideally a physical, emotional and spiritual union. When we begin to realize these and other similar truths, tremendous healing will occur.

• We have confused touching with sex and aggression. Some of us have virtually stopped touching each other, except in one of these two ways. Many people go through their entire lives deprived of nurturing, loving touch. We must find new, safe ways of touching each other in order to survive as a species.

• We thought this life was merely a testing ground to see if we qualified for the next one, which was to be either heaven or hell. Because of this, we have lived for many years in guilt and fear, believing people are basically sinful. This has been the cause of great suffering, and it has caused us to devalue the miracle of existence. Recovery means to begin to realize the heaven that is here now. We must also take responsibility for healing the bits of hell we have created here on earth.

As you claim your worth and value as a physical, intellectual, emotional and spiritual being, you are recovering from these and many other related mistakes in your thinking. Before you can recognize that this planet is your home and that all other species of life are members of your family, you must come home within your own skin. We cannot deny our physical bodies and embrace the planet with love. Taking care of and loving the environment starts with taking care of and loving ourselves. Each of us is the center of our own universe. When we love ourselves, we love the world.

AFFIRMATIONS

- *This body is my home.*
- *This planet is my home.*
- *I am at home in my body.*
- *I accept and embrace all that I am.*
- *My commitment to myself and to the world is to value and care for this gift of life that I am.*

APPENDIX I
AFFIRMATIONS EXERCISE

I. Physical
A. Target areas
  1. Exercise
  2. Diet
  3. Health maintenance
B. New thought/affirmation
  1. I release the need for/to _____
  2. I deserve _____
  3. I am experiencing _____
  4. Negative or contradictory thoughts which arose were _____.
  5. Affirmations to replace these negative thoughts are

  _____
  _____
  _____.

II. Mental
A. Target areas
  1. Openness (to open my mind)
  2. Authority (to claim the authority of my mind over my actions)
  3. Knowledge and consciousness expansion
B. New thought/affirmation
  1. I release the need for/to _____
  2. I deserve _____
  3. I am experiencing _____
  4. Negative or contradictory thoughts which arose were _____.

5. Affirmations to replace these negative thoughts are

_____

_____

_____.

III. Emotional
A. Target areas
    1. Experience (to give myself permission to experience my feelings)
    2. Expression (to openly express my emotions)
    3. Stability (to affirm emotional stability in my life)
B. New thought/affirmation
    1. I release the need for/to _____
    2. I deserve _____
    3. I am experiencing _____
    4. Negative or contradictory thoughts which arose were _____.
    5. Affirmations to replace these negative thoughts are

_____

_____

_____.

IV. Relationships
A. Target areas
    1. Boundaries (to affirm my right to clear, flexible boundaries)
    2. Intimacy (to give myself permission to be intimate)
    3. Openness (to create open communication in my relationships)
B. New thought/affirmation
    1. I release the need for/to _____
    2. I deserve _____
    3. I am experiencing _____
    4. Negative or contradictory thoughts which arose were _____.

5. Affirmations to replace these negative thoughts are

_____

_____

_____.

V. Financial
   A. Target areas
      1. Opportunity (to open my mind to new financial possibilities)
      2. Planning
      3. Managing
   B. New thought/affirmation
      1. I release the need for/to _____
      2. I deserve _____
      3. I am experiencing _____
      4. Negative or contradictory thoughts which arose were _____.
      5. Affirmations to replace these negative thoughts are

_____

_____

_____.

VI. Professional
   A. Target areas
      1. Knowledge
      2. Skills
      3. Development
   B. New thought/affirmation
      1. I release the need for/to _____
      2. I deserve _____
      3. I am experiencing _____
      4. Negative or contradictory thoughts which arose were _____.

5. Affirmations to replace these negative thoughts are

_____

_____

_____.

APPENDIX II:
GUIDELINES FOR RESPECTFUL
COMMUNICATION FOR COUPLES
AND CLOSE RELATIONSHIPS

The Speaker

Connection: I want to talk to you in this way because ... *(I love you, our relationship is important to me, etc.)*

Perception: When I perceive you as ... *(angry, ignoring me, criticizing me, etc.)* or When you ... *(are late, leave your clothes out, etc.)*

Feeling response: I feel ... *(angry, hurt, frustrated, etc.)*

Behavior: So I respond by ... *(arguing, yelling, withdrawing, not talking to you, etc.)*

Underlying Fear: My fear when these things happen is ... *(of being rejected, abandoned, shamed, violated, etc.)*

History of feelings: The way this relates to my childhood emotional experience is ... *(describe related emotional experiences from your earliest memories before this relationship)*

Request: What I really want from you is ... *(state the specific behavior you would like from your partner)*

The Listener

Reflection: To the best of your ability, repeat the exact words of your partner with respect and concern. *("What I hear you saying is . . ." "If I'm hearing you correctly . . .")*

Empathy and validation: Accept the validity of your partner's feelings regardless of whether you agree with them. *("When I put myself in your shoes, I can see why you would feel that way." "When I look at this from your viewpoint, your feelings make sense to me.")*

Understanding: Indicate understanding of what your partner is experiencing. *("I think I can see where you're coming from." "I see what you mean.")*

Support: Express appreciation for your partner's openness. *("I appreciate your telling me how you feel." "Thanks for being open with me.")*

Guidelines for the Speaker

1. Use a calm, pleasant tone; avoid raising your voice.
2. Sit back comfortably in your chair with your arms and legs uncrossed.
3. Breathe deeply into your abdomen. This will help you to remain calm and keep your voice tone pleasant.

Guidelines for the Listener

1. Listen attentively because you will be asked to repeat what your partner has said when s/he has finished to be sure you understand correctly.

2. Look at your partner while s/he is talking to you.
3. Wait patiently while your partner is talking to you. Avoid any nonverbal reactions that might interrupt her/his flow of communication.
4. Don't interrupt.
5. As you listen, put yourself in the speaker's place. Set aside your agenda for a moment. How does s/he feel? What is her/his perspective? How does s/he experience you?
6. If you are unclear or don't understand what the speaker has just said, ask her/him to repeat it. But remember not to comment or respond at this time to what is being said.

APPENDIX III:
RESPECTFUL CONFLICT RESOLUTION FOR WORKPLACE PROBLEM-SOLVING

Step 1: Opening the Door to Communication

Speaker:

- I am talking to you in this way because _____
_____. *("I respect you," "I like you,"*
"Our relationship is important to me")
- When _____
_____. *(describe* specific
behavior or event, being as clear and precise as possible)
- I feel *(felt)* _____ *(mad, sad, scared)* because
_____. *(be brief)*

Step 2: Active Listening

Partner:

- What I hear you saying is that when _____
_____. *(use speaker's*
exact words, as close as you can remember)
- You feel/felt _____ *(mad, sad, scared)*
- Because _____.
(use speaker's words; avoid interpretation)
- Is that correct?

**(Repeat above process until speaker feels accurately heard.
Then the partner continues with the following):**

- As I understand it, this means _____
_____.

(give your interpretation of the situation as you see it—avoid
explaining or defending your position—this is a time for taking
responsibility for your part of the problem)

- The way I feel about this is _____ (*mad, sad, scared, glad*)
  because_____.
- And I also feel _____ (*sad, scared, glad*)
  because_____.
  (*try to end on a positive note here*)

Step 3: The Decision Point

Note to Speaker:
- If you are satisfied with your partner's response, proceed to Step 4.
- If you did not feel heard, or your partner omitted something important, say something like "Let me clarify myself," and repeat all or part of Step 1 and/or 2. Ask that your partner review with you, until you feel you have been heard and understood. Then proceed to Step 4.

NOTE: Only the speaker can decide to move on to Step 4.

Step 4: Developing an Action Plan

Speaker:
- What I would like is _____. (*propose a practical, doable action plan with a concrete timeline*)

Partner:
- You say that you would like _____.
  (*repeat what you have heard them propose*)
- My response is _____.
  (*state your agreement with the proposed plan, or if you do not agree, propose an alternative—this may become a negotiating process—or in some cases you may just have to agree to disagree*)

Speaker:
   • To prevent this problem from occurring again, I propose
   _____. *(this usually involves
   more effective and timely communication processes)*

Partner:
   • You are suggesting that we _____
   (repeat what the speaker proposed) to prevent this from occurring again, and my response is _____
   _____.

Speaker:
   • Now that we have developed our action plan, let's *(shake
   hands, have a cup of coffee, go to lunch, get back to work, etc.)*

PRODUCTS AND
CONTACT INFORMATION

For more information about Dr. DeFoore, his services and products, visit *www.defoore.com,* call his office at 214-764-7930 or 800-322-4773, or e-mail him at *ippd@defoore.com.* Telephone and e-mail counseling and coaching sessions are available. For a free preview and to download all audio products go to *defoore.com.*

All of the following are available for purchase as CDs or as audio downloads.

Healing Anger and Depression: Removing Barriers to Health and Happiness. This dynamic information-packed program will help you to understand and overcome anger management and depression problems. Create dynamic health by becoming healthy emotionally!

Sacred Roles in Marriage: Keys to Creating Fantastic Relationships. This powerful program teaches you how to make your relationship a vibrant resource of love, joy and fulfillment. Become a master of expressing love!

Anger: Deal With It Before It Deals With You. Supplementary to this book, this program gives further information on anger, depression, rage addiction and the inner journey.

Helping Your Children With Their Anger: A Guide for Parents. This powerful program helps parents to help their children ages 4–18 to understand, manage and express their anger in healthy ways. Help your children or adolescents be the best they can be.

Nurturing Your Inner Child. This powerful program guides you on a journey of self-love and self-healing. Includes a guided visualization for healing emotional memories. Use this tool on a regular basis to heal emotionally and learn to truly love yourself.

Affirmations for Well-Being. This highly effective program helps you to develop positive beliefs about your body, mind and spirit health. Excellent for anyone dealing with health issues.

Smoking Cessation. This one-of-a-kind program provides a totally positive approach to stopping smoking. Reprogram your subconscious mind so that you automatically begin making healthy choices to breathe clean, fresh air. Learn to love your body enough to take really good care of it.

Go to *www.defoore.com* for a free preview and to download with no S/H charges!

REFERENCES

Introduction

Bureau of Labor Statistics (2001). *National Census of Fatal Occupai Injuries,* 2000.

Life Stories: The Board Game. TaliCor. *www.toysrus.com,* 2003.

McAdams, Dan. *The Stories We Live By: Personal Myths and the Mak of the Self.* Guilford Press, 1997.

Pearsall, Paul. *Superimmunity.* McGraw-Hill, 1987.

Chapter 3

Elam, P. ivillageHealth, *ivillagehealth.com,* 2003.

Fava, M., and Rosenbaum, J. "Anger Attacks Patients with Depression." *Journal of Clinical Psychiatry.* 60:21–24, 1999.

Speca, M., Carlson, L.E., Goodey, E., Angen, M. "A randomized, wait-list controlled clinical trial: the effect of a mindfulness meditation-based stress reduction program on mood and symptoms of stress in cancer outpatients." *Psychosomatic Medicine.* Sept.–Oct.; 62:613–22. 2000.

Chapter 7

Golding, William. *Lord of the Flies.* Perigee, 1959.

Mehrabian, Albert. *Silent Messages: Implicit Communication of Emotions and Attitudes.* Wadsworth Publishing, 1981.

Suicide and America's Youth. Prevention and Treatment for Teenage Depression. *www.suicide.com,* 2001.

Webb, Wyatt. *It's Not About the Horse: It's About Overcoming Fear and Self-Doubt.* Hay House, 2002.

Chapter 8

Goleman, Daniel. *Emotional Intelligence.* Bantam Books, 1997.

Jung, Carl. *Memories, Dreams, Reflections.* Vintage Books, 1989.

Jung, Carl, and Kerenyi, C. *Essays on a Science of Mythology: The Myth of the Divine Child and the Mysteries of Eleusis.* Princeton University Press, 1969.

MacLean, Paul. *The Triune Brain in Evolution: Role in Paleocerebral Functions.* Plenum Press, 1990.

McAdams, Dan. *The Stories We Live By: Personal Myths and the Making of the Self.* Guilford Press, 1997.

Chapter 10

Castaneda, Carlos. *Tales of Power.* Washington Square Press. 1974.

DiGiuseppe, Ray, and Tafrate, R.C. *The Anger Disorder ScalManual.* Multi-Health Systems, in press.

Shakespeare, William. *The Taming of the Shrew.* Washington Square Press, 1992.

Steiner, Claude. *Scripts People Live.* Grove Press, 1990.

Thomas, S. P. *Women and Anger.* Springer, 1993.

Chapter 11

Bly, Robert. *Iron John.* Addison Wesley, 1990.

Hollis, James. *The Middle Passage: From Misery to Meaning in Midlife.* Inner City Books, 1993.

Stoney, C. M., and Engebretson, T. O. *Plasma homocysteine concentrations are positively associated with hostility and anger.* Life Sciences, Vol. 66. pp. 2267–2275. 2000.

Sullivan, H.S. *The Interpersonal Theory of Psychiatry.* Norton Publishing, 1953.

The ManKind Project. www.mkp.org.

Chapter 12

Bradshaw, John. *Healing the Shame That Binds You.* Health Communications, 1988.

Goleman, Daniel. *Emotional Intelligence.* Bantam Books, 1997.

Samuels, Michael, and Samuels, Nancy. *Seeing With the Mind's Eye: The History, Techniques and Uses of Visualization.* Random House Trade Paperbacks, 1975.

Chapter 13

Ornish, Dean. *Love and Survival: The Scientific Basis for the Healing Power of Intimacy.* Perennial, 1999.

Chapter 14

Benson, Herbert. *Timeless Healing.* Fireside, April 1997.

Castaneda, Carlos. "Portrait of a Sorcerer." *New Age,* April, 1994.

DeFoore, William. *Anger Among Angels: Shedding Light on the Darkness of the Human Soul.* Health Communications, 2000.

Kasparov, S., Davies, K., Patel, U., Boscan, P., Garret, M., and Paton, J. *Journal of Physiology.* Vol. 536: 785–796. 2001.

Klauser, Henriette. *Write It Down, Make It Happen: Knowing What You Want and Getting It.* Simon & Schuster, 2001.

Lemonick, Michael, and Mankato, Alice. "The Nun Study." *Time* May 18, 2001.

McCraty, R., and Childre, D. "The Grateful Heart: The Psychophysiology of Appreciation." Chapter published in: *The Psychology of Gratitude,* edited by R. A. Emmons and M. E. McCullough. Oxford University Press, 2003.

Pearson, Carol. *Awakening the Heroes Within: Twelve Archetypes to Help Us Find Ourselves and Transform Our World.* HarperSanFrancisco, 1991.

Sarno, J.E. *The Mindbody Prescription: Healing the Body, Healing the Pain.* Warner Books, 1999.

Chapter 15

Goleman, D., McKee, A. and Boyatzis, R. *Primal Leadership: Realizing the Power of Emotional Intelligence.* Harvard Business School Press, 2002.

Langone, John. *Violence! Our Fastest-Growing Public Health Problem.* Little, Brown and Company, 1984.

Toch, H, and Karon, B. *Violent Men: An Inquiry into the Psychology of Violence.* American Psychological Association, 1992.

www.questia.com—the world's largest online library

Chapter 16

Bradshaw, John. *Homecoming: Reclaiming and Championing Your Inner Child.* Bantam, 1990.

Fishel, Ruth. *The Journey Within: A Spiritual Path to Recovery.* Health Communications, 1987.

Harris Thomas. *I'm OK—You're OK.* Avon, 1976.

Hay, Louise. *You Can Heal Your Life.* Hay House, 1987.

Whitfield, Charles. *A Gift To Myself.* Health Communications, 1989.

ABOUT THE AUTHOR

William Gray (Bill) DeFoore, Ph.D., is a counselor, executive coach, and president of the Institute for Personal and Professional Development in Dallas, Texas. He speaks and conducts workshops internationally on emotional intelligence and emotional wellness in personal and business relationships. Through his work, Dr. DeFoore helps individuals and organizations bring body, mind and spirit into an integrated focus, leading to enhanced levels of personal and professional integrity. As a consultant and trainer, he has coached and facilitated conflict resolution in management-union disputes, and facilitated trauma resolution in organizational change processes. He is a commentator on Wisdom Radio (*www.wisdomradio.com*), columnist for Wisdom Media (*www.wisdommedia.com*) and an adjunct faculty member at Cooper Aerobics Center (*www.cooperaerobics.com*). He is the author of *Anger Among Angels,* and he coedited and coauthored *The New Bottom Line: Bringing Heart and Soul to Business* and *Rediscovering the Soul in Business: A Renaissance of Values.* He is in the process of completing his next book, *Castles of the Heart: A Guide to the Treasures of the Human Soul,* to be released in 2005. He lives in the countryside near Aubrey, Texas, with his wife and business partner, Cindy, and their two cats and horse Honey.